Alexander Palma di Cesnola, Samuel Birch

Salaminia (Cyprus): History, Treasures and Antiquities

Alexander Palma di Cesnola, Samuel Birch

Salaminia (Cyprus): History, Treasures and Antiquities

ISBN/EAN: 9783744730631

Printed in Europe, USA, Canada, Australia, Japan

Cover: Foto ©ninafisch / pixelio.de

More available books at **www.hansebooks.com**

THE HISTORY, TREASURES, & ANTIQUITIES

OF

SALAMIS IN THE ISLAND OF CYPRUS.

BY

ALEXANDER PALMA DI CESNOLA, F.S.A.

Member of the British Archæological Association, and of the Society of Biblical Archæology;
Hon. Member of the Royal Academy of Medicine, Turin;
etc., etc., etc.

With an Introduction,

BY

SAMUEL BIRCH, Esq., D.C.L., LL.D., F.S.A.,

Keeper of the Egyptian and Oriental Antiquities in the British Museum.

AND

WITH UPWARDS OF SEVEN HUNDRED ILLUSTRATIONS,

AND MAP OF ANCIENT CYPRUS.

LONDON:

TRÜBNER AND CO., LUDGATE HILL.

1882.

THIS WORK IS DEDICATED

TO

EDWIN HENRY LAWRENCE, Esq., F.S.A.,

BY

THE AUTHOR.

London, June 3rd, 1882

HE antiquities discovered lately in the Island of Cyprus, consisting of all the different periods of its civilisation, have certainly cast a new and important light on the history of art, for they form a connecting link between the Greek and Phœnician, or Aryan and Semitic civilisation.

That Cyprus received colonists from the three continents of the old world is undoubted. Evidence of the Phœnician and Greek colonists is proved by the remains of these nationalities found on the coast and elsewhere, while its conquest by Egypt and Assyria has been recorded in the annals of those countries, and their arts have left the stamp of their impression on the sculpture of Cyprus At the time of the eighteenth Egyptian dynasty, fifteen or sixteen centuries before Christ, Cyprus was known to the Egyptians, and had evidently been colonised and inhabited. The Greeks anterior to the time of Homer had peopled portions of the island, and the coast was held by their settlements, the establishment of which was placed at the period of the Nostoi, or return of the Greeks from the Trojan War, and cannot be depressed lower than nine centuries before Christ; and these settlers had evidently brought with them the Cypriote alphabet, invented before that known as the Greek, examples of which cannot be identified earlier than six centuries before the Christian era. Contemporaneously, or later, the Phœnicians had emigrated there, and mingled with the Hellenic population. At the seventh century

B.C., the Assyrian annals shew that Cyprus was held by numerous princes, for as early as B.C. 715, seven kings of Cyprus had sent tribute to Sargon at Babylon, and later, ten kings of Cyprus, amongst whom appears a king of Salamis, propitiated Esarhaddon and Assurbanipal with their tribute. To the Egyptians, Cyprus was "the Isle in the middle of the Great Sea", perhaps the Khaft of the earlier period, and the Masenia of the later age. The arts of Egypt and Assyria had a striking influence upon Phœnician art, and also considerably modified the sculpture of Cyprus. The only question is to decide the period of that influence, if it is to be attributed to the older age of the ninth and tenth centuries B.C., or to the later one of the conquest of the island by the Egyptians just prior to the Persian Conquest, about the fifth century B.C. This is principally to be determined by the arrangement of the head and hair, or the curls and beard, which differ at the period, resembling the Egyptian of the sixth century, or the Persian of the fifth, although there are undoubted evidences of earlier imitations in the bronze bowls and other objects. It is in this respect that the antiquities discovered in Cyprus possess such great interest for the study of archæology. To the later period of Cypriote art belong the sculptures and other objects, which were made after the Greek element obtained a stronger hold on the civilisation. The types, however, still retain an Asiatic tendency, but assimilate more to the art and style of other Greek settlements.

Besides the sculpture, innumerable articles of foreign fabric, the opaque glass toilet vases, made at an early period in the furnaces of Phœnicia, the bronze bowls or cups, with subjects in relief, like those of Assyria and Etruria, poured into the island by the intercourse kept up with the coasts of Syria and Egypt. These vases, which, by the route of commerce, have been found deposited in the tombs of Egypt, the graves of the Greek isles, and the sepulchral chambers of Etruria, and which are now known to be at least as old as the sixteenth century B.C., have also been found in the Necropolis of Salamis, and many beautiful examples are in the Lawrence-Cesnola collection. They are amongst the most beautiful products of ancient art, and the predecessors of the glass *chefs-d'œuvre* of Rome and Venice. Amongst those which the Necropolis of Salamis has contributed is a remarkable egg-cup, with the egg still remaining in it, a type not yet discovered amongst the shapes of Hellenic vases of a later period. But also of unrivalled beauty is a toilet vase of the shape of an amphora, ornamented with peacocks and foliage, painted by the hand, this bird, however, the pride of India, not appearing on works of ancient art till about the first century. Another charming specimen is the lid of a box, with Aphrodite Anadyomene. The first appearance of transparent glass with indications of a date is only about the seventh century B.C., when the vase made for the Assyrian monarch Sargon, which was discovered at Kouyunjik, or Nineveh, exhibits a green transparent glass made with thick sides; and other vases of the same kind have been discovered in Cyprus and at Salamis. A great deal of this transparent glass, but of thinner substance and more elegant shape, is extant, and this kind of transparent glass was continued till the close of the Roman Empire. The quantity of ancient glass found in Cyprus is considerable, and many specimens exhibit a rare iridescence of colours. A large proportion of the glass is, however, of the Roman period, and of the second and third century of the era.

A class of objects, also of Phœnician fabric, are the scarabæi, made of hard stones, such as sard, sardonyx, agate, cornelians, and jaspers imitated from the Egyptian. A most interesting example occurs in the collection, bearing an inscription in Cypriote characters, and illustrating the fact that these scarabæi were made on the island as well as imported. The earlier engraved were followed by the usual Greek intaglios, and many of the period of Greek and Roman dominion are in the collection. These are principally of the later period of art, and probably made in Cyprus, as under the Ptolemies there was a mine in the island. A class of objects peculiar to Cyprus are the cylinders of steatite coarsely glazed, found in the island, this collection being very rich in those from Salamis. These were probably imitated from Assyrian and Babylonian art, the deities and figures represented on them being derived from that source, while the material and glazing were copied from Egypt, cylinders of glazed steatite having prevailed till fifteen centuries B.C. in that country; but the art of these cylinders is so different from that of both countries, that the cylinders were not imported from either, and must have been an indigenous production, and they consequently form a distinctive type of Cypriote art. Many cylinders, however, of hæmatite, chalcedony, and other hard stones, some inscribed with cuneiform Assyrian, and Babylonian inscriptions, and even Egyptian hieroglyphics, have been found in Cyprus, brought thither either by commerce, or introduced subsequent to the conquest of the island by Sargon; while in the Lawrence-Cesnola collection appear other engraved stones of the conical shape which is seen at the Assyrian and Persian period, or the later hemispherical type in use at the period of the Parthian Empire, descending to the third century B.C.

Amongst the objects introduced from Egypt are the scarabæi, which preceded by many centuries the Phœnician, some as early as the fourth dynasty, a period so remote that there is no evidence that Cyprus was then known to the Egyptians; others of the period of the eighteenth dynasty, when Cyprus figures as a tributary to Egypt. Other Egyptian objects in the collection, however, point to a later period, when the Phœnicians and Greeks exported Egyptian objects in porcelain to the isles. From Egypt, too, Cyprus probably acquired the alabaster, or rather stalagmite, of which many of the toilet vases were made; and bronze and porcelain figures of the twenty-sixth dynasty, or between the sixth and seventh centuries B.C., obtained by this means, are in the Lawrence-Cesnola collection.

A considerable series of gold ornaments throw considerable light upon the arts of the jeweller at different periods of the history of Cyprus. Some of these have inscriptions in Cypriote characters, and are probably older than the time of Evagoras, or the third century B.C., and are of the age of the Phœnician and Greek kings, rising to the sixth and seventh centuries. Many of the ear-rings and finger-rings are beautiful examples of the best period of Greek art, while other rings are good examples of the excellence still retained at the time of the Romans. Silver contemporaneous with the earliest period does not retain its preservation so well as gold; but there are many interesting specimens in the collection, and from the stones set in the rings, evidently productions of Phœnician artists, either indigenous or foreign, and apparently of the fourth or fifth century B.C., and as such are objects of great interest.

The leaden remains are not as a rule of the same antiquity as the metals mentioned before, and a large proportion of those discovered generally belong to the class of toys, or little votive objects. Seals attached to merchandise are occasionally found, and the sling bullets of the Greek and Roman armies, with inscriptions in relief, are found, mentioning the division or corps to which they belonged. Other vases of small size, for the eye-ointments of the Roman oculists, have, however, been found in lead. They commence about the time of Alexander, and seems to end at the Augustan era. The Lawrence-Cesnola collection, however, has also leaden plates, anciently rolled up, of a nature similar to the diræ, or imprecations discovered at Athens and Cnidus, deposited under the pavement of the temple, and probably about the fourth century B.C. One of these discovered at Salamis has a Cypriote inscription, and is of high interest, as it probably precedes the supremacy of the Hellenic civilisation. The oldest known objects in lead are probably the archaic weights of Athens of the Æginetan standard, and which may be attributed to the fifth century B.C. But even for weights, lead subsequently was superseded by stone and bronze, and the last appearance of this metal in ancient art is in the bulke, or seals, inscribed with monograms, of the age of the Byzantine Empire, as late as five centuries, and even later, after Christ, examples of which will be found in the collection.

Although the use of iron implements and objects can be traced to eight and nine centuries before our era, the few remains found.

owing to the rapid oxydisation of the metal, are precious, although of a later period.

The bronze portion of the collection contains some remarkable objects—the Phœnico-Egyptian bowl, and the bronze flute, constructed upon a novel principle, probably of the Greek period. Amongst the weapons found at Cyprus are some of copper, which may have preceded the use of bronze, and have been found elsewhere in the island.

The articles of bone and ivory found at Salamis are principally of the later Greek and Roman period, comprising spoons, hairpins, and small objects; but the ivory box found, protected by a lead box and two paterœ, is most remarkable, and of an earlier period; along with the ivory must be mentioned the box in shape of a shell, with a Cypriote inscription, which was employed for the purposes of the toilet. Bone is, no doubt, a later substitute for ivory, as proved by the numerous plaques, tickets for the amphitheatre, and tesserœ of gladiators, portions of caskets, knife-handles, and hairpins found all over the ancient world at the time of the Roman Empire. The use of ivory, indeed, is of the most remote antiquity, that beautiful, soft, and elegant material having been at the earliest period adapted for objects of decorative art.

The numerous sculptures in stone, although not of the largest size, exhibit the principal vicissitudes of Cypriote art, as it passed through the transition of Egyptian, Phœnician, and Greek and Roman influences; the material employed for this purpose was principally a kind of fine limestone, resembling modern Caen stone, which easily yielded to the chisel, and has retained a worn colour on the surface, producing a pleasing effect after centuries. The very facility of working it instead of marble, more stubborn to the chisel, without doubt, modified the art, and, to some extent, prevented it rivalling the soaring genius of Athenian art or that of Asia Minor. Yet some of the effects of the Cypriote sculptor are undoubtedly happy, especially those made at a later time, when his labours were untrammeled by hieratic influences, which had the effect of producing a pseudo-archaism more interesting to the archæologist than pleasing to the general spectator. Criteria, however, are not wanting for determining even the relative place of these sculptures as revealed by the appearance of the laurel or other wreaths upon the head, and rings upon the fingers, in costume, or the treatment of the hair, the brows, eyes, and beard, in the representation of the countenance. But at Salamis have also been found those small naked female figures of Dædalic fabric found elsewhere distributed through the Isles of Greece, perhaps some of the oldest remains of Carian art, or Phœnician sculpture in stone.

The inscriptions from this site are precious from their rarity and their belonging to the different epochs. The Cypriote have been illustrated by Professor Sayce; one at least presents either a new letter or new form of a known letter of the Cypriote alphabet, and is on stone. The precise date of the first appearance of this early attempt to write the Greek language is unknown, and has to be determined from the bas reliefs and coins. Although its appearance is supposed to be first amongst the ruins of Hissarlik or Troy, the doubts and difficulties are too great to enable that alone to decide the epoch. Unfortunately, in Cyprus, the character continued in use to the exclusion of the more recent Greek alphabet, till the fourth century before our era. The reform of Evagoras, no doubt, effected the substitution of the Greek alphabet for the complex and ambiguous Cypriote; but there are no bilingual inscriptions, either Cypriote and Greek, or Cypriote and Phœnician, which can be assigned earlier than the fifth century B.C.; and that is certainly not the earliest date of Cypriote inscriptions, for the golden bracelets of Eteander, contemporary of Sargon, must be as old as the seventh century. Some of the lapidary inscriptions look older. The terra-cotta figurines and vases were undoubtedly made on the Island, and are amongst some of the oldest productions of the potter's art. The statuettes found of the oldest Assyrian or Persian style, the middle period of the history of the Island, are succeeded by the Phœnico-Egyptian, then by archaic Greek, and finally by such as were made at the time of the Roman Empire. Some of the earlier ones are incised with Cypriote inscriptions, apparently the names of the donors or persons represented. Amongst the most remarkable of the archaic kind are dogs and lions inscribed with Phœnician and Cypriote characters. One remarkable terra-cotta, representing a Genius on a cock, is dedicated to Cleopatra, but to which queen of that name is uncertain. Of the Roman period is that inscribed the Goddess of Rain, or a Naiad; and to the same period belong the numerous Cupids or Genii, which swarm on the sarcophagi, and other objects of art of the second century. Analogous to the statuettes are the lamps of the Roman period of terra-cotta, hundreds of which were found at Salamis. These are the chief contributions to the antiquities of a later period.

The vases discovered on different sites have a different type of decoration and character from those exhumed in Italy, Greece, and the Isles. An immense quantity belong to the oldest period of the fictile art, and have some analogy with those of Rhodes and Ialysus. The back grounds are pale-yellow; the ornaments geometric, plain bands, and annulets. Vases ornamented with plain bands, annulets, circles, vandykes, and similar decorations, belong to the earliest period of Greek art; some have been found in Cyprus, occasionally with Phœnician inscriptions burnt in, and others with Cypriote inscriptions incised, and consequently belong to the earlier period of the fictile art, but these are not all of the earliest age, as one remarkable vase in the collection bears the name of Arsinoe, the wife of Philadelphus, B.C. 284.

The great peculiarity of early Cypriote art is the employment of birds in its earliest development. These are often of large size, and occupy the greater portion of the area. The human figures, introduced by degrees as subordinate to ornament, exhibit all the peculiarities of the infancy of art. This is the style peculiar to Cyprus, especially the quaint figures of birds and trees. Corinthian vases, with maroon figures on a yellow ground, are however found in Cyprus; and another peculiar ware of red clay, resembling the so-called Samian, but ornamented with archaic annulets and other patterns, and found under circumstances demonstrating their high antiquity. The vases of the Greek style of the last period are rare, but many interesting specimens of the Roman period, and a great number of lamps, are in the collection.

The silver currency of Cyprus consists principally of didrachms on the Persian standard, and is as old as the sixth century B.C.; and amongst the earlier examples are those of Evelthon, king of Salamis, who flourished about B.C. 530, inscribed with Cypriote characters, which were in use at that period. The other coins of the supposed Euanthes and Pygmalion may also be of the same place and period. Those of the Phœnician kings, which exhibit Greek art and the same standard, and which are supposed to have been struck from B.C. 448 to B.C. 332, are contemporaneous with the Greek rulers, commencing with Evagoras, who issued gold pieces on the Attic standard, as well as silver, apparently at Paphos. They are beautiful examples of Greek art, inscribed with Greek inscriptions. After Nicocreon in B.C. 312, the Ptolemies established one of their mints in Cyprus, and struck coins at some of the principal cities, Salamis included. The political vicissitudes of the period, as well as the state of the art, are reflected by the currency, and after the acquisition of Cyprus by the Romans, the currency, which was bronze, became that part of the provincial issue known as imperial or provincial. In fact, at no period of its history, was the island governed otherwise than by kings, the institutions being always monarchical.

The dominant civilization was undoubtedly Greek, and so was the language of the principal cities; and the character in which it was written, although perhaps modified by Asiatic influences, cannot be traced with any amount of probability to any other known source. This is the more remarkable, as there is every evidence that the Phœnician population divided the possession of the island with the Greek, and that in some of the chief cities they held an undoubted supremacy; while as late as the Ptolemies, official and other acts were recorded in Phœnician as well as Greek. And this is the historical teaching of the antiquities found in the island, and their contribution to our knowledge of that portion of its former condition.

c

The present work shows the results of the long and laborious excavations of Major di Cesnola in Cyprus, extending over a period of three years, chiefly at Salamis, one of the most important towns in the island, and colonised by Phœnicians and Greeks. This is the third town in the island the Necropolis of which has yielded such important archæological results, and extended the knowledge of Anatolian Greek art, as distinguished from that of a purely Hellenic character. The success which has attended the efforts of the excavator is due to his perseverance and discernment, added to his experience of the position and appearance of promising sites, his acquaintance with the native character, and requisite resources for conducting the operations to a successful issue. Hence the acquisition of adequate results, which must be admitted to have been obtained in the Lawrence-Cesnola collection.

S. BIRCH.

PREFACE.

RE the reader takes up the following pages, I beg leave to say a few words about the book, and the explorations it describes.

An Italian by birth, and a soldier by profession, I passed the greater part of my early life in the service of my country, and remained in this profession until soon after the last war of Italian independence. It was due to many circumstances of no public interest, that a few years later on I found myself in the East, and concerned in archæological researches. But I made no profession of archæological knowledge, nor does my book even now pretend to be more than a simple narrative and description of explorations in the Island of Cyprus. These pages have been prepared, in order to place before students and the public the principal relics which I discovered; but it is not expected that they can exhaust the interest and associations of those remains. My own position is that of an enthusiastic digger-up of antiquities. I went to Cyprus in the year 1873, and remained there until the end of 1874. After an absence of about eighteen months, which were spent in London, I returned to Cyprus.

During this interval my days were freely spent in the British Museum, the vast oriental treasures of which are arranged in a scientific manner, prodigiously to the advantage of those who, like myself, diligently study them. It was while thus occupied that I had the honour of making the acquaintance of Dr. Samuel Birch, the all-accomplished and learned keeper of the Oriental

antiquities in the museum. This acquaintance ripened, on my
part at least, into a very devoted friendship, and I am at this time
indebted to Dr. Birch for the abundant aid he has given me, in
writing the introduction to the following chapters. My previous
engagement in Cyprus having been broken, not through my own
wish nor my consent, but by others, I accepted the generous offer
of Mr. Edwin H. Lawrence, F.S.A., to supply a sum of money to
enable me to commence digging on my own account, a condition
being, that if I succeeded in forming a collection of antiquities of
sufficient importance, it should be offered to England before any
other country. On arriving in Cyprus at the end of July 1876, I
engaged the same house and servants in Larnaka I had before,
and also a country house at Ormidia, the latter being near to
Kitium, Idalium, Salamis, and other localities which are rich in
ancient monuments. In the month of August I was ready to
resume researches, and had collected, partly in Larnaka and partly
in Dali, twenty skilled workmen, putting at their head an
excellent aged digger, who soon proved himself an affectionate
and faithful assistant. My intention was to secure a collection
of vases and glass, so as to have one or two specimens of every
shape and kind used by the ancient Cypriotes. The vases being
mostly funereal were not difficult to discover. My men and I
knew where to search, all that was required were patience and time.

As to the glass, the case was not so simple; some of the
natives, and even my own men, were disheartened. Very little
glass had been found, they declared, within the last two years; but
I am happy to say that in the end I obtained a large number of
specimens, and a vast variety of glass relics, as well as terra cotta
vases, the number now in the Lawrence-Cesnola collection, which
is hereinafter described, being about four thousand of each material. Many specimens, among this multitude of ancient art-relics,
are remarkable for their shape and character. With objects in
glass, coins are always found, therefore I have been able to obtain
a most valuable and exceedingly interesting collection of more
than one thousand six hundred examples, which include specimens

in gold, silver, and bronze of every dynasty which has occupied
the island in ancient times; the reader will, amongst other descriptions in my book, find an account of the more important of these
relics. As coins are found with objects in glass, so lamps are
found with terra cotta vases, and I thus collected more than two
thousand lamps, of which two hundred bear makers' names
stamped upon them in Greek or Roman characters. All excavators have a fancy for one particular kind of relic, and I was not
exempt, my ambition being to find inscriptions in the Phœnician
and Cypriote languages; therefore my men had strict orders to
bring to me everything which bore an indication of an inscription,
and I also was always on the look out for such things. The
result of these efforts the reader will find in many interesting
examples as described in this book, for the translations and explanations of which I am greatly indebted to friends, but most
especially to the learned and Rev. Professor A. H. Sayce, of Queen's
College, Oxford. The first objects I found with inscriptions were
two vases in terra cotta, bearing Phœnician lettering, such as was
used for cinerary urns. Inside one of these vases I found burnt
matter, probably the remains of a child: the only differences
between the two vases were in respect to the places where they
were found, and the inscriptions they bear. One came from
ancient Kitium, and has a Phœnician inscription, the other came
from Idalium, and is enriched with Cypriote letters. Another
vase which I found in the village of Athieno, has Cypriote letters,
and was probably used as a family cooking pot.

From the end of June until October 1876, I was obliged to
suspend work on account of the heat of the weather. I occupied
this interval in an excursion to Salamis, and with the aid of some
natives of two villages, I dug near to the ruins of the ancient city;
but I was deceived, and after much outlay and trouble left the place
without finding anything of great importance. Although I lost
money in this research I did not regret it, as I met there two very
intelligent natives, who were large proprietors of land in the ruins
of Salamis, and well informed about digging. Having furnished

them with money, and incited their diligence with many promises
of future payments, I left them, to seek tombs at Salamis. I
think, and my men had the same opinion, that neither I nor
those who worked before me among those ruins, had failed to find
the proper place for successful explorations. I may explain here why
I sought the site of the tombs in Salamis before commencing any
other diggings. The manner I adopted was that of my predecessors.

Be it noticed, that there are two methods of exploring the
antique world,—digging in the ruins of the cities, and digging
in the tombs of their inhabitants. Tombs are found generally
near ruins. Digging in ruins is always uncertain, and can only
be carried out at great expense, which sometimes may be continued for months without producing anything of importance; but
if the excavator should find but one fine object, it will pay more
than all the expenses incurred. When digging in ruins I always
sunk shafts at the spots which bore indications of temples, palaces,
or other large buildings. These shafts were sunk a few feet apart,
and were made more or less deep, the depth of each being dependent
on the men finding rock or virgin earth. When either of these
substances was reached, I knew there was no hope for researches
in these directions, therefore abandoning the pits, I tried other
parts and dug again. When the shafts disclosed a foundation or
pavement, I continued working in the direction indicated, feeling
sure that something would surely be found there. I have many
times hoped to find a famous temple and other remains, and was
often ready to draw plans, and began to take measures for the
elucidation of these *chateaux d'Espagne*, but all of these visions
ended in nothing except foundations of common buildings. It is
only an excavator who can enter into my feelings. At the
moment of expectation, the excitement of a digger can only be
compared to that of a gambler. I must, however, say that if a
digger has many disappointments, he has great pleasures and
much satisfaction in the progress of his work, and this satisfaction
I experienced in mine, especially at Salamis. Searching for tombs
was conducted nearly in the same manner as among the ruins, the

only change in the manner of seeking being due to the different constructions of the tombs, and this depended upon the people who had buried their dead in them, for of course the antiquities were in accord with the people to whom they had belonged. In digging in the tombs I always recovered antiquities to the full value of the expenses incurred, because the objects found are generally gold.

My system of work was generally to divide the diggers into small parties of three or four each to work in the tombs, and one party in the ruins, I myself remaining with the latter, ready to run to the spot when my men opened a fresh tomb. In this manner also, if I found it necessary to have more men in the ruins, I could easily call for those who were working in the tombs. To the workmen I generally paid the fixed wages of one shilling a day, paying them every Saturday also for the objects they had found at a rate fixed beforehand by my foreman and the workmen. The gold was paid for by weight, adding sometimes a little more when there was art in the work. Under this system I continued digging for about three years. I will take this opportunity of stating that all this time of my diggings, I was never cheated, nor had I any trouble with these poor workmen (as many excavators in other countries have had), but, on the contrary, I received from them most faithful work; and on their part, they had confidence in me. If I had occasion for complaints, it was not against Cypriote people; and it must be remembered that, although I always employed men of both religions, orthodox and Mahommedan, I could not say which of the two was more faithful. I had great confidence in men of both classes, and have sometimes left in their hands large sums of money, and never experienced misgivings about its safety; and I do not think there is any other island or country where the people are more honest or trustworthy than the folks of Cyprus are. When I parted from them it was with great regret.

In October and November of 1876, I was digging at Timbo, Ormidia, and other villages, and I collected in those places a very

large number of vases and fine specimens of glass. It was at this
time that I sent two parties of five men each, the one to Curium,
and the other to Soli; but they came back with very few spoils
of the spade and pick. This was the last time I sent out independent parties of diggers, for I found it better to discontinue this
system, and to keep all the men with me. I returned home to
Larnaka for the winter, and began to pack the relics which had
then been unearthed for conveyance to Mr. Lawrence in England.
My first cargo consisted of six large cases despatched in an
Austrian Lloyd's steamer. For the success attending this ship-
ment, I am indebted to Messrs. Osmiani Brothers. At Alexandria
the cases were passed to another company, en route to Messrs.
Moss and Co., Liverpool, who, in their turn, delivered them safely
in London.

My life in Larnaka was very solitary, and I received very few
friends. My time was taken up in sorting the antiquities, and
arranging and studying them. I was, and am, greatly obliged for
many explanations given by my dear friend, Mr. Demetrius
Pierides, a great antiquary and numismatist, who is thoroughly
acquainted with Cypriote monuments, which he has studied inde-
fatigably for about half a century. He is an honourable gentleman, whose presence adorns the island of Cyprus. The reader
will see that the kindness of Mr. Pierides towards me was not
limited to the time that I spent in Cyprus, but that it continues
now; for in reading this book it will be observed how kindly he
has aided me in many things, I thankfully remember, too, the
kindness of H. E. the Bishop of Larnaka, of the Archimandrite
himself, and of the Venerable Dr. Valsamacchi, and the goodness
of others, who were the only friends I received during this
winter. In March 1877, I visited Paphos, and while on the way
thither spent many hours in the ruins of ancient Marium, visiting
the spot where the learned German, Dr. Sigismondi, met his
death while examining a tomb. These ruins were one hour's
distance from Limassol, and half-way between Larnaka and
Paphos. I received kind hospitality from M. Teodoro Peristiani, a

learned lawyer from the University of Paris. This gentleman was
in every instance most obliging towards me. During my stay in
Limassol I visited two collections of Cypriote antiquities, one
belonging to a native, and the other to Dr. Gastan, but I could not
succeed in buying either of them. The first of these collections
comprised many objects that I liked, especially three pieces of a
patera, with Phœnician inscriptions ; but I could not obtain it, on
account of the great price set upon it by the owner, and because I
thought the inscription was not of one patera, but of three different specimens put together as one ; and in spite of some savants
in Paris, who said it was but one inscription, I retain my opinion.

I stayed at the Lusignan Castle, in Colosso, and received
very kind attention from M. Lobianco, proprietor of a large estate
in Limassol. At Paphos I remained ten days, and dug in several
places, where I found some fine gold objects and vases of a particular form, which are found only in this locality. I obtained at
a village near Paphos-Nova a beautiful Cypriote inscription of
three lines, and I there bought four other inscribed stones.
Paphos is an excellent locality for digging in the ruins; but it is
an extremely expensive place, and difficult to explore, because the
ruins have been buried and re-buried by earthquakes, so that it
requires many men and very deep shafts to reach them.

In April 1877, I returned to my country house, and extended
my diggings to Riso-Carpazzo. I remained in this line of mountains until July 1877, and collected there many very rare relics
in gold, glass, vases, and inscriptions. It was at this time I found
a square well, partly of brick and stone, which was full of
fractured statuettes of a new form, and mixed with earth. I put
together of these about two hundred statuettes ; the reader will
find illustrations of some of these in this book. This well was
about two miles distant from Salamis. The statuettes probably
belonged to a temple of the latter town, and were placed in this
well in the early part of our era. The statuettes were found
thus : first those of very ordinary and rough work ; in the centre
were those of much better art ; and in the lowest stratum they

exhibited most beautiful art. No news came to me from Salamis, but I knew that the man who was excavating there for me was keeping his promise, and working hard in our joint interest. On my return from Carpazzi I saw him, and bought from him some very good ancient Greek glass, such as is called Phœnician in Cyprus. He said to me, "No tomb yet; but I hope very soon to have news to bring you." In August I went again to Limassol; but only passed the ruins of Kurium, and began digging with ten men in the same spot in which one of my predecessors found a treasure, which is now in the New York Museum. I recovered many relics, principally in gold or silver,—fibulæ, rings, earrings, and a beautiful necklace. After a fortnight's work, I was advised by a friendly Turkish officer and others in the village, that people in the coffee-houses were beginning to speak adversely to my operations, while one of the proprietors thought it would be better to inform the Kaimakan or Chief of the Province of Limassol, with a view to stopping my work. On hearing this, I decided to leave the place for a time, and went back to Larnaka. I left only one man to continue the work at Kurium.

After a month this man returned with many very good objects in silver and bronze, and twenty or more fine earrings. I must say that in this circumstance, as during all my digging in the island, I was most obliged to the Turkish authorities. If I have succeeded in gleaning the Lawrence-Cesnola collection from Cyprus, it is due to the kindness of the Turkish officers, from the simple zaptieh or policeman, to the Governors-General; and I know that this kindness continued, although some jealous persons and others did their utmost to deprive me of this indulgence and regard. This, however, was not the same when, at a later time, they tried to injure me with the new Government. This jealousy was not limited to the authorities of the island; but resulted in a communication to the Minister of Foreign Affairs in Italy. In thinking of how much other diggers and archæologists have had to suffer in foreign countries, principally in the East, before me, for instance, Botta, Layard, Schliemann, and others, I cannot but feel that my lot was not so hard as theirs, and so I continued my work without paying much attention to what was said and done against me. I always worked with the countenance and indulgence of the authorities and public officers. I had, indeed, made application in Constantinople for a firman, but never received a positive answer, so I continued digging without it. It is on this account that the reader will not find in the Lawrence-Cesnola collection many large monuments of the statuary class, such as my predecessors had been able to obtain. It was not because I did not find any, or made no researches for them; but I was unable to treat them like small articles which are easily removed. If I had tried to remove large works, it would not have been to my advantage; but, most probably, advantageous to others, and possibly they would have stopped my work. It is certain that if I had succeeded in obtaining a firman, England might have obtained some fine statues and monuments, and had no cause to regret what it has lost. Mr. Edwin Lawrence would, in that case, have had all his wishes fulfilled. In November 1877, my workman came from Salamina to Larnaka, and brought three statuettes in terra cotta, one with a Greek inscription on it, which he had found in a tomb there. He brought, also, several pieces in marble and stone bas-reliefs, from a spot at which he hoped explorations might prove very successful. I ordered all my men directly to Salamis, and followed immediately, took a house in a village near the ruins, and remained there until the British occupation of the island. My collection at that time was not a third of what it afterwards became, in consequence of this discovery in Salamina.

On bringing to England the mass of the relics I had recovered from the soil of Cyprus, an exhibition of the whole was arranged, where it still continues, in Holland Park, in the mansion of Mr. Lawrence; but very few general visitors have seen it, on account of its display at a private residence.

Fortunately, no necessity of selling this collection exists, as many other collections have been sold at public auction, and for the sake of realising their money value; and, certainly, no one would desire to disperse this one, until every means had been used of securing these works of antiquity to the public use in the fittest manner, and I should be glad, if it were possible, that they could be exhibited in a public museum.

The student will find every piece described in this book, with the name of the place where found; and this has been done so as not to fatigue the reader with a long preface. During all my diggings I have never sold a single antiquity. I have, on the other hand, presented many things, principally to English and American visitors, who honoured me with visits while they were passing through the island; but I always refused to sell anything.

I embarked on the *Lloyd* steamer from Cyprus in February 1879; and returned to London the 22nd of May 1879, after having stayed in Italy some time, in order to re-establish my health. Six months after, the collection was arranged in cabinets in two large rooms, in the house of Mr. E. H. Lawrence, 84, Holland Park, where they still remain. Many Englishmen and foreigners of learning have visited the collection. I invited Dr. S. Birch and Professor C. T. Newton, C.B., of the British Museum; and Mr. Wallis and Mr. Thompson, of the South Kensington Museum, to see the antiquities; which they did. In 1881, with Mr. Lawrence's consent, I offered to exhibit the collection in the South Kensington Museum, and for the benefit of art students. After four months I received an answer from the authorities, who placed at my disposal six small cases in a room near the Water Colour Department. I took the advice of many friends; and all agreed it was impossible to make a favourable exhibition in so small a place. I therefore declined the offer, hoping for a better occasion at a later time. At the end of the same year I offered to lend the greater part of the collection to the British Museum for temporary exhibition; but the offer was not then brought to a successful conclusion. With these offers I feel I have completed my duty to students and amateurs in antiquities. The Lawrence-

Cesnola collection is too large for a private museum. It is my ardent wish that some day it may be in a public one.

Before ending this preface I heartily thank many learned friends, besides those I have previously mentioned, who have helped me with counsel and aid in this work, and I especially thank Professor E. Renan, Mr. F. G. Stephens, and Mr. Walter de Gray Birch, F.S.A.

After this explanation, I leave my book in the hands of the reader, begging him to show all leniency and benevolence towards my many shortcomings.

A. PALMA DI CESNOLA.

DESCRIPTION OF THE PLATES.

COLOURED PLATE.

PLATE I.

Fig.

1. Necklace with a Pendant, on which is the Head of Phœbus Apollo rayed.
2. A Child's Bracelet of small dimensions. There are several in the Collection.
3. Portion of a Necklace with cut stones, and Pendant in form of a Satyric face or Mask.
4. Adjustable Bracelet with punctured inscription now illegible.
5. Snake-ring.
6. Plain ring.
7. Finger-ring : two Erotes wrestling.
8. Filigree ear-ring of elegant and elaborate design—one of a pair.
9. Ear-ring of fine design : Cornelian in centre ; three Ruby Pendants.
10. Ring, with Pendant of blue and white mosaic in solid setting, perhaps part of a necklace.
11. Ring of similar style ; solid chased setting.
12. Ear-ring of very fine work ; bulla-shaped ornaments.
13. Ear-ring ; Pearl Pendant.
14. Ear-ring ; Cornelian centre ; six Amethysts in Pendant.
15. Model of a Right Hand, ringed ; the thumb protruded between the first and second finger.
16. Ear-ring ; large Pearl in centre.
17. Crescent-shaped Ear-ring ; three Pearl Pendants on Chains.

18. Ear-ring ; Glass in centre ; three Pearl Pendants.
19. Ear-ring ; pendants of Pearls and Filigree.
20. Ear-ring, twisted wire ; Pendants.
21. Ear-ring ; two Emerald Pendants.
22. Ear-ring ; paste setting with a youthful face ; two pear shaped Pendants.
23. Ear-ring ; four Pearls set on pins.
24. Ear-ring ; leaf-shaped ornaments.
25. Ear-ring ; Amethyst Pendant and centre. Two pairs of this pattern were found.
26. Ear-ring ; Lotus-shaped Pendant.
27. Ear-ring, lunated form ; two pendent drops.
28. Ear-ring ; massive bud-shaped Pendant.
29. Ear-ring, set with two Emeralds.
30. Ear-ring ; Filigree work ; glass centre ; two Pearl Pendants.
31. Ear-ring ; chain pattern ; two Pearls.
32. Ear-ring ; Turquoise in a rosette ; Pearl Pendant.
33. Ear-ring ; elegant rosette and drop.
34. Ear-ring ; five Pearls set in a quatrefoil pattern.
35. Ear-ring ; ball-shaped Pendant.
36. Lion's tooth, set in gold.
37. Lion's tooth, the setting lost.
38. Ear-ring ; two Pearls.
39. Heart-shaped Ear-ring.
40. Ear-ring ; Cornelian centre ; Pearl Pendant.
41. Ear-ring ; circular plaque with bust to the left in relief.

PLATE II.

SILVER OBJECTS . *Face page* 48.

1. Snake Bracelet, five turns.
2. Large Ear-ring ; Paste Pendant, a Lion and Crescent.
3. Reverse of Fig. 2.
4. Ear-pick or Scoop.
5. Spoon, circular bowl.
6. Pin, rosette centre.
7. Spoon, circular bowl.
8. Spoon ; bowl in form of a Pomegranate.
9. Fibula.
10. Model of Human Lips, perhaps a Spoon-bowl.
11. Ear-ring, in form of a Bull's Head.
12. Plain wire Ear-ring.

13. Ear-ring of a very commonly recurring kind.
14. Adjustable plain wire Bracelet.
15 A-I. Various portions of a Bracelet, Pendants, etc.
16. Pin, in form of a Swan.
17. Finger-ring; Paste setting.
18. Finger-ring.
19. Scarabæus set as a Finger-ring.
20. Finger-ring; rectangular Bezel.

PLATE III.

BRONZE OBJECTS .   .   .   . *Face page* 54.
Fig. 1, 2, 3. Parts of a Tripod, with ornaments in form of Bulls' heads.
   A. Bronze parts. B. Iron parts.
4. Part of a Tripod or Stand, in form of a Bull's leg. A. Bronze.
   B. Iron.
5. Lion's claw, part of a Stand. A. Bronze. B. Iron.
6. Figure of Eros, with screw for fixing to a lid or cover.
7 A-D. Tools and Weapons.
8 A-E. Arrow-heads and other Weapons.
9. Part of a piece of Harness, on it a winged figure.
10. Part of a Breast-band for a Horse.
11. Axe with two cutting edges, ornamented with Friezes of Lotus and
   other designs.
12. Early form of Axe or Celt.
13. Crucible or Pot.
14. Cylindrical Box.
15. Key.
16. Key, on a finger-ring of wire.
17. Loop with two balance weights of Human Head and Bust.
18. Handle of a *Situla*.
19. A Weight in form of a Human Bust.
20. Part of a Lock, or of Harness.
21. Part of a Lock or Staple-fastening.
22. Leg of a Tripod or Stand, triple claw.
23. A Strigil.
24. A Finger-ring with Bezel in form of a Key.
25. A Strigil.

PLATE IV.

1. Group of a Large Jar, showing repairs; *paterae*, *phiale omphalotos*, and drinking vessels.
2. A-E. Mirrors.
3. A Patera or Plate, *Pinax*.
4. A-D. Weights, one with three triangular holes.
5. Egyptian Figure of the Goddess Isis.
6. Egyptian Figure of the God Osiris, mummied: head-dress of plumes; in the hands the usual emblems of flail and hook; beneath the feet the tang to fasten the object to a plinth.
7. Head of a similar figure.
8. A-E. Hairpins and objects of Toilet.
9. A-I. Nine Pins of various forms.
10. A-C. Three Tripods or Candelabra.
11. Egyptian *Situla* or little Bucket; uncertain religious subject in relief.
12. Part of a Chain or Manacle.
13. A Pendant.

PLATE V.

1. Sword, leaf-shaped blade. *Iron.*
2. Sword, rivets on the tang. *Iron.*

3, 4. Spear-heads. *Iron.*

5, 6. Knives. *Iron.*

7. Axe or Pick, of remarkable shape. *Iron.*
8. Arrow-head. *Iron.*
9. Group of conglomerated Arrow-heads. *Iron.*

10, 11. Finger-rings. *Iron.*

12-20. Strigils of various shapes and dimensions. (18, *Bronze.*)

21. Tweezers or small Pliers. *Iron.*
22. Arrow-head with a tang. *Iron.*
23. Boss and Ring. *Iron and Bronze.*
24. A Lock and Hasp. *Iron and Bronze.*
25. Calipers. *Bronze.*
26. Hasp of a Lock. *Bronze.*
27. Stylus. *Bronze.*

PLATE VI.

LEADEN OBJECTS . . . . *Face page* 64

1. A-D. Portion of a Toy Chariot. The wheels oval; the spokes resemble in arrangement those of the chariot wheel painted on the celebrated Panathenaic amphora found by Mr. T. Burgon at Athens, and considered by Mr. C. T. Newton, from its archaic lettering, to be the oldest extant example of the style of vase.
2. Bullet, with Greek inscription in relief.
3. A-C. Bullae with monograms in relief.
4. Engraved Frames.
5. Reeded Jug, perhaps a toy.
6. Jug resembling an Amphora or Situla.
7. Alabastrum or Bottle, grooved body.
8-11. Bullae, with devices, monograms, and inscriptions in relief.
12. Funnel-shaped Vase, perhaps a toy.
13. Covered Pot or Box with contents, glass drops.
14 A. Two-Handled Bowl or Plate.
15. Flat Box with lid.
16. Fibula.
17. Feeder.
[18.] Indented Box.

PLATE VII.

IVORY AND BONE OBJECTS . . *Face page* 70

1, 1 A. Portions of a carved Box.
2. A. B. Finger-ring, carved with a Female Head in profile to the left, perhaps Arsinoe. *Bone.*
3. Spoon, carved handle.
4. Handle of a Spoon.
5. Spoon.
6. Ring.
7. Ring, set with Crystal Bezel.
8. Ring with rectangular carved Bezel.
9. Handle of a Knife, carved in form of a Lion. *Bone.*
10. A Pin-case, or *Etui.*
11. A Die.
12. Two Female Figures, between a term or column. *Bone.*
13. Bridge, or Fret of a Lyre or Musical Instrument.
14. Ornamental Hairpin: a Head.
15. Ornamental Hairpin: a Bust.

16. Carved Hairpin.
17. Carved Torso, part of a Hairpin.
18. Hairpin, with globular top.
19. Hairpin, with pear-shaped top.
20. Carved Hairpin, with Stud.
21. Hairpin, with rectangular Stud.
22. Hairpin, with rectangular head.
23. Carved Head of a Hairpin.
24. Part of a Musical Instrument.
25-28. Studs for Hairpins.
29. Key of a Musical Instrument.

PLATE VIII.

PLATE IX.

1. Carved Christian Tympanum. (*See* pages 109, 110.)
2. Sarcophagus. (*See* pages 100, 101.)

PLATE.

PLATE X.

1. Draped Female Statuette.
2. Draped Male Statuette.
3. Female, seated on a chair, holding an infant.
4. Female, seated in a chair, at her side a fawn.
5. Statuette of a Shepherd wearing conical hat, carrying a Ram over the Shoulders.
6. Squatting Figure, the wrists bound with a thong.
7. Upper part of a Female Statuette.
8. Statuette of a Venus, the arms folded over the head.
9. Base of a Bowl, the feet carved in the form of heads.
10. A Lion's Face, perhaps the Spout of a Fountain.
11. Model of a Sarcophagus or Altar, with archaic ornamentation of zigzags and lozenges.
12-14. Altars or models of Altars.
15-17. Cups, Chalices, or models of Cups.

PLATE XI.

PLATE XII.

PLATE XIII.

PLATE.

PLATE XIV.

1-8. Vessels of pale colour with dark brown ornamentation.
9. Grotesque Figure.
10. Lamp, in form of a Fish.
11. Lamp for two wicks, ornamental design.
12. Grotesque Figure.
13. Rhyton, a Goat's Head.
14. Tetine or Sprinkler, in form of a Goat.
15. Lamp, in form of a Dog.
16. Tetine, in form of a Bull.
17. Lamp, in form of a Ram.
18. Portable Calidarium or Warmer.
19. Lamp for two wicks, in form of two Female Feet cut off at the
Ankles.
20. Portable Warmer.

LIST OF ILLUSTRATIONS.

f

287, 288. Mould of a Lamp. *Terra-Cotta*   .   .   283
289, 290. Mould of a Lamp. *Terra-Cotta*   .   .   ib.
291. Early Cypriote Coin—a Sphinx. *Silver*   .   .   287
292. Early Cypriote Coin—a Ram. *Silver*   .   .   288
293. Coin of King Evelthon. *Silver*   .   .   .   ib.
294. Early Cypriote Coin—a Ram. *Silver*   .   .   289
295. Coin of Azbaal, or Baal-Melek, Kings of Kitium. *Silver.*   ib.
296. Coin of Azbaal. *Silver*   .   .   .   .   ib.
297. A Variant. *Silver*   290
298. Another. *Silver*   .   .   .   .   ib.
299. Early Cypriote Coin—a Ram. *Silver*   .   .   291
300. Early Cypriote Coin—a Demi-Lion. *Silver*   .   .   ib.
301. Early Cypriote Coin—a Lion's Head. *Silver* .   .   293
302. Cypriote Bilingual Coin of Nicocles or Nicocreon. *Copper*   ib.
303. Cypriote Coin of Nicocles or Nicocreon. *Silver*   .   294
304. Early Cypriote Coin. *Silver*   .   .   .   ib.
305. Early Cypriote Coin. *Silver*   .   .   .   ib.
306. Cypriote Coin. *Silver*   .   .   295
307. Cypriote Coin. *Silver*   .   .   ib.
308. Early Coin. *Silver*   .   .   ib.
309. Coin of Cyprus. *Copper* .   .   ib.
310. Coin of Cyprus. *Electrum*   .   296
311. Coin of Alexander the Great. *Gold* .   ib.
312. Lycian Coin. *Silver*   .   .   ib.
313. Coin of Antiochus II, King of Syria. *Electrum*   297
314. Coin of Corinth. *Silver* .   .   ib.
315. Coin of Eretria in Euboea. *Silver* .   ib.
316. Uncertain Greek Coin. *Silver*   .   ib.
317. Coin of Ephesus : Lysanias the Magistrate. *Silver* ib.
318. Coin of Celenderis in Cilicia. *Silver*   .   298
319. Coin of Miletus. *Silver* .   .   ib.
320. Coin of Soli in Cilicia. *Silver*   ib.
321. Coin of Judæa. *Copper* .   .   ib.
322. Coin of Rhodes. *Silver* .   .   ib.
323. Coin of a Phœnician City. *Copper* .   299
324. Coin of Attaleia. *Copper* .   .   ib.
325. Hoard of Coins in a Jar. *Terra-Cotta*   301
326. Cover of Fig. 325. *Stone.*   302
Larnaka (Kitium)   303
Coin of Cleopatra   310
Cypriote characters   . 313-15
Statuette. *Terra-Cotta*   .   316

Coin of Nicocles and Salamis.   *Silver.*

" O Salamina, o reggia
  Splendente d'Evagora !
  O del prudente Nicocle
  Alta regal dimora !—
  Or giaccion frantumate
  Tue moli smisurate ;
      E sul terren, che Cérere
  E Bacco fean che s'apra
  Di frondi al festeggiar,
  Si vede or ruminar
  L'irsuta capra."

                B.

CHAPTER I.

SALAMINIA.

HE ruins of the ancient city of Salamis[1] or Salaminium, in the island of Cyprus, are distant about one hour's journey from the shore, and about a quarter of an hour's journey from the remaining vestiges of the ancient and celebrated harbour of Salaminia, which has now almost wholly disappeared beneath the shingle thrown up by the sea. It is situated in the middle of the eastern coast of the island, somewhat north of the river Pediæus.[2] The powerful agency of earthquakes—frequent in the island—may also account in some measure

[1] This site must not be confounded with the island of Salamis off the West Coast of Attica, from which it is separated by a narrow channel. This is said to have been called *Salamis*, from the name of a daughter of Asopus, a Greek River God. It was colonised at an early period by the Æacidæ of Ægina. Telamon, son of Æacus, fled thither after murdering his half brother Phocus, and obtained possession of the island. The old city of Salamis, which gives its name to the new Salamis in Cyprus, stood on the south side of the island opposite Ægina; but this was afterwards deserted, and a new city of the same name built on the east coast, opposite Attica. Salamis is chiefly remarkable on account of the great battle which took place just off its coast, when the powerful Persian fleet, brought down by Xerxes for the destruction of the Greek Empire, was signally defeated by the Greeks in the year 480 B.C.

[2] The Pedias, Pedœius, or Pediæus, is the principal river; it rises on the range of Mount Olympus, and in its course irrigates the plains of Lefkosia and Messaria, finally discharging itself into the sea on the east coast at this ancient port of Salamis.

for the subsidence of the ancient buildings. The harbour and the city were, doubtless, connected, as is the case in many Greek sites, by a long and straggling village, now entirely passed away. It was probably destroyed by the earthquake which took place during the reign of Constantine, and entombed many of the inhabitants. At the present day there only exists one monument which may be considered to belong to the first epoch. This is a wall; perhaps a part of the ancient wall bounding the interior area of the harbour. It is now used for a Greek church or chapel. The method which has been employed in the construction of this wall, of which so small a fragment is left, has no parallel except in the composition of the walls of the temple of Baalbec in Syria; like this, the wall of Salaminia consists of a mass of masonry measuring thirty-four feet in length and eighteen in breadth. There is a Greek tradition, of little or no importance, which, indeed, I do not think worth while to discuss, and merely allude to because it has been taken seriously by several distinguished archaeologists and historians, in which it is related that Salaminia was constructed by Teucer[1], the hero of Troy, son of Telamon and Hesione, after having been driven out by his father because he did not wreak vengeance upon those who were concerned in the death of his step-brother Ajax. There is also another legend, to the effect that Belus, king of Sidon, conquered the island of Cyprus and made a gift of it to the hero Teucer, who thereupon founded the city of Salamis, not long after the Trojan war.

We have still extant an Assyrian monument as old as the reign of Sargon, B.C. 800. of which the inscription records the name of a king of Salamis. Herodotus in like manner makes mention of several royal per-

[1] Teucer is related to have married Eune, the daughter of Cyprus, by whom he became the father of Asteria.

sonages, reigning in Salaminia from B.C. 566 to B.C.
495. The Greek invaders appear to have descended upon
the island in parties, under the leadership of small or
petty chiefs, who seized upon the quiet bays, wherever
the scenery of the coast held out an inviting prospect, and
speedily brought their armed ships to land. Then they
made their way into the dense forests, hewed down the
trees, and, after constructing entrenchments, awaited
with shield and spear to see whether the natives of the
island, who had assembled in the distance, would dare to
attack them. All around the coast similar inroads were
continually repeated, until at length the invaders, em-
boldened by constant successes, ventured further up the
course of the rivers, and there established their infant
colonies, which became the nucleus of a petty state. This
Greek occupation of the island of Cyprus lasted for a considerable period, in concert with the presence of Syrians
of Phœnician or Jewish descent, until at length the two
races became assimilated both in speech and customs, and
formed but one people. Certain inscriptions, according to
Von Löher, that have been found in the island, were at
first quite impossible to decipher, because they were
attributed to some very ancient people, older even than
the Phœnicians. Further examination of them has, however, resulted in the discovery that the language is of
Græco-Cyprian origin. For a considerable length of time
the city of Salamis was subject to the sway of Amosis,
King of Egypt, about B.C. 540. Upon the downfall of
the Egyptian supremacy, it passed under the dominion of
the Persians, until Evagoras, who claimed to be descended
from Teucer, the Greek founder of the colony of Salaminia, in B.C. 410 captured the city by surprise, after a
sanguinary battle, and thus rendered the island of Cyprus
an independent kingdom, he himself being King of Salaminia. Evagoras succumbed to a tragic fate, being assas-
sinated by an eunuch, who at the same time despatched

his eldest son. Nicocles, the second son of Evagoras, succeeded his father in the year B.C. 374, and was put to
death by Ptolemy in B.C. 310. Passing over intermediate events, we find the Romans in the year A.D. 60
in possession of Salamis, converting the whole island into
a province of the Roman empire, and delivering it into
the jurisdiction of Cato.

During the reign of the Emperor Trajan, Salamis experienced considerable destruction at the hands of the
Jews, who revolted against the oppression of their Roman
masters, who organised a great massacre of these unfor-
tunate people. Since that time no Jew has ever established himself in the island. Probably the motive of
their absence is more owing to the fact that there is
hardly any trade in the island, for, in fact, where trade does
not prevail Israelite communities are never to be found.

Under the dominion of Constantine the Great, Salaminia became a town of considerable importance, from its
commerce; it developed itself as a mistress of the whole
Mediterranean; its harbour was rich in exportations
and a centre of the grain trade; so much so, that Salaminia eventually became the wealthiest town in the
island of Cyprus. It was, as recorded above, during the
reign of the Emperor Constantine that Salamis was destroyed by earthquake, and the inhabitants rendered
homeless and houseless. The Emperor assisted in the
loan of the money required for the rebuilding, and the
former residents constructed a new town out of the
greater part of the ruined walls, in token of gratitude
endowing the new city with the name of Constantia; but
the new city in its turn fell a prey to subterranean dis-
turbances, and is now lying in ruins.

" From the middle of the seventh," says Von Löher, in
Mrs. Joyner's excellent translation, " to the middle of
the tenth century, the hand of man caused fearful de-
vastation. Hordes of pirates appeared upon the coast,

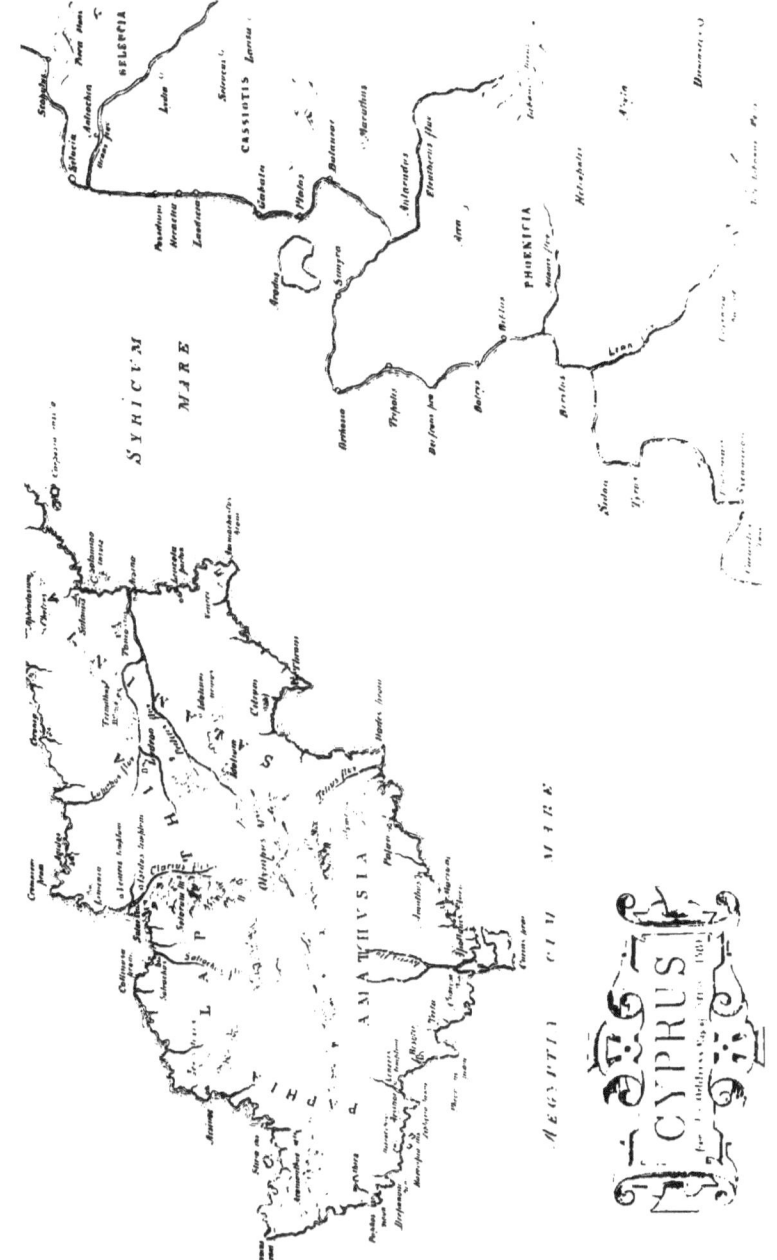

who, landing at every available place, set fire to the towns and villages, and when the inhabitants fled to save themselves, laid hands on everything within their reach. Money and fruit, men and cattle—all were hurried on board their ships. Swiftly as they had come, they departed. In vain the fleet sent out by government endeavoured to follow them.

" Among the islands and havens of the Grecian Archipelago concealment and shelter were easily obtained ; the only resource was to place watchmen upon commanding points of the coast, from whence they could see to a distance, and to build towers and beacons, whence signals could be made by means of fire and smoke as soon as any suspicious craft made its appearance. On seeing this signal, all the inhabitants of the coast fled into the interior, taking their children and cattle and their money and valuables with them ; and there they remained concealed until another signal from the watchmen told them that the coast was clear. Next came robbers of a still worse description. The former only sought for what could be readily carried off in their ships ; these others were land robbers. The pirates only struck down or burned whatever hindered them in their proceedings ; the others destroyed for destruction's sake, and, collecting men like sheep, drove them into slavery. These were Arabs. From their sandy and rocky deserts, they brought with them a savage hatred against all religious edifices ; which they levelled to the ground. It was now that the ancient buildings of Cyprus suffered. The old temples were reduced to ruins, the towns were destroyed, and everything Greek or Roman perished. The Arabs wished to establish their new Government in the island, and for this purpose they only required bare ground."

It appears that the town of Arsinoe was anterior in point of date to Salaminia, and from the former the town of Salaminia was colonised. Among the ruins of Sala-

minia a village gradually arose, and rapidly increased in
size, which afterwards acquired, as has already been said,
the name of Constantia.[1] Upon the ruins of this, in its
turn, the city of Famagusta was built. Famagusta, too,
fell under the power of the Turks. In fact, the village of
Varoscia, which represents it now, is daily spreading in
size ; and if Famagusta were gifted with a harbour by its
new inhabitants, very soon a Victoria might arise upon
the ancient site of Salamis.

And now that I have briefly recounted the traditions
and historical records concerning Salamis and other Cypriote sites, I shall proceed to lay before archæologists
and students an account of my discoveries in those places,
and relate simply my impressions, and as far as possible
endeavour to describe the exact details of the spots where
my excavations were carried out.

[1] The *Istoria di Cipro*, by Florio Bustron (*Brit. Mus. Add. MS.
8630*), speaks of discoveries of antiquities in the author's day (seven-
teenth century) at Salaminia. He says: " Near to Salaminia was a
town called Costanza or Costanzin, a large and strongly fortified town,
and very rich, with fine palaces with marble columns. In removing the
earth, were found many medals in gold, silver, and copper ; rings, earrings, necklaces, bracelets in gold and silver, and other ancient monuments in terra-cotta or stone. It is not very long ago that the tomb of
St. Epiphanius was found with a Greek inscription. Now it is all in
ruins, and people call these ruins Old Famagusta." The excavations,
which I was the first to carry out on this site systematically, confirm
this statement.

CHAPTER II.

GENERAL IDEA OF CYPRIOTE ANTIQUITIES.

NTIQUITIES found in Cyprus comprise fictile vases, statues in terra-cotta, bronze, and stone, glass vessels. bronze implements and arms, alabastra, ornaments in gold and silver, gems of precious stones, and coins of different epochs. Most of these objects have been discovered in tombs. Numerous sculptured statues and bas-reliefs were found among the ruins of temples or in walled enclosures, into which, after being broken, they were thrown by pious converts to Christianity, in obedience to an edict of Constantine the Great. Some recent excavators in Cyprus have fallen into what is, I think, the error of supposing that wherever sculptured remains have been discovered there is the site of a temple. This is certainly not always the case, for I have examined many similar places, and dug there in search of plans and buildings, endeavouring to learn if any structures had existed there; but I found only shallow foundations of large squares and enclosures, with no indications of temples, no columns, nor any signs of wells. In these enclosures the broken statues lay in heaps. In a hollow of the mountain side, not far from the Temple of Apollo, in Kurium. I unearthed a number of fragments of statues which had been thrown together. The heads were in the lowest

layer, the torsi in the middle, and the feet of the statuettes on the uppermost layer over all, at about a yard below the surface. A little later, in a dried-up stream near some ruins, which appear to be those of the city of Throni, an enclosure forty feet square was discovered, containing parts of more than a thousand statuettes in terracotta, of a type representing priestesses bearing offerings. Of these, I reconstructed about two hundred entire figures, of which the tallest was three feet high. They are beautifully decorated, particularly their crowned or turreted heads ; but I saw neither columns nor bas-reliefs to indicate the site of a temple, while the walls of the quadrangle were thin, a fact which confirms the notion that they were built for the sole purpose of forming an enclosure. In obedience to the above mentioned imperial order, many temples were destroyed, while others were appropriated to the worship of the Christians. Even now may be seen ancient hypogea, which have been converted into Greek chapels. In them traces of their first use may sometimes be discovered ; others, which were probably used in a similar manner for Christian worship, were stripped of their Pagan appendages, and have fallen into decay, so as to leave no vestiges of the statues buried in their ruins. Beneath the *débris* of temples, and in tombs, many articles in bronze have been discovered, including armour, weapons, and implements, such as bucklers, axe-heads, and spear-heads, statuettes, mirrors, pateræ, strigils, and such objects. A few pateræ are decorated with sculptures in relief, and in rare cases some were found which had been incised with mythological and other representations. The alabastra are of different forms, but, generally speaking, in a poor state of preservation. Very few bear inscriptions. Gold personal ornaments have been discovered, such as earrings, finger-rings, bracelets, armlets, necklaces, and buttons ; also mortuary chaplets of a flimsy foil or leaf of gold, with embossed ornaments. Some children's finger-rings have letters pricked in outline with a votive inscription.

Intaglios of clumsy work, some of which were artistically engraved, have been found with inscriptions, which are generally personal names. Glass is frequently found among Cypriote antiquities; the majority of the examples are remarkable on account of their beautiful iridescence, and for the variety of their forms. Coloured glass comprises articles of blue, purple, and canary tints, and now and then painted unguentarium covers occur, representing Venus, Bacchus holding a bunch of grapes, and other subjects. Some objects of this nature are inscribed with mottoes and artists' names in relief; these are eagerly sought after. The glass vessels discovered in Cyprus belong, in my opinion, to the periods of the Ptolemies and of the Roman domination in the island.

This opinion is confirmed by the dates of the copper coins that were found in the tombs with the vessels. Cippi sometimes occur in the same tombs with works in glass, and the latter bear the names of their owners and an invocation. These sepulchral relics are believed to be of Christian origin and due to periods of persecution. I have not yet been able to convince myself what period should be assigned to those objects of opaque and enamelled glass which by some excavators have been called "Phœnician," on the ground that they were found with terra-cotta amphoræ bearing Phœnician inscriptions in black or red. These examples in glass are of two kinds, viz., those which are shaped like amphoræ, and those which are enamelled and pear-shaped; the latter are of a greenish colour and very thick. Not having found any coins in the same tombs with these vessels, I am unable to say to what age the latter belong; but it is my intention to examine further into this subject in the chapters devoted to this branch of the work. In point of variety and value, antiquities of glass may be divided into groups as follows:—

1st. Those with embossed figures, ornaments, and inscriptions : those having the shape of the human head; and those representing animals, fruit, etc.

2nd. Unguentarium covers with subjects painted in black on white or red grounds; these are exceedingly rare.

3rd. The so-called Phœnician examples, of which I have already spoken.

4th. Those of large size, of rare form, and fine iridescence, as well as vessels of coloured glass.

On the inscribed specimens in glass, the letters are Greek, which was, and is, the language prevailing in the island. The inscriptions on these articles consist of the names of the makers, or of the persons to whom the relics had belonged, or to whom they were given. A few glass cups have been found with inscriptions round the rim in high relief; on one vessel the owner is desired to keep the maker in remembrance. The iridescence, as is well known, is produced by the gradual decomposition of glass, which occurs when the material has been covered with earth, or has contained a liquid which has afterwards hardened. In the first case, decomposition is in flakes ; in the second, it is granular; the latter being of rarer occurrence, is the more prized. Vessels with granular iridescence are generally found resting on rocks, slabs, or in sarcophagi ; empty vessels deposited under similar conditions become brittle, but not iridescent. With regard to examples of Greek and Roman origin, I carefully examined a site near Larnaca, yet I found with them only Ptolemaic coins, principally of the later monarchs; therefore I am inclined to think that these vessels belong to the epoch of 200 or 300 years B.C.

Of the coins found in Cyprus, those in copper are most abundant, but they are generally illegible and much corroded. The series represented in this metal are coins of the Ptolemies; Roman in general, and Imperial Roman of Cyprus with Greek legends; and Byzantine. In gold we have coins of Cyprus, with Cypriote, Phœnician, or Greek letters, including staters of Philip and Alexander; scyphati of the Latin kings of the island: all these are rare; the Byzantine instances are less so. Gold solidi, which are flat and concave, were kept in families, and suspended round the necks of children, in order to bring good luck to the wearer. The silver coins found are the early ones of the island, as above, and due to Alexander, or to the Ptolemies; or they are Roman in general and Imperial of Cyprus; besants of the Latin kings of Cyprus occur; likewise Venetian coins. The early coins of Cyprus are rare. We now and then meet with coins in billon, which belong almost entirely to the time of the Crusades, and are of the Lusignan dynasty.

CHAPTER III

GOLD OBJECTS.

FRONTALS — NECKLACES — HAIR PINS — EAR-RINGS — FINGER-RINGS — NONDESCRIPT OBJECTS, AND PARTS OF PERSONAL ORNAMENTS.

HE relics of this precious metal consist of frontals and other parts of face-masks for the dead, such as eyepieces and mouthpieces, besides necklaces, hairpins, earrings, finger-rings, nondescript objects, and parts of personal ornaments. Some of the engraved gems are hereafter described with the finger-rings. A few more occur in the class of nondescript objects.

It must be understood that many golden antiquities found in the tombs of Cyprus and in other countries, such as Etruria and Greece, are obviously of too fragile a nature for use by the living. They are sometimes so small that children alone could have worn them, if, indeed, they were worn at all. It is evident that a considerable proportion of these relics, like those found in other sites, were constructed for mortuary service only, that is, they were designed for the grave alone ; and it is likewise beyond a doubt that these are substitutes or *fac-similes* in all other respects but solidity[1] of the prototypes which remained above ground with the survivors.

FRONTALS.

No class of golden relics discovered in Cyprus or elsewhere, not even the diadems or so-called "minds" which

[1] In tombs of the Cyrenaica, sham jewels of lead were often found.

occur in Ireland and other lands of the Celts, equals in interest those face-masks, to the very limited number of which known to be existing I have been fortunate enough to make some very important additions, which were gathered in a new field, and exhibit characteristics of their own. Dr. Schliemann, the celebrated excavator of the Troad, who based some very remarkable theories, and historical as well as personal deductions, on the fact, found such masks at Mycenæ. Gold frontlets were discovered by him on the site of his "Ilion"; others were exhumed at Kertch, Olbia, and other places in the Khersonese—sites which had contributed much wealth of antique golden works to the matchless collection in the museum at St. Petersburg. Such masks have also occurred in Phœnicia and in Mesopotamia, that yet but half-explored world of treasures of ancient use and beauty.[1]

The relics of this kind, however great may be their antiquity—and there can be no doubt they range within considerable spaces of time—are exceptionally interesting, because they exhibit distinct traces of primitive ornamentation of the nature hereinafter described in respect to each example. Among others, I found a frontal indented *en repoussé*, with lines marked in a pattern which illustrates the art-history and geographical situations of Cyprus, as it was alternately subjected to the influence of Egypt, Assyria, Phœnicia, Greece, or Rome. Lying, as the island does, on the highway between the East and West, at times an *entrepôt*, and occasionally impressed by the taste or education of more than one of these nations at the

---

[1] Writing of his discoveries in that vast metropolis of the dead, Warka, in Lower Chaldea, Mr. Loftus, in his *Chaldea and Susiana*, p. 211, stated, of the corpses he exhumed with their slipper-shaped coffins : "Thin gold leaf sometimes appears to have covered the face like a veil ; and one or two broad ribbons of gold not unfrequently occur on each side of the head." "Gold laminæ, with archaic reliefs, were found in *quasi* Etruscan tombs at Monteroni."—See *Cities and Cemeteries of Etruria*, Dennis, 1878, i, 223, note.

same time, it is not wonderful that relics which were found in Cyprus are of an extremely complex character in respect to the art they display, and that in not a few cases it is absolutely impossible to discriminate between these influences, and thus to decide without a doubt to which nationality they severally refer. This uncertainty affects our judgment, and often compels us to hesitate about the very age of certain relics, which we cannot with certainty attribute to one more than the other of the powers which have successively dominated in the island.

Broadly speaking, however, I cannot be wrong in ascribing the greatest antiquity to the remains in which the older forms of Egyptian designs occur; the next to that class which bears traces of Assyria; the third to those in which we recognise the marks of Phœnicia. In the last case, however, there is this difficulty, that Phœnician designs, as such, can hardly be said to have existed independently and without any reference to Egypt on the one hand, and Assyria on the other. As might be expected, the art-works of Tyre and Sidon, which undoubtedly abound in my collections, are distinguishable from others by the presence of the combined influences of the eastern and southern neighbours of the greatest trading and manufacturing people of antiquity. In fact, where we find Egyptian modes corrupted by Assyrian admixture, or Assyrian modes affected by *quasi* Egyptian rendering, we recognise what is universally ascribed to Phœnician makers. The fourth order in antiquity among Cypriote remains comprises works which are very numerous, and, generally speaking, unusually beautiful, and emphasized by Greek taste, skill, and learning, in design. The fifth order is Roman, which, strange to say, is hardly ever unaffected by that Greek spirit which thus proves to have been for ages domiciled as paramount in Cyprus. As to later orders than the Roman it is not necessary for me to be concerned at present, beyond what may be required to enable me to state, that in the rich collection of coins which I have formed are specimens of Byzantine, or later Greek manufacture, of Gothic, Venetian, and even Renaissance origin.

I have been led into this disquisition by means of the indented pattern on the gold relic which is here engraved (fig. 1), and displays very distinctly the Egyptian influence on the Assyrian type of ornamentation.

These remarks are applicable to the art-works of Cyprus of all kinds, not to golden instances alone. But the difficulty of discrimination, to which I have referred, is greatly increased by the existence of a numerous body of nondescript antiquities, especially terra-cottas, to which we are accustomed to ascribe a purely native origin, and cannot group them with either of the classes in question

Fig. 1.   Frontal, with Archaic Ornamentation.   Gold.

above. They are generally rude and uncouth, disproportioned, and without distinguishing style. They are represented by numerous instances in the Lawrence-Cesnola collection; in that which enriches the Metropolitan Museum at New York; Dr. Schliemann found the like on his "Trojan" hill, and was much exercised by their peculiarities; they have been found in Greece; and in Etruria. As to the last-named place, the museum at Bologna, and other provincial collections in the north of Italy, are by no means poor in respect to these quaint and rude, if not invariably primæval relics. We must never forget that mere rudeness of execution does not absolutely affirm the extreme antiquity of any object.

To return to the golden frontals of this collection, I

may indicate one example (fig. 2), which is more elaborately decorated, and, perhaps, not so old as the above-named example. It comprises a punctured and engraved pattern of a border of alternate broad and flat, and thin and narrow leaves, arranged like the elements of the well-known echinus moulding, and between lines of punctured dots; within this border are what look like bunches of grapes *en repoussé*, in groups of three each, forming twelve in all. At the angles of this plate of gold are holes, intended, doubtless, to attach the strings, by means of which it was secured on the face of the deceased.

From the same tomb comes a mouthpiece with a similar punctured border to the above, but without the grape-like granulations. All these objects came from Idalium

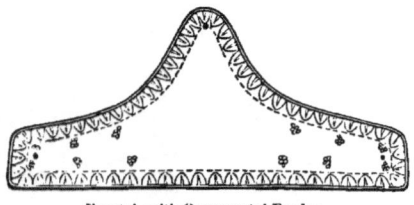

Fig. 2.   Frontal, with Ornamental Border.   *Gold.*

(Dali), with another narrow mouthpiece without ornaments of any kind. Like the frontal last represented, the other objects exhibit holes for strings. I have specimens also of oval plates of thin gold intended for eyepieces, the former bears on its edges indented radial lines which may have been intended to represent the eyelashes of the wearer.

Of pure gold there were found during excavations nearly a dozen flowers of beaten metal, cut to the shapes of leaves, and grouped in cinquefoils, quatrefoils, and trefoils, and severally indented *en repoussé* to reproduce the fibres and veins of foliage (figs. 3, 4, 5, 6). Exemplary specimens are parts of mortuary chaplets and

very beautiful instances of a class of ornaments which is
fairly represented in many European collections, as for
example, in the Louvre, and in the museums at Naples
and Rome. In the British Museum is a fine bronze helmet
of Etruscan form, of the purest type, about which appears
the golden wreath worn by the warrior to whom this
piece of armour belonged. Other examples of the same
kind exist elsewhere.

I have also an eye (fig. 6a) and a mouthpiece (fig. 6b)
decorated by the same means as that mentioned above,
and with volutes of a very simple, if not primitive Ionic
character; so simple indeed are they, that we seem to
trace in their plain forms something which may be called

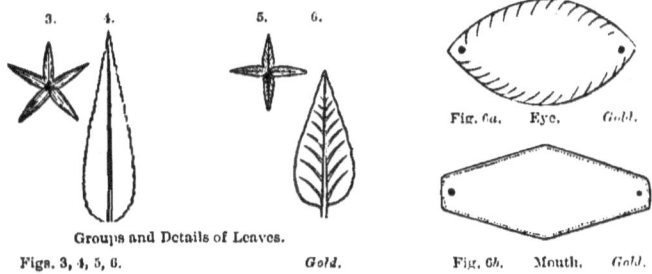

3. 4. 5. 6.

Groups and Details of Leaves.
Figs. 3, 4, 5, 6. Gold.

Fig. 6a. Eye. Gold.

Fig. 6b. Mouth. Gold.

the archaic Babylonian or severer Assyrian mood; these
volutes are made to issue from little vase-shaped stems,
and were probably designed by a local artist of Cyprus
while under Phœnician inspiration. This pattern is en-
riched by a border of |⁻|_|⁻|_|-shaped fret. There is,
from the same site as that illustrated by the last-named
relic, another fragment of gold-leaf, which exhibits
double scrolls of more distinctly Greek character and,
probably, later date than any of the above, the execution
of the ornaments being more advanced than that of those
mentioned before. In the same class are fragments of a
mesh indented with patterns of a nature similar to that
which has already been described.

D

NECKLACES.

There are several fine examples of this class in the collection, and more fragments of such ornaments, being pendants and separate beads. The first which I shall mention consists of a linked chain of gold wires and oblong cornelian beads, the angles of which are, after a fashion which frequently occurs in Etruscan as well as in Greek works, chamfered off (fig. 7). To this is attached an oval Greek gem representing Ceres, and of a good style

Fig. 7.   Gold and Cornelian Necklace.

and period of design. On the back of the gold setting of the stone is the same lattice-like ornament which we observe in the cornelian pendant of the necklace itself. This may be said to attest the idea that the antiquity of the ornament is, comparatively, not very considerable; for the style it exhibits is somewhat indefinite, probably Roman derived from Greece, as was commonly the case in many good instances of the same kind and origin. With this the worn state of the surface

of the gem agrees well enough, because it contrasts with
the sharpness of the state of the oblong beads; it may
be, however, that the gem is a comparatively recent
addition to the carcanet, with which it is now associated.
There is also a smaller example than the last, which
is unquestionably due to the same period and mode of

Fig. 8.   Gold and Enamel Necklace.

art; it consists of alternate beads of cornelian, or sard,
and twisted links of gold wire. Another necklace which
I have found is composed of a group of fragments of
several carcanets, probably including some relics of widely
differing dates, brought together here for convenience of
exhibition and preservation; among the objects in question is one of the conventional grapes, or granulations,

en repoussé, and a pendant of spiral flutings, which may be of late Greek or Romano-Greek origin; there are double cones of gold which suggest the Assyrian type of jewellery, to which the mode they illustrate undoubtedly pertains.

It appears to me that these cones show traces of provincial art, of the period of the Assyrian domination in Cyprus, which may be called ancient even with regard to the exceptional antiquity of works in gold. Similar types appear in another specimen, which comprises, with many other examples of differing types, two very curious sexual emblems, male and female, very delicately and neatly modelled, evidently designed, like numerous similar relics found elsewhere, to be used as personal ornaments. I have no doubt these phallic emblems are pure Greek, and

Figs. 9, 10, 11, 12.   Pendants of Necklaces.   *Gold.*

of the best period of the art of that country. They show, with the conventional treatment which could hardly be dispensed with, even in Greece of old or Cyprus, where there would be few scruples as to the use of such ornaments, a fine order of execution and a great amount of naturalistic character. To the same grouped necklace is appended a lotus flower of gold, with hollows designed to hold enamel or coloured pastes. It is doubtless Greek, with Egyptian characteristics, the latter being more distinctly marked in the choice of the subject than its execution (fig. 8).

Similar jewels have been found in Lower Italy, Greece, and Egypt. Cyprus furnished similar relics to the Metropolitan Museum of New York; and it is certain that necklaces, either whole or fragmentary, have been found

in other parts of Cyprus, which, from the designs and
devices exhibited by the pendants and other details, may
be compared with the specimens that were discovered
during the progress of my own excavations at Salaminia.[1] The well-known works of Sir Gardner Wilkinson,
Mariette, and other writers who have treated on the
jewellery and goldsmiths' work of the Egyptians, do not
fail to inform the student of the extreme closeness of the
likeness which may be recognised between a very large
proportion of the relics of that category which have been

Fig. 13.   Necklace.   Gold.

found in Cyprus and those of Egyptian antiquity generally. The museums at Alnwick Castle, Naples, and
London, abound with such instances as might well have
been discovered in Cyprus, instead of on the banks of the
Nile. In speaking of earrings, and other works of personal ornament, I shall have occasion to refer to this
similitude, which may almost be taken to attest the
common origin of very considerable numbers of these

[1] See figs. 9-12, p. 20.

articles. Several circumstances, to which I shall allude
by-and-by, prompt the notion that we ought to look to
the goldsmiths of Tyre rather than to those of Egypt or
Cyprus, for the origin and manufacture of the greater
portion of these beautiful relics, as the examples display
Egyptian or Assyrian types of subjects, and are not of
the highest order in art.   The art-work of the Greek
goldsmith, of course, surpassed all others, except its con-
gener, the marvellously modelled and exquisitely laborious "Etruscan" works, or rather those which appear to
be Phœnician and are found in Etruria as well as other
Mediterranean countries.   The museum at Leyden contains a noble collection of Egyptian jewellery which might
profitably be compared by the student of Cypriote antiquities.   The British Museum is rich in personal ornaments attesting the fact to which I have alluded, i.e.,
the similitude of much Cypriotic and Nilotic gold
work.   Nor is it thus with regard to works in the
precious metal only: at Alnwick, at Leyden, are numerous objects, such as toilet-boxes carved in wood, or
moulded in earthenware, in the forms of ducks, geese,
fish, and other things, which closely resemble specimens
in the collection before us.   Bronze and earthenware
vases found in Thebes, or represented by wall-paintings
at that place, depart, in but small respects, from those
which I can place before the reader as brought from
Cyprus.   There is a picture in the British Museum, brought
from Thebes, which represents a party of Egyptian ladies
at what may be called an "afternoon tea", eagerly dis-
cussing their ear-rings, the patterns of which are very
like those which occur in gold in this collection, and are
reproduced in the statuettes of terra-cotta, to which I
shall, farther on, call attention, as illustrating in a
very complete, curious, and perfectly veritable manner, the Cypriotic fashions in personal decorations with
gold and other precious materials.   "The jewels of

silver and jewels of gold" which are represented in this collection, may be taken to be of the kind occasionally alluded to in the Scriptures, and like them to be due in no inconsiderable numbers to those Syrian and Sidonian artificers[1] whose skill undoubtedly had much to do in furnishing models and types of inestimable value in the development of Greek art, which, of all the classes in question, is the noblest and most pure.

Besides the phallic and other emblems, *i.e.*, the lotus

Fig 14.   Statuette shewing manner of wearing Necklace.   *Terra-cotta.*

flower, etc., there are two differently shaped beads of cornelian. The mode in which the objects of this group have been attached to each other, proves that they were intended to be worn as a group, as in Fig. 14.

The surfaces of the beads have suffered by attrition. Among other articles included with the necklace which contains the phallic emblems to which I have drawn the attention of the reader, is a very small pomegranate in gold. A pendant similar to this is in the New York Museum. Both these articles are likely to have been made by the same goldsmith; they closely resemble

[1] See Ezekiel's denunciation of Tyrus, Chapters xxvi, xxvii.

each other. and they were found in the same city.
Another in this group is very curious and valuable; it is
a small model of an archaic type of gold, reproducing
the great club of Hercules, which appears as if encircled
by two bands intended to strengthen the weapon; the
knots on its surface have been given in enamel in a manner like that which is known as *cloisonnée* (fig. 8). Representations of Hercules, generally of the skin-clad, satyr-
like type, and imbued with a certain element of satyric
grotesqueness, will be found in this collection among the

Fig. 15.   Gold and Sard Bead Necklace.

numerous terra-cotta statuettes. The club of this hero
is no unfrequent subject in the Greek artistic antiquities,
but this minute model in gold, or perhaps *electrum*, is one
of the most curious of its order. Another club is used
as the pendant of an ear-ring.

Another necklace (fig. 15) comprises dark sard beads of
an oblong form, similar to those which have been already
described in the same terms, and strung on their original
gold wires. With these is a tear-shaped bead of glass,

now oxidized and beautifully iridescent, and enclosed in a frame of gold closely fitting its shape. This frame, or setting, has a delicate line of punctured dots by way of border. The exceptional character of this little relic suggests that it was a personal relic, a souvenir designed to commemorate some pathetic event, some death, or event of love. Attached to this carcanet is a pendant of very lovely design, doubtless originally an ear-ring, and including within a lyre-shaped frame a very delicate fern, or acanthus leaf, cut from a plate of gold, modelled with rare artistic tact, and designed with spirit. Three cylindrical beads have terminated this pendant in a sort of fringe ; of these beads a piece of emerald, or glass, remains in the centre, while, at the sides, only the wire on which the now missing beads were strung, exists. Two other stones, out of three, are enclosed by gold settings in this pendant.

There is also a wedge or obelisk of crystal, pierced for suspension, and retaining the wire by means of which it may have been supported as one of the pendants of a necklace. Likewise a second crystal obelisk, which is of octangular section, whereas the section of its companion here is oblong ; it is still supported by a carefully applied band of gold, to which was attached the little chain or wire supporting the object in its place among the pendants of a large carcanet for the neck, or bandeau for the head, such as the before-named Egyptian women wear in the picture which was brought from Thebes. There was found also an object which is undoubtedly a pendant, like that which is described above, and the companion ear-ring to the latter. It comprises the fern-leaf and similar cylinders of glass or green stone, and, by way of companion for them, a small pearl.

In the same group is an oval sard set in a square tablet of gold, and furnished with a hook for suspending it with some other objects of personal adornment.

Another class of pendants appear in the gold or electrum sheathing of the tooth of a beast, which may be a trophy of prowess or good luck in hunting. Another similar object belongs to two similar remains, both mounted in the above manner; these teeth are furnished at the back with little tube-like appendages or hollow rods; the last seem to have been used to attach strings to the mounting of the teeth.

There was found, in the course of my diggings, a

Fig. 16.   Gold and Jewelled Necklace.

necklet of gold, with a circular pendant disk of the same metal, and embossed with a full face of Phœbus of Greek workmanship; found at Salamis, this article, like most of its fellows from the same city, attests that place was the most Greek of all the towns of Cyprus. In the collection there is also (fig. 16) a composite circle of beads of glass, amethyst, cornelian and other materials, some of which are engraved and moulded, and disks of gold, which exhibit the concentric ring pattern so frequent in the archaic works of nearly all nations, and recognisable as Egyptian, Assyrian, Greek, or Scandinavian, according to the locality in which they have been found. Such concentric rings occur on terra-cotta vases, personal jewellery, arms, and, indeed, nearly everywhere. Herr Helbig, in the *Annali d'Inst. Arch.*, 1875, page 221, seems to have supposed that this pattern is due to metal-working artificers. It appears to me that this is archæological criticism of a somewhat fanciful sort. A pattern of concentric rings is exactly such as would almost suggest itself to any one seeking to decorate an object of any material which admitted enrichment by impressions from tools or fingers while being manufactured in a lathe, or subjected to the use of stamps; indeed, stamps capable of being used to produce such impressions on clay have been found in Egypt and, if my memory does not deceive me, in Assyria. After the chevrons of the almost universal chevron ornament, the primitive type of decorations, were exhausted, the concentric ring arrangement was the next resource of the aboriginal decorator : we need not trouble ourselves with cumbrous affectations of learning on this point, nor send primitive " Indo-European" artists to the East for such crude notions as they, or any one not absolutely imbecile, could be relied on to apply out of their own heads. Undoubtedly this ring pattern very often occurs in works of metal, but, in another mode of application it is the most common of all decorations to vases, pateræ, and other vessels of all countries, and, one might say of all ages, from the completely barbarous to the most cultivated.

Another specimen which I have was found at Salamis, and is, as usual, very Greek. It consists (fig. 17) of prisms of emerald glass, strung on knotted wires of gold and having a pendant, like a fir cone, or rather bottle, a tiny amphora, in fact, not intended, of course, for use in holding scent, but simply as an ornament of a kind illus-

trated by innumerable examples. Pendants, which may
have been applied to ear-rings as well as to necklaces,
appear (see Plate I, fig. 34), where amethysts are set in
little oblong boxes of gold, with triangular groups of
grape-like disks of dark blue glass suspended from them
in their turn, each of which is enclosed in its proper
frame of gold. Amethysts are not uncommon in this
mass of jewellery, but less so than carbuncles, still less
so than cornelians and sards. This is generally the
order of such remains of antiquity, and it is due to the

Fig. 17.   Gold and Emerald Glass Necklace.

frequency of the materials themselves in the countries to
which I refer. There are a few pearls, most of which are
of irregular shapes. Amber, which is so extremely frequent
in Egyptian, Assyrian, Greek, Crimean, the more ancient
Etrurian, and Roman jewellery, and is the most common
of the *quasi* precious materials in northern graves, such
as British interments and otherwise, does not occur. The
fact that most of the ancient amber was brought from
the coasts of the Baltic, which still yield great quantities

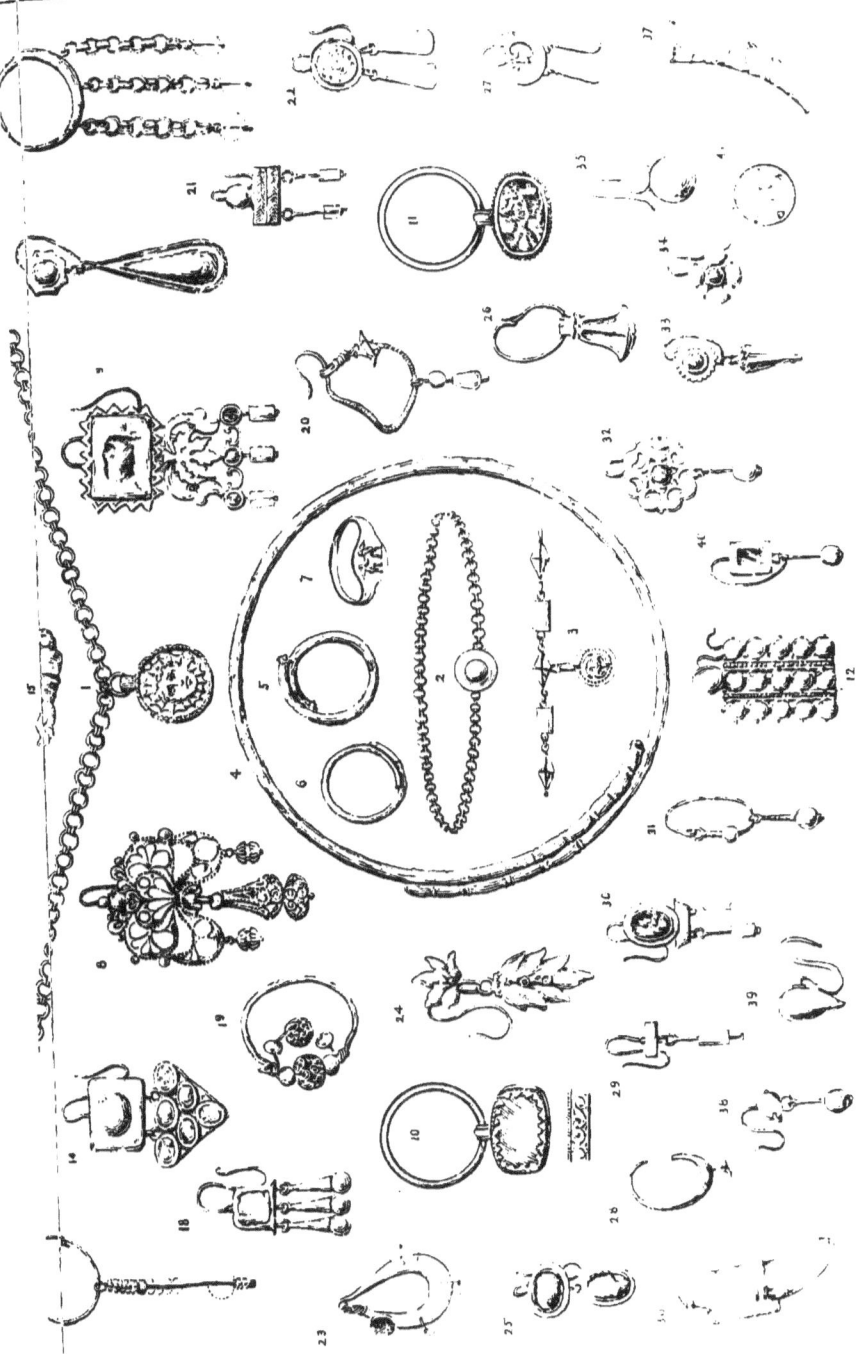

of the material, allows us to account for the characteristic abundance of the substance in northern antiquities.[1]

Homer mentioned the offering of a Phœnician trader, "Beads of bright amber, riveted in gold," to the Queen of Syra.[2] Nevertheless, and quite contrary to our expectations, amber has rarely been found in Cyprus, and I found none.[3]

I have been compelled by considerations of convenience to group here with the necklaces certain fragments of jewellery which may have belonged to ear-rings; on the other hand, the reader will find among objects described in the class of miscellaneous relics a few which probably were parts of necklaces.

HAIR PINS

Are represented in the collection by numerous examples, formed of several materials, such as glass and ivory. Among the superior works is one the head of which is composed of a disk of cornelian, sculptured to represent

[1] So abundant is amber in British graves, that in one series of excavations made in a cemetery of no great extent in Norfolk, not fewer than seven hundred beads were recovered. In England, Denmark, and Scandinavia, it would be an exceptional circumstance to find a group of interments without any amber.

[2] *Odyssey*, xv, 560.

[3] Signor Castellani, in his valuable tract, *Orificeria Italiana* (Roma, 1872), described the archaic jewellery found in the Etruscan provinces, and noticed the great quantity of amber which, with some silver and less gold, has been discovered at Veii, Cervetri, Corneto, Chiusi, and Bologna, ancient cities of the "pre-historic" people whom he designates as "Tyrrhenes", as well as in places not inhabited by the Etrurians, between whose works and those commonly attributed to the "Tyrrhenes" a great difference is recognisable, to the disadvantage of the former. He is inclined to ascribe the superior works to the Phœnicians, who were always renowned as goldsmiths, workers and dealers in metal. Amber is not mentioned in the English version of the Scriptures. "On amber found in Etruria", see *Cities and Cemeteries*, by Dennis, 1878 (new edition).

the full face of a chubby child, surrounded by well-grown hair ; the stone is encircled by a flat ring of lead, probably the matrix of a gold or silver ornament from which the more precious metal has perished in course of time. The reader should refer to what is said of the use of lead in Greek jewellery, as shown by excavations in tombs

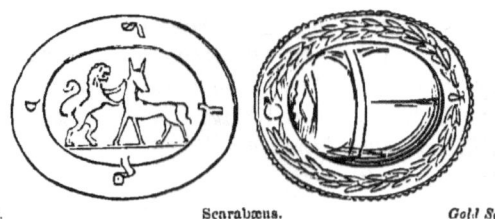

Fig. 18.   Scarabæus.   Gold Setting.

of the Cyrenaica. There is also, among these miscellaneous gold objects, a scarabæus (fig. 18) of green stone, set in a gold band, enriched by a wreath of laurel of exquisite workmanship, in very fine Greek taste.

Of Earrings,

The number in this collection is greater than that of any other class of personal ornaments. It is the same in all other collections. This may be not wholly due to the fact that such jewels were usually worn in pairs, for this was by no means invariably the case. One earring is said to have been part of the costume of a slave, and examples occur which illustrate the practice of wearing a single ornament of this kind. I may refer to the account given below of the spirited and admirably-modelled black terra-cotta lamp, which, while representing the laughing face of a young negress, retains in its right ear a gold ring of the lion's head type, which is so common in Phœnician, Assyrian, and Greek jewellery, and has been so often found in Egyptian tombs.

[1] See the *Ancient Egyptians* of Sir J. Gardner Wilkinson, the chapter on ornaments, and the index to that work.

All the forms of this class of jewellery were found in Egyptian remains. Some represent Assyrian types, but with a "difference", as the heralds say, which, as has been hinted above, seems to suggest that a considerable number of the specimens are by Tyrian workmen, who supplied the ladies of the Nile, and those who resided in "Chittim", or the Isles of the Sea, Cyprus among them, with innumerable personal ornaments. These were alluded to in the terrible denunciation of Ezekiel:— "Thus saith the Lord God to Tyrus; Shall not the isles shake at the sound of thy fall? Every precious stone was thy covering, the sardius, topaz, and diamond, the beryl, the onyx, and the jasper, the sapphire, the emerald, and the carbuncle, and gold" (xxvi, 15; xxviii, 13).

The number of earrings in this collection is not only relatively but actually considerable. The variety of their patterns is probably as great as the difference of their ages, which extend from very early times to the Byzantine period; at least, the later class includes examples which exhibit Byzantine fashions as in Venetian use to a date which is, in relation to others, quite modern.

It is noteworthy that the extreme simplicity of the forms of some of these relics does not allow us on that account alone to declare the age of many of the works to be great, or even to predicate that they are archaic in their origin. On the contrary, the flat lunettes, which were evidently cut from plates of gold, sometimes from mere films of the metal, are simply of indefinite antiquity; the works may be, so far as this peculiar pattern enables us to affirm, of almost any age. These specimens are chiefly interesting as illustrating popular goldsmiths' work as it was in vogue in Cyprus, and all other countries in the east of the "Great Sea". Other instances of these peculiar types may also be recognised. For example, there is a pair of lunette-shaped earrings, of which the grape-like granulations of gold remind us of the so-called granulated jewellery attributed to the ancient Etruscans, of which so much gold work is preserved in the British Museum (fig. 19).

The next class, as regards simplicity of form and design, and as to age and origin, doubtless of equal diversity with the above-named lunettes, are earrings of tube-like contours, crescent-shaped, and tapering at each end, to form the usual loop and pin which, being joined at the extremities, secured the ornament when in use. Of these, several have wires remaining, on which beads were placed (fig. 20). Most of these relics are of thin gold and hollow. They were made thus for cheapness, as well as lightness. An example has been found of a modified form of the same type as the above, to which, by way of pendant, is attached a little disk of gold, which is chased with a

19.

20.

Figs. 19, 20.   Earrings.   Gold.

satyric mask of free and energetic designs, and doubtless of Greek origin and provincial manufacture. The ring itself is of bronze, covered with thick leaf gold, through which the more perishable alloy within has forced its way, since fracture of the gold covering by some mechanical means exposed the bronze to the action of the atmosphere, causing extensive oxydisation, so that the green oxyde burst forth and spread itself, rending the gold as it did so.[1] A very large number of objects of this kind occur in collections of antique jewellery. The deteriorating effect of the process in question has been very great. While thus describing the condition of gold encrusted bronze objects, I may as well add that examples of the commoner sorts of goldsmiths' works sometimes

[1] See Plate 1, fig. 27.

prove to have been formed on clay or gypsum bodies, other specimens on silver-gilt; others again consist of lead bodies, encrusted with thick gold.

I found, among others, a wire earring of gold or electrum, on which is strung a pear-shaped bead of green glass —another specimen of popular jewellery, and as such very interesting to the student of the "ways and means" of antiquity. A similar wire earring retains its little pendent cylindrical bugles, one of which, being of glass, is splendidly iridescent. It is in this respect a small example of the effect of decomposition of glass when exposed to certain influences of the same kind which have affected large numbers of glass vessels of many ages and forms, which it will be my pleasure to describe further on. There are

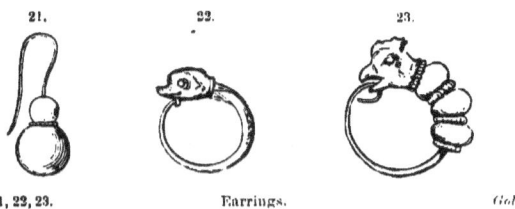

Figs. 21, 22, 23.   Earrings.   Gold.

other instances to be classed with the last-named earring. Many of these ornaments are so small that they must have belonged to children, if they were not, which is equally probable, merely designed for mortuary use. Earrings of great varieties of design and age occur in this collection.

Here (fig. 21) the pendants are little balls of gold strung on stems of twisted wire of the same metal, and accompanied by disks of the like material, which are enriched with granulated work of no great fineness. One of the most numerous classes of earrings is that of which many specimens have been found by excavators in Assyrian sites, as well as in Egypt, Mesopo-

F

tamia, Sardinia, and Etruria. These beautiful objects have
at one extremity of the ring proper the head of a bull.
Other specimens of the same category (figs. 22-26), terminate in the heads of goats, cocks, and dolphins.

More frequent than the latter are the earrings, which,
in the same fashion, bear the heads of lions (fig. 27) of
exquisite workmanship and noble designs. Bracelets
with lions' heads have been found at Kurium and elsewhere. They were believed to have been of Assyrian
origin, but the dispersion of jewellery of the like
character and closely resembling the above in artistic
style, has led observers to attribute these relics to the
famous Tyrian artificers, whose works would be borne all
over the ancient world in the ships of Phœnicia and the

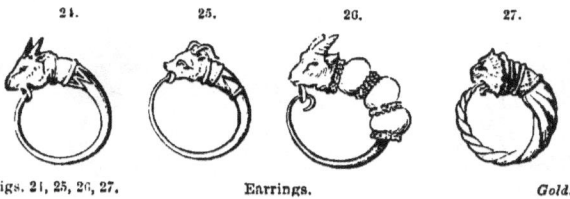

Figs. 24, 25, 26, 27.   Earrings.   Gold.

merchants who attended Sidonian markets. "The merchants of Sheba and Raamah, they were thy merchants:
They occupied in thy fairs with chief of all spices, and
with all precious stones and gold." " What city is like
Tyrus, like the destroyed in the midst of the sea?
When thy wares went forth out of the seas, thou filledst
many people; thou didst enrich the kings of the earth."[1]

The heads pertaining to these earrings are not all
derived from the forms of animals. The largest and
finest of this collection is, in the usual way, made of
twisted gold wire, enlarging to form a body of some
bulk, and terminating at one extremity in a female head,
furnished with ample tresses, and of a noble aspect;
on the wire are strung four rings of gold, enriched

[1] Ezek. xxvii, 22, 32, 33.

with granulations in the so-called "Etruscan" mode, together with two dark red beads, and one of variegated colour (fig. 28).

A similar object, of inferior quality, if not greater antiquity, is accompanied by three beads, two being of green glass, while the third and central one is composed of layers of that material, the one kind being white, between two that are black. This bead may have been intended to imitate an onyx. Of course, the existence of a bead made in this manner at once suggests the place of its manufacture to have been identical with that from which issued those pretty amphora-shaped bottles of alternate stripes of dark blue or black and white, or yellow vitreous material arranged in chevron, of which many examples

Fig. 28.   Beaded Earring.   *Gold.*

are in this collection. They are universally accepted as Phœnician, and they illustrate a peculiar handicraft, of which I have more to say when treating of beads, the well-known "Druids' Beads", any example of which it was the custom to describe as an *Ovum Anguinum*, or adder stone.

Some examples in the cabinet are of like character. They are probably late Greek, or even Roman, but they preserve the so-called Assyrian type of the ball and lion-headed examples above named. If this idea of the age of these works is correct, the earrings are curious illustrations of the survival of ancient forms in jewellery, exactly as two examples in the cases, in having pendants

of the Egyptian lotus pattern, as represented in the
"Phœnician" mode, may bring before our memories the
histories of successive invasions of Cyprus by diverse
peoples, each of which in its turn influenced the natives
of the island.

The collection also contains an earring with a long hoop
of twisted wire (fig. 30), comprising a little gold figure
of a winged genius, Eros, or Cupid, similar in design and
treatment to those which were found at Kurium; and
two with the youthful heads of Eros or Cupid in high
relief, set in bands of gold (figs. 29, 31).

The most elaborately wrought examples of this class
are a pair of charming earrings of sculptured gold, each
of which is furnished with a delicate "honeysuckle"

29.   30.   31.

Figs. 29, 30, 31.   Earrings.   Gold.

pattern of great beauty, and sustaining three pendants of
open work, a sort of filigree enriched with granulations.

Some doubts having been cast on the idea that ornaments of this category are not earrings, it is well to dis-
prove such questionings.   This may be done readily,
and on the simple evidence, among others, of a black
terra-cotta lamp of a laughing negress's head,[1] to
which I have before alluded as still retaining in the
lobe of the right ear a tiny earring of this order, and
most exquisitely wrought in spirals of "granulated"
work, terminating in the head of a lion.   The single
earring indicates that the wearer was a slave.   To wear
one earring is still the practice of Oriental slaves.

[1] See further on, under the description of the lamps, in the chapters
devoted to the consideration of the terra-cottas.

The next object which I shall describe is a beautiful relic, with a pear-shaped pendant of flat gold plate; this portion may have been the backing of a large stone. The body of this jewel is a circular disk of cornelian, deeply cut with the head of an infant Genius, of beautiful character and very animated expression. At the side is the name of "Eros" in Greek letters. This example corresponds with another which was found not far from it.

FINGER-RINGS.

There is a very large number of these objects in the Lawrence-Cesnola collection, and they comprise—1. Simple gold rings, with tablets, like modern signets; but,

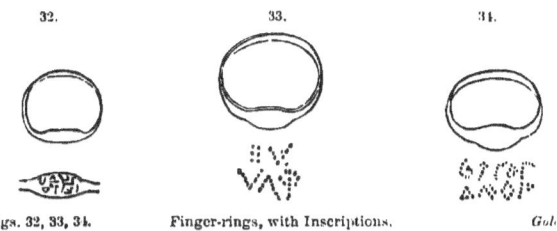

Figs. 32, 33, 34.   Finger-rings, with Inscriptions.   Gold.

with some exceptions, these articles, unlike the modern examples, bear no intaglio work fitting them for use as seals. 2. Another class consists of relics which bear stones and jewels of diverse materials, such as onyx, carbuncle, and cornelian, sculptured and unsculptured.

Of the first class, I have two examples unusually substantial; for, as in other jewels of antique production found in tombs, it is evident that a large proportion of these relics were designed for mortuary service only, and not for personal use. The exception to this is that kind which shows on the tablet punctures or indentations of a small tool, which have been grouped so as to produce a Greek inscription[1] or benediction on the part of the giver

[1] Fig. 33 reads ΨΕΦΑΥ; fig. 34, ΕΡΩΣ ΑΜΟΡ, in letters which appear to be of the first century after Christ.

to the owner (figs. 32-34).   Another bears in intaglio
two winged infant Genii embracing; being small, solid,
and somewhat worn, this appears to have been used
on the finger of a Salaminian lady.   The style of the
figures informs us that the jewel was made by a Greek
artist of a fine period, if not of the best of all the phases
of Greek art in gold.

2. The second class of finger-rings is more numerous
and important than the first.   The sculptures exhibited
by the relics which it comprises are mostly human figures.
In the collection there is a cornelian ring, which shows a
man dancing, and holding an implement, which resembles
a fir-cone or thyrsus.   Another (fig. 40), of black and
blue onyx, bears the effigies of a man standing and

Fig. 35.   Finger-ring with Engraved Gem—Discobolus.   *Gold.*

holding in one hand a patera with offerings of fruit,
and, in the other hand, nondescript objects, which resemble pine apples, but are, doubtless, fir-cones.   Four
examples of interest exhibit sculptures of the same order,
which, being in intaglio, were doubtless designed for the
private signets of the owners.   An onyx shows a Discobolus in the attitude of the Townley statue, and an illegible inscription (fig. 35).   The reader will observe with
interest the position of the head of this disk-thrower,
and consider it in reference to the attitude of the head in
the famous statue in the British Museum, and he will
thus be able to derive light on a subject which has been
freely and laboriously discussed by many antiquaries, who
have maintained that the restoration of the head of the
statue is wrong, and shows defect of perception on the
part of the modern sculptor who 'restored' the figure.

Several rings are enriched with settings of scarabæi, such as were worn during many ages by the people of the Mediterranean countries, who were more or less influenced by Egyptian fashions, and who employed the sacred Nilotic emblem in jewellery without attaching any sacredness to the gems they affected. Fig. 36 is an example of a rare and fine kind, unusually bold and good in its

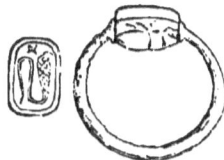

Fig. 36.   Finger-ring. Scarabæus, engraved with an Uræus.   Gold.

character, and of much older date than the gold setting which accompanies it. The scarabæus is Egyptian, and its device, the uræus, appears on another ring in the collection (fig. 37).

The other scarabæus is one of these reproductions of this famous symbol, which, owing to their inexact and perfunctory sculpturing, are supposed to be of Phœnician

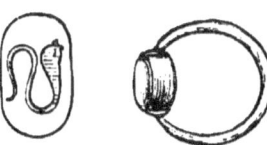

Fig. 37.   Finger-ring, engraved with Uræus.   Gold.

manufacture for exportation, and designed to serve as personal ornaments, without regard to the sacred significance of the emblem itself. This scarabæus is set on pivots, and the prettily-designed gold hoop to which it is attached is moulded to resemble a double braid of twisted wire, and very tastefully modelled at the pivots, on which the stone was intended to turn. Another ring consists of an oval carbuncle, set in con-

centric mouldings of gold, and very bulky. It appears
to be of the Assyrian type, although its general character
reminds us of rings which have been found with episcopal and other interments of mediæval dates (fig. 38).

Primitive types of personal ornaments survived in use
from age to age, and during enormous periods of time.
Apart from this, it is no uncommon thing for jewels of
extreme antiquity, having been found in tombs, to have

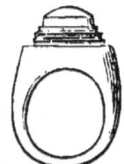

Fig. 38.   Finger-ring, set with a Carbuncle.   *Gold.*

been worn again by members of nations who were almost
wholly ignorant of the very names of the races to one of
which the resuscitated relics belonged. Antique gems
are often found in mediæval service, and curious legends
attributed magical virtues to Egyptian, Greek, or Roman

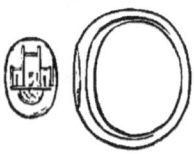

Fig. 39.   Engraved Ring.   *Gold.*

onyxes, cornelians, or sards, which were innocent of anything beyond incontestible power to charm antiquaries by
means of their historical associations, artists on account of
their artistic merit. Signets of Carlovingian, Frankish,
and French monarchs, and wonder-working fragments
found in the treasuries of cathedrals, bishops, and kings,
are often real antiques. Paste imitations of such gems
even found places in sacred and royal utensils and ornaments.

The ring in fig. 39 encloses a cornelian, on which is engraved the outline of a building, composed of a central tower and two lower wings, with indications of doorways. It represents the Temple of Venus at Paphos, which was a frequent subject with the Cypriotic artists. The reader may refer to a similar representation noticed in the account of a bronze disk, which is included in the chapter dealing with works of that material in this collection.

Fig. 40.   Gem Ring.   Gold.

One interesting example of ring represents the whole-length figure of a bull, with a star in the same position as that which appears in certain Cypriotic coins, where a horse is represented (fig. 41). The history of the coins

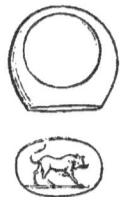

Fig. 41.   Finger-ring. A Bull.   Gold.

of Cyprus, which is to be found further on, treats of other examples of the use of this emblem. The bull's action of pain and wrath is very finely represented.[1] The execution is of excellent quality.

Another finger-ring consists of a cornelian, with a draped female figure, holding a cornucopiae and a wreath.

[1] This bull is found on silver coins of Thurium, and is repeated on those of Augustus.

There is also a ring, which is similarly enriched by a cornelian, on which is engraved a winged and draped female figure, holding a palm and wreath. This is probably a Victory; the gem is doubtless Greek; the execution is not equal to the design. We are, therefore, led to suppose that the latter element was derived from a fine model; indeed, there are plenty of examples of the finest class which would have sufficed to supply what was wanted here. The execution was doubtless due to a provincial artist.

The elements of the category of nondescript objects and parts of personal ornaments are numerous and various, and, in their several natures, curious. Among them is a cornelian, originally part of a finger-ring, which is engraved with a very spirited figure of a lion *passant*,

Fig. 12.   Bead of a Necklace.   Gold.

with a ball or star above it, as on the above-named ring. The execution here is very rude, not to say primitive, and the artist seems to have been a provincial workman rather than a skilled goldsmith.

Comprised in the group of beads from a tomb at Kittium is a scarabaeus of amethyst, and also a second scarabaeus of green stone, on the back of which is a winged figure in intaglio. Both of these relics are doubtless of Cypriotic manufacture. Attached to this group of objects is a rudely-shaped disk of massive gold, very like a button in its form, and perforated, so that it may have served as a bead of a necklace or bracelet. One face is blank, and shows signs of wear. On the other face are (fig. 12) deeply engraved in intaglio three dolphin-like figures, which are not unlike the bull-headed earrings mentioned above in the descriptions of those objects in this collection. These figures are arranged like the spokes of a wheel revolving, and remind us of that ancient heraldic bearing—the three legs borne on the shield of the Isle of Man. They are to be more closely associated with the very ancient cognizance of Trinacria, the Island of Sicily, in which there appears, at the meeting point of the legs, a human face with a grotesque expression. On the gold disk to which I refer are likewise represented three other objects, which resemble so many antique oars, disposed in the intervals of the so-called dolphins. This relic has occupied the close attention of those distinguished antiquaries, Dr. Birch, Signor Castellani, and Mr. Newton.

Figs. 43, 44.   Female Figure arranging   Ape.   Gold.
          the Hair.

In this class there are two little figures of noteworthy interest. The first represents (fig. 43) a nude female, at full length, standing erect, and in the act of arranging her hair, which, in long tresses, hangs behind her back. Between her feet is what appears to be the remnant of a figure of a dolphin. It is doubtless Venus Anadyomene, who is thus represented in gold, and by a rude sculptor of her native isle. The other figure is that of a cynocephalus, or ape, with exceptional emblems, the head of which is much injured (fig. 44). This figure resembles other examples of the same animal which exist among the terra-cotta objects in this collection, and, as such, described below.

Two or three small gold bottles of conical shape, and
intended for pendants for necklaces, occur in this section
of the body of relics before us. The same form is represented also in crystal among the objects which will
be noticed hereafter. One of these gold bottles was
found at Salamis. I place in this class a rudely-sculp-
tured scarabæus, or rather polypus, of pale green stone,
or glazed terra-cotta, and evidently not Egyptian in its
origin. The material is frequently found in collections of
antiques. Some characters which this example bears
resemble Hebrew. Another object of this category is a
much oxydised pendant of deep blue glass, moulded
to represent a lion's head of fine character. Two female
heads of the same nature and material, and, doubtless, of
Greek origin. The head of a child-genius, carved very

Fig. 15.   Wire Fibula.   Gold.

delicately in white stone, and highly polished. It belonged to an earring of the class represented by others in
my collection.[1] A seated figure of Cybele, crowned with
towers, and made of pure deep blue glass, was also found
during my diggings. In this group of objects are to be
reckoned two large bracelets for female use, the overlapping ends of which are moulded to represent a soft substance bound by double ligatures. On the former are
punctures arranged in the way of an inscription, which is
not legible. These ornaments are of bronze, thickly
coated with gold. They are of that class of ornaments
to which I have already alluded as showing the ancient
practice of economising the more precious metal by uniting
it with the almost universal alloy.

[1] See what is written above, under the head of Ear-rings.

A very considerable number of fibulæ of gold wire
occur in this collection. They are formed by bending
wire like hoops, with overlapping ends, and they doubtless answered the purpose of modern pins when employed
to attach portions of garments to each other. The ends,
and even the folds of drapery, were often thus joined
together for the convenience of the wearers. These
objects are represented extensively in the collection (fig.
45). Some larger examples of this class bear Cypriote
inscriptions. See figs. 46, 47, 48.

Some of the larger instances of the same articles show,
by the outbreaking of the inferior alloy of which their

Figs. 46, 47, 48.   Inscribed Fibulæ.   Gold.

bodies are composed, that, like the bracelets described
just now, they are of bronze, thickly coated with gold.
Other relics of this class prove that a material in value
even inferior to bronze has been employed to strengthen
or back up thick coatings of gold. There is, for instance,
among the earrings, one, of which the pendant is shaped
like, and about the same size as, a modern musket ball,
and filled with clay, now revealed by the breaking of the
golden crust.

CHAPTER IV

SILVER OBJECTS.

LTHOUGH anciently the number of objects in silver used for personal adornment and in domestic service must have immeasurably outnumbered those which were formed of the more precious metal, the ratio of proportion between the respective classes of relics in these materials has been entirely reversed, so that the number of articles in silver is very far indeed from equalling that of those which are made of gold. This is one of those facts which serve to show how prodigious has been the loss to art of the countless pieces which had occupied the silversmiths of antiquity. Among the fine examples of silver-work which still remain, there is more than enough to prove that beautiful design and fine sculpture were lavished on silver, with not inferior profusion to those which distinguished works in gold.

The destructive action of time, and powers of atmospheric corrosion, fully account for this complete reversal in the number of precious objects remaining for the world. In the collection, the modern rule of proportion more than holds its own, for the articles of silver are few indeed compared with those made of gold, and to which I have already referred. As in Assyria, Egypt, Greece, and Rome, and even in the comparatively recent Scandinavian hoards, so it is with regard to Cyprus, where, indeed, we might expect such a result to have been due to the moisture of an insular climate.

Oxydisation has unfortunately caused destruction or disfigurement of nearly all the silver relics of antiquity. For this metal appears to be particularly sensitive to the acid vapours which come in contact with it when exposed to the air, and to the various kinds of moisture with which it is frequently associated when lying hidden in the ground. The museums of Rome, Naples, Paris, New York, and London supply illustrations of the same result from the same cause, almost the only exception being the so-called Treasure of Varus, the camp equipage of a Roman commander, all the pieces of which are made of fine and richly-chased silver, which, strange to say, were found and still exist in a perfect state of preservation.

The silver articles to be found in the Lawrence-Cesnola collection, of far greater antiquity than these Roman relics, have shared the more common fate, and are but the sparse survivors of an innumerable class of the little household treasures of the middle and inferior orders of the people of Cyprus. Generally speaking, these remains show the same forms as those which obtain in gold. The finger-rings, although they are blistered and distorted nearly out of shape, retain enough of their original aspects to prove that they were nearly identical with the above-mentioned types in the more precious metal. One example in the cabinet, formed of iron, coated or covered in some way with silver, has held a stone in a plain annular setting, fitting it for a finger-ring. Another finger-ring has a flattened plate. It also has lost nearly all the silver coating of the iron body. Another is a ring of simple form. There are earrings of silver in the collection, which bear bulls' heads, like those already spoken of in the chapter devoted to the gold objects. Parts of spoons, of the shape of those known as mustard-spoons,

were also found. Several specimens have bowls smaller
than those of the last objects, and it has been conjectured
that these may have been employed for taking or trans-
ferring scented or costly fluids from one bottle to another.

There is one form among the spoons which was evidently designed to remove marrow from long bones.
Similar implements to this have been found in the drift
and in bone caves of greater antiquity than those Cypriote
relics. Silver hairpins appear to have been in common
use. Of these, one was found, embossed with a six-foil
rosette; another has a rosette, the petals of which
retain traces of gilding. I found, among other silver
relics in the tombs of Salaminia, a small plaque, bearing
a female head *en repoussé*. A fibula, which, in a far
more charming condition than of yore, retains its now
splendidly iridescent glass ball. Parts of a necklace
of twisted silver wire, with beads, were found. The
bead on the former is of the class called " Druids' Beads"
in this country, or " Adder Stones", of which larger
examples are described under their proper heading
among the articles in glass. With the silver, on parts
of the same necklace, they comprise beautiful pearls,
and a large silver oval object, of which portions remain. The larger portion has been beaten up of a
peculiar form, which might readily be mistaken for that
of a human mouth.

Such votive offerings have been common in all ages;
their types survive in every church in Italy, where
models of legs, arms, eyes, lips, and ears abound. The
British Museum, and its fellow institutions on the Continent, contain numerous votive sculptures of breasts,
hands, lips, and eyes, and other members of the
human body, the offerings of sufferers of antiquity for
cures believed to have been effected by divine inter-
ference with the course of nature. It has been suggested that, as this relic was found in a tomb at

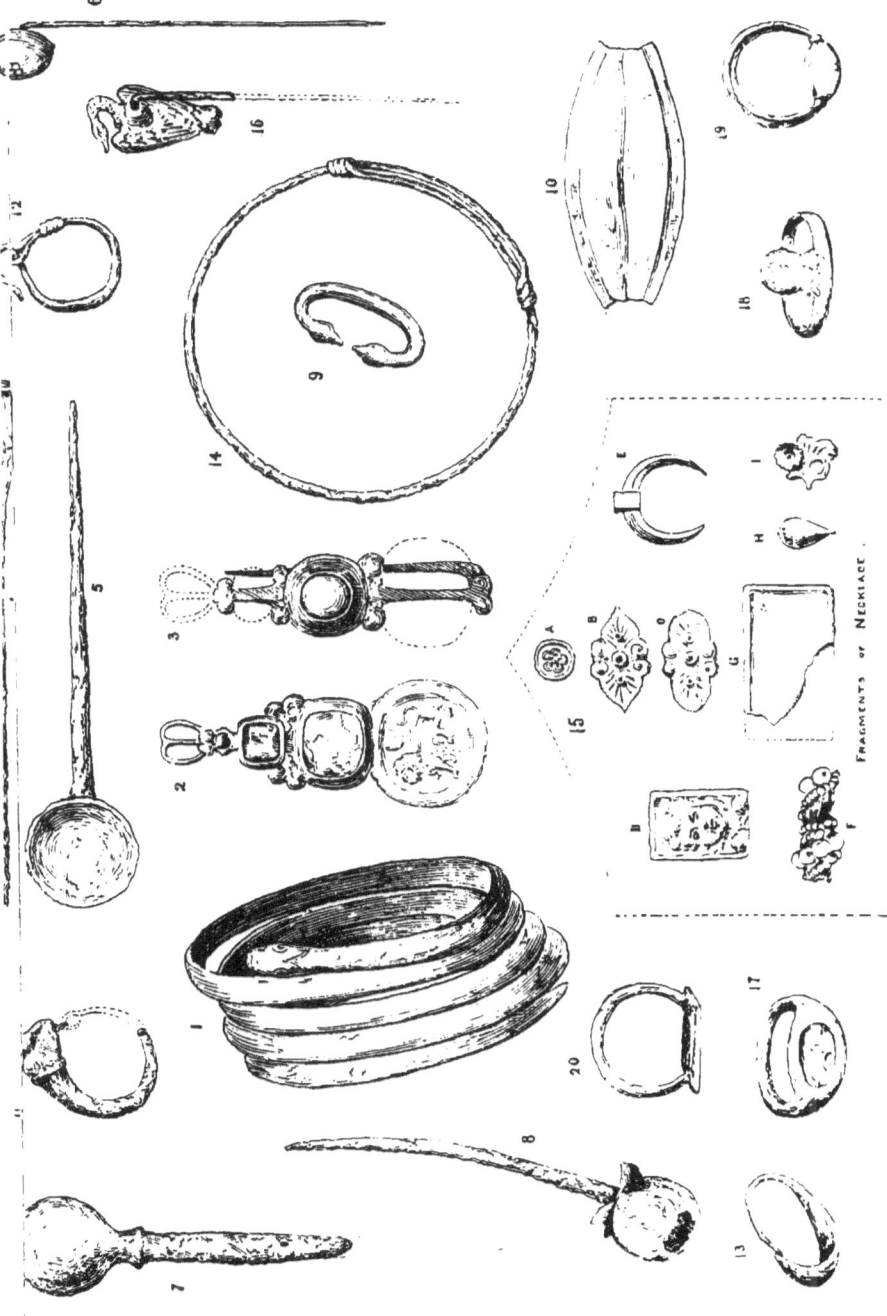

FRAGMENTS OF NECKLACE.

Salamis, it may have belonged to a face-mask, such as those already described with other golden objects. On this point, it is worth while to notice that the art employed to represent the mouth[1] (or bowl, if this is part of a spoon) is not archaic, but of a very far advanced kind.

In addition to these remains are several extremely curious and uncommon articles in silver, bracelets, formed of stout wires, the overlapping ends of which are fur-

Fig. 49.   Finger-ring, with engraved Cornelian.   Silver.

nished with rings. These, sliding on the body of the ornament, enabled the owner to enlarge or reduce its circumference at pleasure, so that it might be adapted

Fig. 50.   Finger-ring, with engraved Cornelian Scarabæus.   Silver.

to the arm of a lady or of a child, of almost any diameter.[2] Among the silver fibulæ, two examples are very similar in form and character; each one having attached, below the setting which includes the iridescent bead, a disk of glass, on which is impressed a figure of a lion *passant*, with a lunette represented over its back

---

[1] Plate II, fig. 10.   [2] Plate II, fig. 11.

4

in the corresponding position to that of the star over
the back of a bull, which has been described among
the finger-rings in the chapter on the gold objects.
Such symbols remain to be considered among the coins
of Cyprus, of which I have yet to give an account.
There are three beautiful rings, set with scarabæi, of
cornelian. On the stone of one is the figure of Pasht,
or Sekhet, an Egyptian goddess, with two pairs of wings
displayed, crowned with a disk, and holding an uncertain
object in each extended palm (fig. 49). Another bears a

Fig. 51.   Finger-ring, with engraved Cornelian.   *Silver.*

griffin, with large wings extended. On the back a male
figure sits astride, in a mantle, wearing a rayed crown,
such as often appears in Cypriote statuettes, and carrying a staff, with a ball, or fir-cone, at its upper extremity
(fig. 50). I shall say more of these crowns in the chapter
devoted to a consideration of the terra-cottas. The third
has a bull, standing with wings expanded (fig. 51).

CHAPTER V

BRONZE AND IRON REMAINS.

PATERÆ—MIRRORS—BOXES—RINGS—ARMOUR—MISCELLANEOUS OBJECTS.

BRONZE.

N this material there are about a thousand examples in the gathering. They consist of vases, parts of vases, mirrors, both Greek and Roman, bowls, strigils, weapons, such as lance-heads and daggers, pins, and pateræ of different forms, ornaments for horse-trappings, fragments of a tripod, and other miscellaneous objects.

In detail, it may be mentioned that there are pateræ of no less than twelve forms. The first and finest which claims attention is a patera (fig. 52) engraved with Phœnician and Egyptian figures, and of great antiquity (fig. 53). Dr. Samuel Birch, Keeper of the Egyptian and Oriental Antiquities in the British Museum, to whom I am indebted for much valuable information upon my collection of relics, has given me the following account of this fine patera :—

"The bowl is very much decayed and covered with ærugo, so that the figures are scarcely discernible. The subject is Phœnico-Egyptian, and arranged into two portions, that in the centre, or medallion, represents a Phœnician or Egyptian monarch, wearing on his head the attire known as the *atef*, which consists of a conical crown formed of withes tied round the apex, and sur-

mounted by a disk, thrice repeated, flanked by ostrich
feathers, and placed on the horns of the sheep or goat.
The single form of this cap is that found on figures of
the Egyptian deity Osiris; the triple form is usually
placed on the head of the Egyptian Horus and of kings,
especially the youthful Ptolemies, in the character of
Horus '*pa neb ta*', 'the Lord of the World'. Round his
loins is the royal '*shenti*', or tunic. The rest of his form
is undraped, and it is uncertain if he wears sandals.
The hair of the monarch shows the rounded form which
came into use at the time of the Twentieth Dynasty, or
about B.C. 600; his head is bound with a fillet or
diadem. This figure faces to the right, and has the left
foot, in the Egyptian style, advanced (the Egyptian

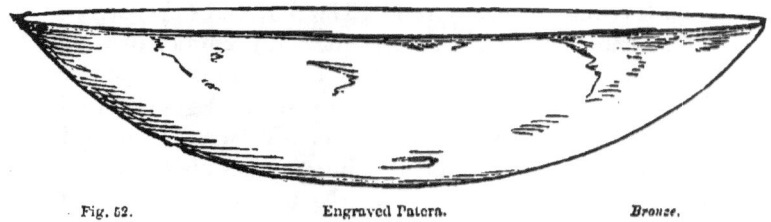

Fig. 52.   Engraved Patera.   *Bronze.*

always marching or walking with the left foot advanced);
his right is raised on the toes. He is in the act of
striking with a mace in his right hand three enemies,
who wear short hair, and have a slight tunic round the
loins; their hands being raised above and behind them.
The prisoners are not bearded, and their short costume
shows that they are enemies, of the white or Libyan race,
rather than of the Semetic nations. Before the king
stands the god Ra or the Sun, hawk-headed, wearing the
Sun's disk, draped in a *shenti*, or tunic, stretching out his
right hand, in which he has probably held the *khepsh* or
scimetar, and holding his left hand pendent as though
he were holding a symbol of life. This action intimates

that victory is accorded to the monarch by the Sun God, the Phœnician Baal Reseph, or Reseph Mical, a form afterwards converted by the Cypriotes to the Apollo Amyclaios. The prisoners or enemies of the king are, as in Egyptian style, of smaller proportions. So also is the

Fig. 53.   Inside of Engraved Patera.   Bronze.

attendant of the monarch who stands behind him facing in the same direction, but he is not in purely Egyptian costume. Around his loins is a short garment, perhaps a kind of '*shenti*' or Egyptian tunic; but he wears on his head a pointed helmet like the Assyrian, or the cap pointed like the Persian *kidaris*, or as it is called in the Cypriote dialect, the *kittaris*. His left hand holds a bow, his right is placed upon his breast as if he held an arrow. At his left side a quiver is slung. In the exergue of this scene is a representation of something, but it is difficult to say what it is. The whole of this belongs to the category of Phœnician art.

"Separated by a funicular border, the frieze or scene running round centre offers more relation with Greek art, although it is treated in the Egyptian manner. It is, however, Cypriote in some respects; entertainments and similar diversions being represented on other cups of the kind published by M. Ceccaldi, and belonging to the collection of General di Cesnola. The triclinium, or repast, dance, music, song, and offering, form a kind of Dionysiac scene mixed with erotic subjects; the men are shorn and draped in short tunics like the Phœnicians on the Egyptian monuments. The women are either naked or in very transparent garments, and their hair is in the Egyptian style. It is difficult to make out the due sequence of the scene, which offers a representation of Cypriote sensualism. The central figures may, however, be considered those which are seated or reclining, at an entertainment, on couches and chairs. To the right a man, recumbent on a couch, facing right, addressing a draped female seated on the couch, and drinking with a cup in his right hand; under the couch is a footstool; at the foot of the couch is a *krater* on a stand; behind the *krater* an *oinochoos*, or youth, serving wine with a jug, *oinochoe*, in his right hand. He stands at the foot of another couch, the figure of which is indistinct; behind this couch is a draped female with a child, seated on a chair. Behind the seated group, and recumbent on the couch on the left, is a man seated on a chair and drinking out of a cup, then a stand, following

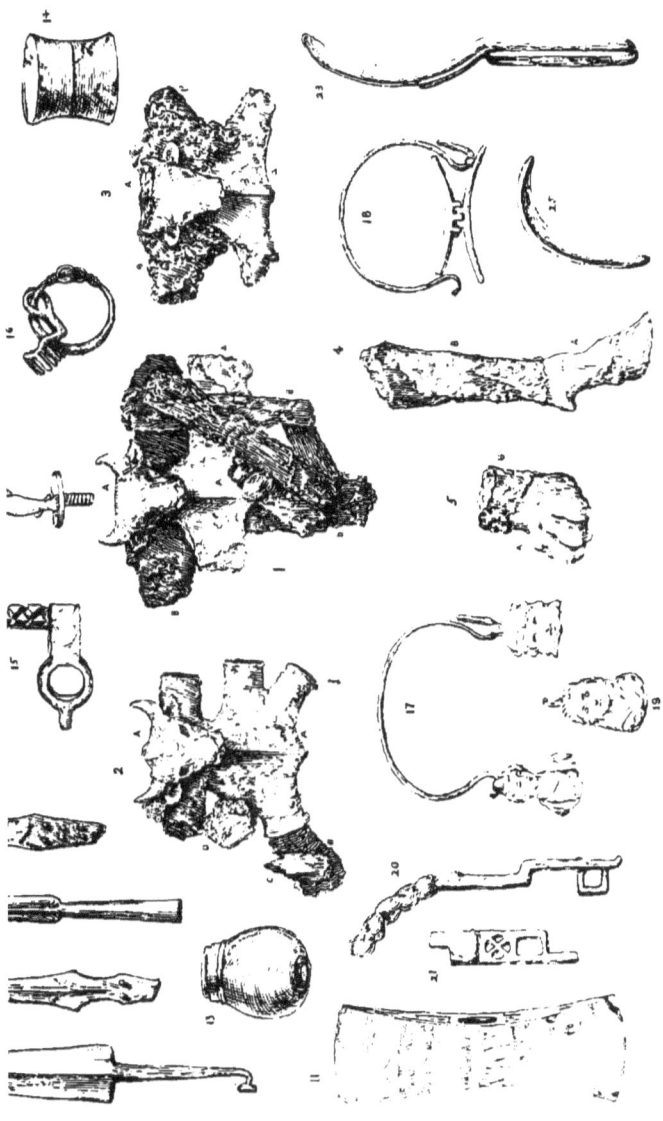

which is a man carrying a female; a couch with footstool, and recumbent figure on the couch; and two men looking back, carrying a kind of bucket, or *situlus*, on a pole. These are figures connected with a symposium, and of which they are the accessaries. Behind the seated figure on the left are figures also connected with a symposium, chiefly the musicians; the first, a female holding her hands down; the second, a man with hands raised, perhaps, a musician, but imperfect; the third, a man holding up an ornament or uncertain object; the fourth, a female holding or playing on a tambourine; the fifth, is a female in Egyptian style holding a cup and lotus flower; behind her is a water plant. This cup, no doubt, possesses in some of its aspects an erotic sentiment, like the Greek symposia which are found not uncommonly depicted on the later vases of the Basilicata, of which the date may be placed about B.C. 300."

There is also a very ancient pipe of remarkable form, formed, it would seem, of two sliding cylinders, so that some of the holes may be shut off if necessary. It is about twenty inches long, perforated in eleven holes on the one side, and three on the other side (fig. 54). Another remarkable bronze relic is a very ancient serrula (fig. 55), or spoon-saw, its slightly concave body being furnished with a serrated edge, and intended to be employed for ladling the blood of sacrifices, and cutting through the stronger tissues of the small creatures that so frequently perished at the altars of the many deities who were venerated at Salamis. It was found in a tomb at Kittium. A small box, or *étui*, of bronze (fig. 56), was found, containing a pin and needles, formed of an alloy of copper and tin, or silver. The latter are about two-and-a-half inches long, made with eyes perfect in form, and carefully pointed. With these were discovered some fragments of

linen thread, so that this curious relic remains almost as
the owner left it many hundreds of years ago
at Salamis. A similar *étui*, which has not yet
been opened, exists in this collection with the
above. A large armlet of bronze (fig. 60), in
the shape of a snake, the eyes being clearly
defined, comes from another tomb. It is remarkable because, having been laid up with
linen cerements, the patina on its surface
retains unmistakeable traces of the threads of
the fabric which accompanied it in the tomb.
In the tomb which yielded this armlet I found
two silver finger rings (figs. 57, 59), the oval
bezel of one of which formerly held three oval
stones, or pieces of glass; the central one is
now remaining in its setting. Two large
fibulæ (figs. 61*a*, 61*b*, 61*c*), a large pin (fig.
63) with an open eye and wire twisted about
its head, a pair of tweezers (fig. 64), or small
tongs, a bronze ring (fig. 58), and a buckle (fig.
62) were found with the above-named articles,
as well as the serrula already described.

I found also several portions of a large
tripod at Kurium, the remaining fragments
of which are now deposited in the Metropolitan Museum at New York. Three of
these are beautifully-modelled heads of bulls,
of a fine Greek type.[1] The eyes of these
sculptures are hollow, and have been filled
with glass, like many other sculptures of Greek
as well as Roman origin. Two pieces come
from the feet of the tripod; one is the claw
of a lion, the other the hoof of a bull.[2]

The miscellaneous bronze antiquities comprise torch-
holders, candelabra on tripod bases, and weights of

Pipe.
Fig. 51.
Bronze.

[1] Plate III, fig. 1, A, B, C.   [2] Plate III, fig. 1, D, E.

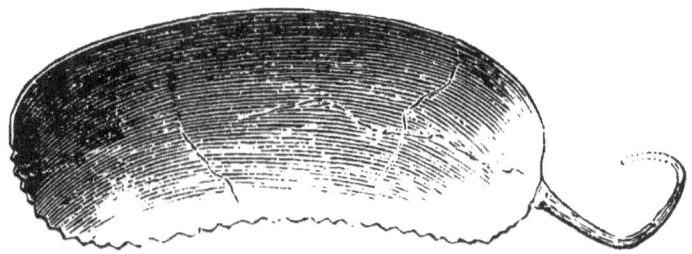

Fig. 55.   Serrula, p. 55.

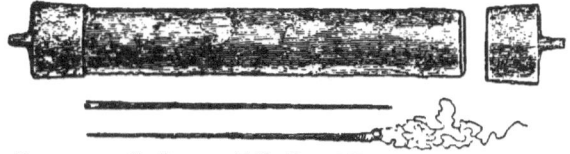

Fig. 56.   Needle-case, with Needles and Thread. p. 55.

(Silver.)   (Silver.)
Figs. 57, 58, 59.   Rings, p. 56.

61c.   60.   61b.

61a.   62.   63.   64.
Figs. 60, Armlet; 61a, 61b, 61c, Fibula; 62, Buckle; 63, Pin; 64, Tweezers.
p. 56.

BRONZE ANTIQUITIES, ETC., FROM A TOMB AT SALAMINIA, CYPRUS.

1

exactly the shape still employed in Cyprus. Among the
latter, two weights adhere by the oxidising of their surfaces. The latter is a disk, perforated by three triangular
holes. A group, or compacted mass, of iron and bronze
objects was found at Salaminia, on the top of a sarcophagus. Most of the articles in the mass were of use for
the bath. This group is a very remarkable one indeed ;
the articles are all massed by means of the oxidisation of
the surfaces of most of them. They comprise a large
iron strigil, with a great ring of the same metal, and

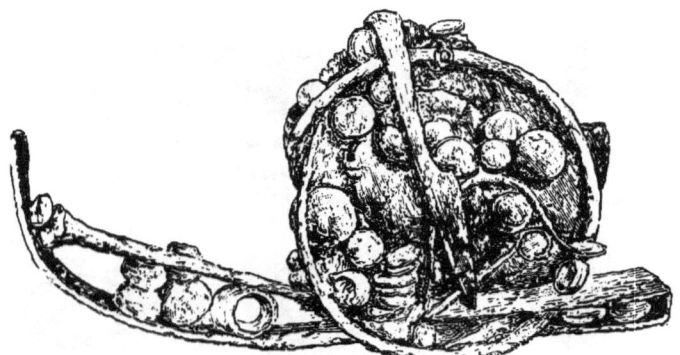

Fig. 65.   Mass of Iron and Bronze Utensils for the Bath, etc.

a pair of shears, a spur with a prick point in the middle
of the heel, a large nail, or, perhaps, the staple of the
large iron ring, and two smaller nails, a fragment of bone,
possibly human, and three finger-rings, one of bronze
and two of iron, one of the latter showing the socket for
the stone which it originally carried. The large iron
ring passes through the two iron finger-rings. It is, of
course, not a complete ring. It retains portions of
bronze, which look very much as if they had belonged
to a casing of that alloy (fig. 65).

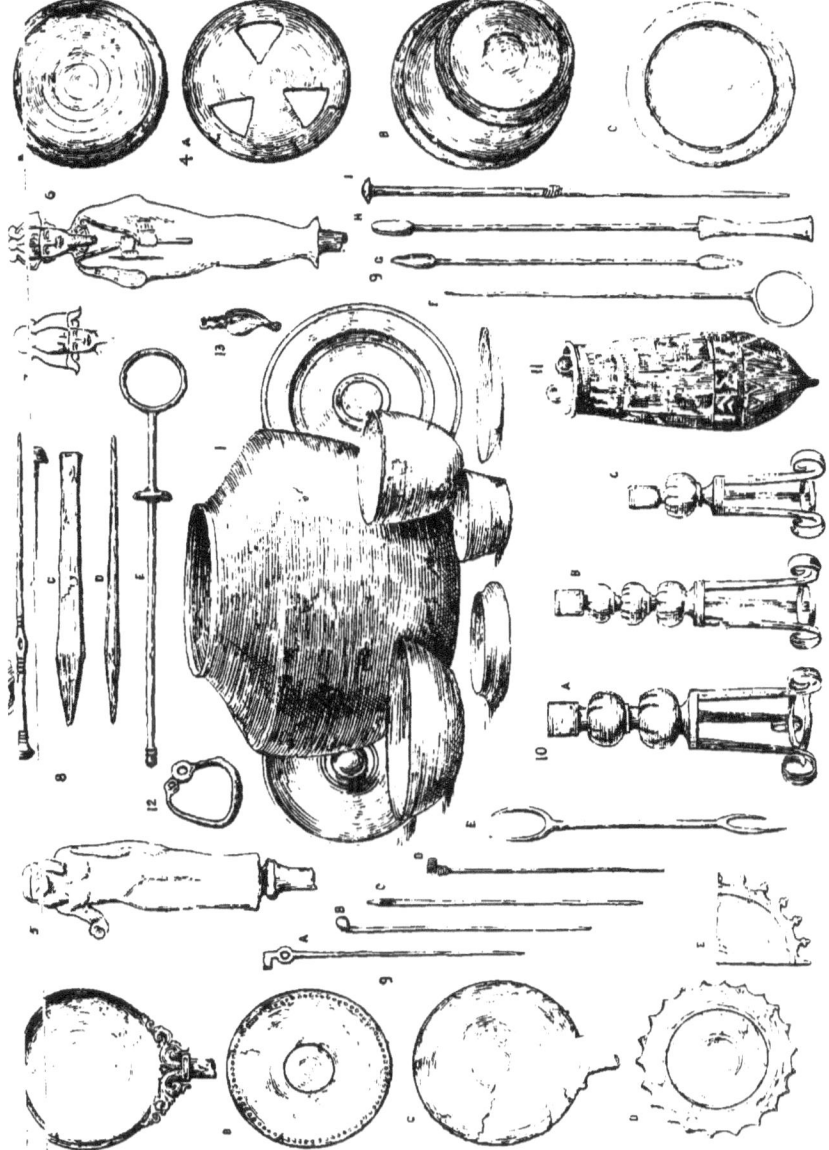

In addition to the above bronze relics, there are three bronze mirrors, one of which (fig. 66) has an engraving, representative of the Temple of Venus at Paphos,[1] with a hatched foreground, and not fewer than forty coins of bronze, which have been oxidised out of all form. It is evident that these articles are of great antiquity, but, in default of the inscriptions on the coins, there is nothing in the group to enable us to state positively to what period they are to be assigned.

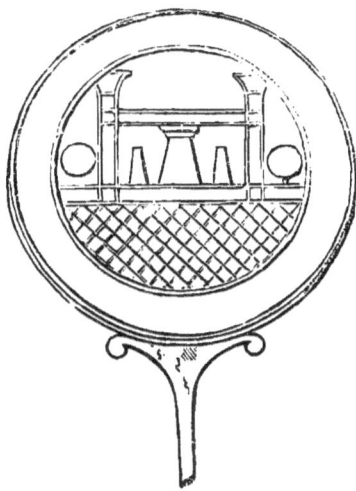

Fig. 66.   Engraved Mirror—the Temple of Paphos.   Bronze.

I found also two bucket-shaped vessels of bronze, the former of which bears a deeply-incised Egyptian scene and inscription. The letters of this inscription are supposed to have been filled with enamel, of which there are, however, but slight indications. Dr. Birch describes the other as " an Egyptian vase, in form of the Roman *situlus*, used

---

[1] This is a favourite subject of the art of the engraver. See page 11, and fig. 39, p. 40.

for carrying holy water, much corroded, with two small
eyes for a loop-shaped handle to pass through, by which
the little vase was carried in ceremonies. This example
is so much corroded that the subject which is on its sides
in bas-relief is difficult to make out. The reliefs are in
four rows. In the first or upper row are seen Boats of
the Sun proceeding through the heavens. In the second,
a procession of several female deities of the Egyptian
Ritual, crowned with the disk and horns, and holding
papyrus sceptres. The third row is illegible. Below
this, a frieze, or row of ornaments, in shape of the petal
or calix of the lotus flower. In the Egyptian *situlus*, the
form of the god Khem, or Ammon Horus, is generally
depicted at the head of the procession of deities whom
the worshipper adores. These vases are not of a very
early period."

IRON.

During the course of my excavations at Salamis, I
came upon a box containing a curious collection of
weapons of iron. These were, perhaps, formerly worn
by a warrior, slain in one of the numerous battles
which took place in his native island. There are two
swords, with leaf-shaped blades and short cross-handles,
by which that material was secured in its place. With
these are two lance-heads and a leaf-bladed knife; two
finger-rings and as many arrow-heads forming a group.
Iron rings have been mentioned in the account of the
bath rings and other objects found at Salamis. The
rapid oxidisation and decay of this metal no doubt
account for there being fewer relics of iron than of
bronze found in digging into sites so ancient as the
tombs of Salaminia. The accompanying plate gives
representations of the principal iron objects that I have
been enabled to gather from the ancient cemeteries
and burial cities of Cyprus.

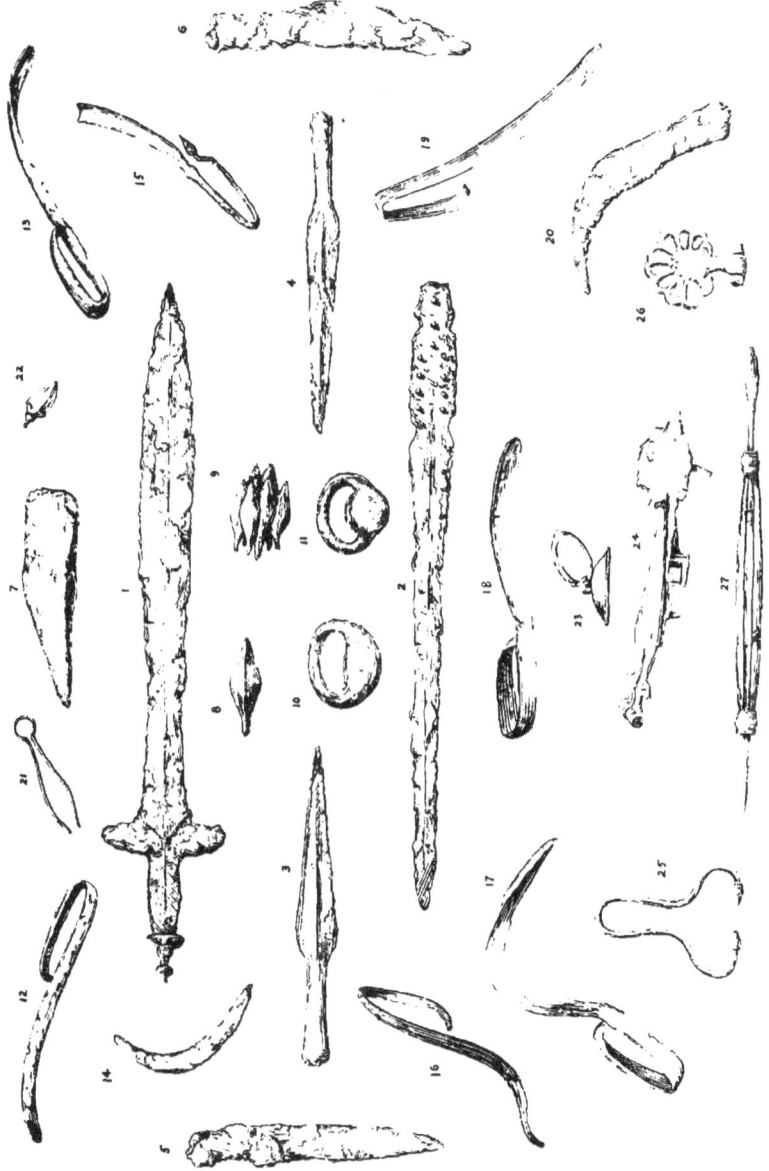

CHAPTER VI.

LEADEN ANTIQUITIES.

GROUPS—PLATES—SLING-BULLETS—BOXES—INSCRIBED ROLLS—SEALS OR STAMPS.

EADEN remains, from their liability to corrode and crumble away into dust when exposed to certain conditions of the adjacent earth, are naturally not very numerous in any collection of antiquities. Nevertheless, I was so fortunate as to secure, during the course of my investigations among the tombs of Salaminia, a not inconsiderable number of relics composed of this metal, which are, indeed, from the peculiarity of their types, worthy of consideration in this place.

Among the most notable remains in lead preserved in the British Museum, mention may be made of plates with Greek and Roman inscriptions, finger-rings, the Roman coffins found in England, the series of bullæ of Sicilian and Byzantine personages, of the Popes, the Doges of Venice, and the early noblesse of France, dating from the seventh century of the Christian era, if not earlier. Many of these antiquities manifest a high degree of preservation, while others, by no means the oldest, have suffered in some measure from the injurious effects of London air.

GROUPS AND PLATES.

Among the moulded objects in this material are the
fragments of a group, in very low relief, of a gladiator,
(fig. 67) clad in breeches and buskins, whose head indicates that he is of African descent.   He is in combat with
a lion, has a cloth about his left arm, and a falchion
in his right hand.   The moulding of this plaque appears to
belong to the Roman period, and it has been suggested
that it was intended to be attached to another object by
some mechanical means of adhesion, exactly as orna-

Fig. 67.   Gladiator in combat with a Lion.   *Lead.*

ments of no dissimilar character and appearance are
still attached to the surfaces of earthenware vessels.
With these figures are two vases of elegant form.   I
found no less than six square plates of lead, moulded
for an unknown purpose, embossed with delicate patterns, and perforated with large circular openings, as
if they formed parts of the covers of caskets.   If they
are not so, it is difficult to say for what purpose they
were designed.   Although these relics have been found
in tombs, it is possible that they are not of any very

remote antiquity. They closely resemble portions of
modern mountings for the frames of miniature portraits.

SLING BULLETS AND BOXES.

An almond-shaped or glandiform object, bears, moulded
in relief, an inscription in Greek characters, perhaps the
name of the maker. It is a missile for a sling. Such
objects are found in tombs of military persons, and are
not uncommon among Greek relics. They do not often
bear inscriptions such as this one.[1] The figure of a
horse, made of a flat plate of lead, and several pieces
which appear to have formed parts of a toy-chariot,
were also found. It would be hard to determine how
old they are.[2]

The custom of using lead, which, next to gold, is,
when not exposed to acid air, the least perishable
among the metals employed by the nations of antiquity, is illustrated by the account given, in the subsequent chapter upon the ivory relics, of a finely-carved
casket of ivory, enclosed in a little box of lead, the
form of which suggested that it had been made to
contain the other relic.[3] Besides this box, there is a
second similar one of lead in the collection, which has
the form of a large cylindrical box. On being opened,
this was found to contain a considerable number of
glass drops. Of these, one at least is of a deep sapphire blue, and now incrusted with an iridescent film of
oxidised material; another is of a clear rather dark
brown tint; and a third has a greyish tint. The infil-
tration of water charged with lime through the space
between the lid and body of this box had been sufficient,
notwithstanding the extreme narrowness of the interval,
to fill the interstices of the drops of glass with fine

---

[1] See Plate VI, fig. 2. Ficoroni has figured several inscribed *glandes*
from Sicily and other localities of the Byzantine Empire.

[2] See Plate VI, fig. 1.   [3] See Plate VI, figs. 14, 15.

calcareous matter, exactly such as had, by similar means,
filled from the floor to the roof the caves beneath the
temple at Kourium, which are said to have contained the
most precious part of the antiquities which now enrich
the Metropolitan Museum at New York. The drops
of glass were thus cemented in a close but friable mass,
which crumbled at the touch of the fingers, leaving the
drops themselves distinct. It has been conjectured that
this little box and its apparently almost valueless contents belonged to the grave of a child, whose toys the
pretty little button-shaped drops had been—toys placed
in the sepulchre, beside the scant remains of some dear
one, who could delight in them no more. There are
about thirty drops altogether.[1] It has, on the other
hand, been suggested that the variously-coloured drops
of glass were intended for use by a seal or gem cutter.

INSCRIBED ROLLS.

A still more curious and important discovery of the
use of lead in Cyprus was made at Salamis under the
following circumstances. During my excavations in the
ancient cemetery of that city, one of the diggers came
upon a toy made of this metal, and brought it to me.
Adjustment of the various pieces in their former positions showed that this relic was a rough toy in the shape
of a chariot, the two wheels of which, from whatever
cause it would be difficult to determine, are not, as one
would have supposed, circular, but undoubtedly oval.
The strangeness of this fact prompted me to desire the
workmen to preserve very carefully whatever leaden
articles might turn up in the course of their future
labours. The very next day was fruitful in relics of
the same kind, and several pipe-like portions of the
metal were put into my hands. As these articles did
not associate themselves with the chariot-toy, towards

[1] See Plate VI, fig. 13.

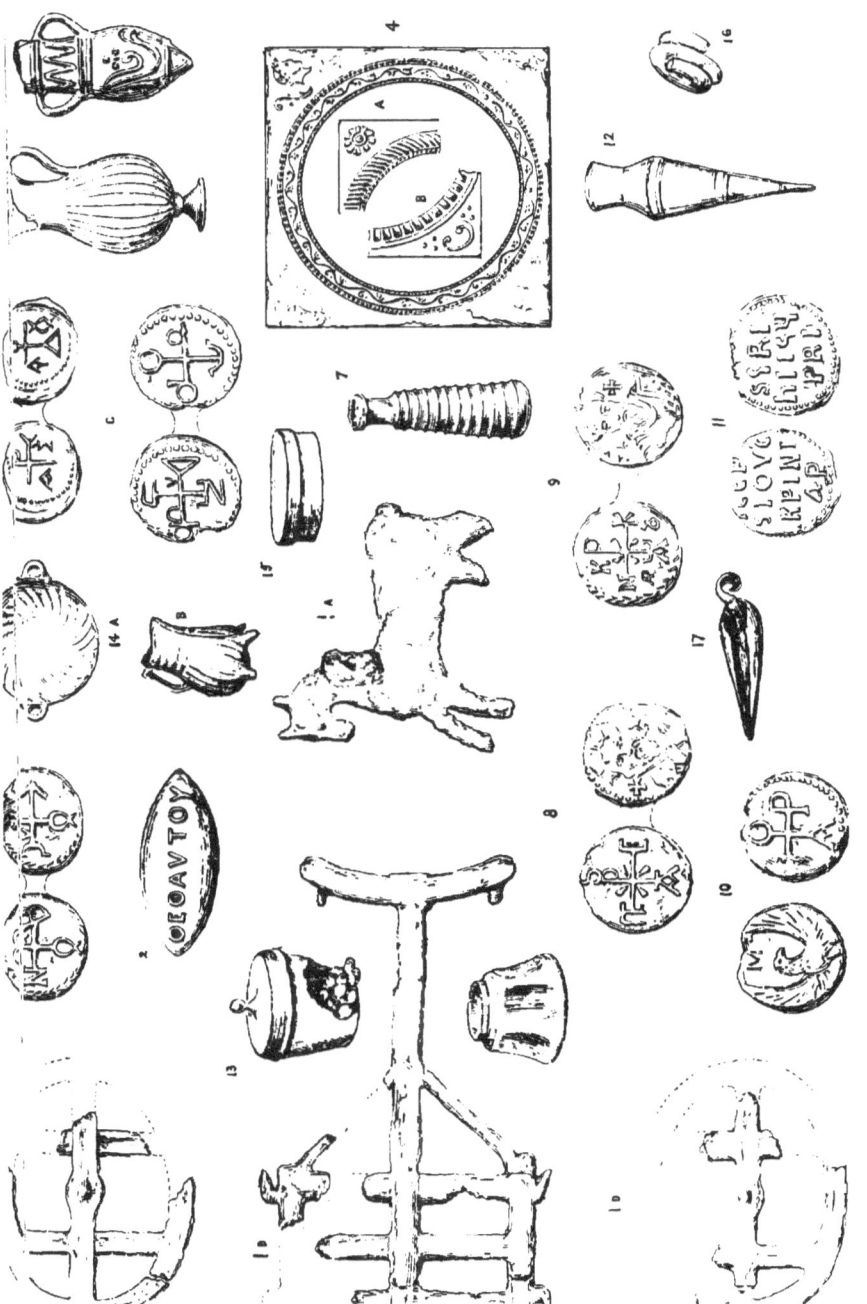

which my attention was then directed, I did not give much attention to them at the moment, but laid them aside in a corner of my tent. It must be confessed that, knowing the frequency with which lead was used for water-pipes by the ancients, I hastily concluded that these newly-found objects had been employed for that purpose, or otherwise applied by way of solder, so as to unite frustra of columns with iron pins, or, possibly, to bind shafts of pillars to their bases.

On the evening of that day, I took one of the supposed tubes of lead, in order to make it a temporary receptacle of some small relics of gold which had been discovered at that time. On trying with my knife to remove from the surface of the metal its earthen incrustations, I found that it was not a pipe at all, but a rolled sheet, resembling a scroll of paper. I called for a smaller piece of the metal, which might be more easily opened than the somewhat bulky one to which I had originally had access. This not being procurable at the moment, and night approaching, I determined to defer further inquiries, and, meanwhile, I put the metal in one of my pockets, and left it there till the next morning. When this time arrived, I returned to my task with the roll. The warm temperature had rendered the metal more pliable than it had been during the many ages it had lain in the earth of the cemetery. It was thus less difficult to open the roll than had been the case the night before. Accordingly, I succeeded in raising the edge of the sheet of metal from the body of the scroll, and, however brittle time had caused it to become, it soon became apparent that, with extreme care, and cautious handling of the scroll, for such it already proved to be, it might be opened, and thus made to give up the records it contained. At any rate, it might be made to give some account of itself.

Profiting by the hint of the softening of the metal

K

under the influence of warmth. I exposed it gently to the
heat of fire, and, after about two hours of careful mani-
pulation, succeeded in unrolling the object. The reader
may conceive how greatly I rejoiced when, on carefully
examining the inner surface of the unrolled plate, I found
that it bore a long inscription in Cypriote characters.
Since that day, I took great care to collect and secure all
the lead which came in my way, because it was easy to
see that this common but almost imperishable metal
might add to our knowledge that which would be more
precious than gold or silver, unless, indeed, these nobler
metals preserved forms of priceless antique art.

It was by means of this fortunate sequence of acci-
dents, and the inquiries they have suggested, that—
being specially indebted to the courtesy and learning
of Professor Sayce of Oxford for the translation he has
generously given me—I am able to put before the reader
the following details of this ancient Salaminian relic :—

Fig. 68.   Inscribed Roll found in a Tomb.   Lead.

Professor Sayce reads the above inscription in the
following way :—

ye si lu se ri mo ta sa ka se o le ke o te re no a to
to a sa mi te a me to to se le su se go a te to
po ro to a to pa ni yi se lo to pi si pu o

Transposed into Greek characters, this would become—

Θεάτωρ Θεοκλέος Καατάμικρις (or κάς Δάμορις) λύσιγε
τόν έχος αύλης τῷ ἑόμε(ν) ἄει,(ν) (ῑ)μίαν ἀνθ' ά'(ν)
ά Πεσίπτολος γιναπᾶ τῷ ά(ν)θμέπφ

The English equivalent is as follows :—

"Theanor, the son of Theokles Kastanoris, (or and Damoris), shall atone for this pollution of sacrilege by giving in full one half of that which (i.e., in return for that which) Pusiptolos charges against the man."

"The forms of many of the characters," writes the Professor, " in this inscription are very remarkable. Thus we have new forms for *a*, *yi*, *o*, *lu*, and *ye*. The use of σύλη for 'sacrilege', of the future λύσιγε and of γινπᾶ (from ἐνιπάω) in the sense of *bringing a charge against* is also to be noticed. The purport of the inscription is curious in other respects."

SEALS OR STAMPS.

Classed with these ancient remains and municipal documents are eight leaden seals from Salamis. They are of Byzantine and early Venetian origin, and they bear monogram inscriptions, or, rather, merchants' marks, very like those familiar to all students of mediæval antiquities.[1] On one, a representation of St. Nicholas;[2] on another, the head of St. Peter, appears. This is the reverse of a stamp, similar to another in the same collection. A third bears an eagle;[3] a fourth bears the inscription, *obv.*, + CEPΓIOT CKPINIAP[IOT] ; *rev.*, SCRINI : KVPRI.[4] Each of these seals is pierced with transverse holes, through which a cord could be passed, so that the seal might be used to bind baggage or other goods in the manner still in vogue ; the lead, being pressed down on the cord, secured the package. These relics have been sought for and treasured up in later times by the ignorant people, who found them, and believed they must needs be charms, because such things were beyond the scope of their knowledge of trade and

---

[1] See Plate vi, fig. 3. [2] *Ibid.*, figs. 8, 9. [3] *Ibid.*, fig. 10.
[4] Sergius, Scrivener of Cyprus. See Plate vi, fig. 11.

property. By these persons the seals were again pierced, and attached by strings, so that they might be hung about the necks of their children, and thus do duty as amulets against the Evil Eye, whereas they were designed centuries ago to keep light fingers from surreptitiously conveying goods of value from the rightful owner to another who had no claim upon it.

The accompanying illustration (fig. 69) shows a relic

Fig. 69.   Youthful Head.   Lead.

in lead, representing a very elegant head of a youth enclosed in a cabled border, which, in its turn, is encircled by a beaded rim or circlet. It was perhaps a badge or ornament, for application to the dress or to a small work of art. The way in which the hair is represented on this head very closely resembles the treatment of the hair on the heads of Eros or Cupid, as shewn in the terra-cotta and bronze figures of that divinity.

CHAPTER VII.

IVORY OBJECTS.

SEALS OR RINGS—CARVINGS—BOXES—SPOONS—ARTICLES FOR THE TOILET,
ETC.

MONG the relics in this material are two to
which I may, in the first instance, call
attention. They are large seals or rings,
and were, doubtless, intended for securing
amphoræ, or other vessels, by impressing
wax with the private marks of the owners of the vessels.
In Nineveh, it was found that a similar practice of sealing had been in vogue. Certain chambers were found to
have been closed by placing lumps of clay against the
doors and their jambs, and impressing on the soft
material the official or state seals of the proper officers.[1]

[1] The Lord answered Job out of the whirlwind, "It is turned as clay
to the seal".—(*Job* xxxviii, 14.) The use of seals is amply illustrated in
the Scriptures, especially in the Book of Revelation. Daniel was sealed
up in the lion's den (*Dan.* vi, 17); and in another place the same
prophet was bidden to "shut up the words, and seal the book" of the
record.—(*Dan.* xii, 4.) "Is not this laid up in store with me, and sealed
up among my treasures?" is one of the demands of Moses.—(*Deuteronomy*
xxxii, 34.) The custom of carrying seals in rings on the hand or
attached to bracelets, is often shown in the same collection of records of
manners and customs. "Set me as a seal upon thine heart, as a seal
upon thine arm", occurs in Solomon's Song (viii, 6). Judah asked of
Tamar, whom he did not know : "What pledge shall I give thee?"
And she said : "Thy signet, and thy bracelets, and thy staff that is in
thy hand." Afterwards, she said : "Discern, I pray thee, whose are
these, the signet, the bracelets, and staff?" The stone of the sepulchre
of Christ was sealed : "So they went, and made the sepulchre sure,
sealing the stone, and setting a watch."—(*Matthew* xxvii, 66.)

Amphorœ of wine have been found still bearing the
impressions of the owners' seals upon their mouths, and
within retaining traces of the fluids thus guarded during
more than twenty centuries.

The collection contains a similar ring to that which
has just now been mentioned. In it is set an oval disk
of green glass.[1] Another bears the head of a woman in
bas-relief; it is probably a cameo of Arsinoe.[2] The other
articles include the pin of ivory, on which one of the
strings of a lyre has been turned; and parts of ivory
boxes, severally sculptured with a Cupid and a lioness,
both in animated actions.[3] Scarabæi of ivory are mentioned below. Some curious rods of ivory were exhumed, having staples or little braces of bronze. They
were designed for attaching the strings to a lyre.[4] In the
chapter of this work which contains an account of terra-
cotta figures of musicians, other notices of similar objects
are given. There are, also, spoons of a kind similar
to those of silver which have been already mentioned in
the chapter which treats of articles formed of that metal.
One hair-pin, round which a woman's tresses were wound,
bears a figure of Venus at its extremity.[5] The handle of
another ends in a coronetted head. Among miscellaneous
objects are a die, an ear-pick, fragments of pins, or bod-
kins, which retain parts of their ancient coating of gold,
and afford additional examples to many others which
illustrate ancient devices for making a little of the precious metal go far. There was found also the engraved
head of a hair-pin, of the kind represented more than
once in the collection, which is a nearly perfect relic.[6]

During the course of my excavations, I had given
particular directions that objects of terra-cotta should
be brought to me whenever they were taken from the
ground. In such remains, owing to the varieties of their

---

[1] See Plate VII, fig. 7.   [2] *Ibid.*, fig. 2.   [3] *Ibid.*, fig. 1.
   Ibid., fig. 13.   [5] *Ibid.*, fig. 15.   [6] *Ibid.*, fig. 14.

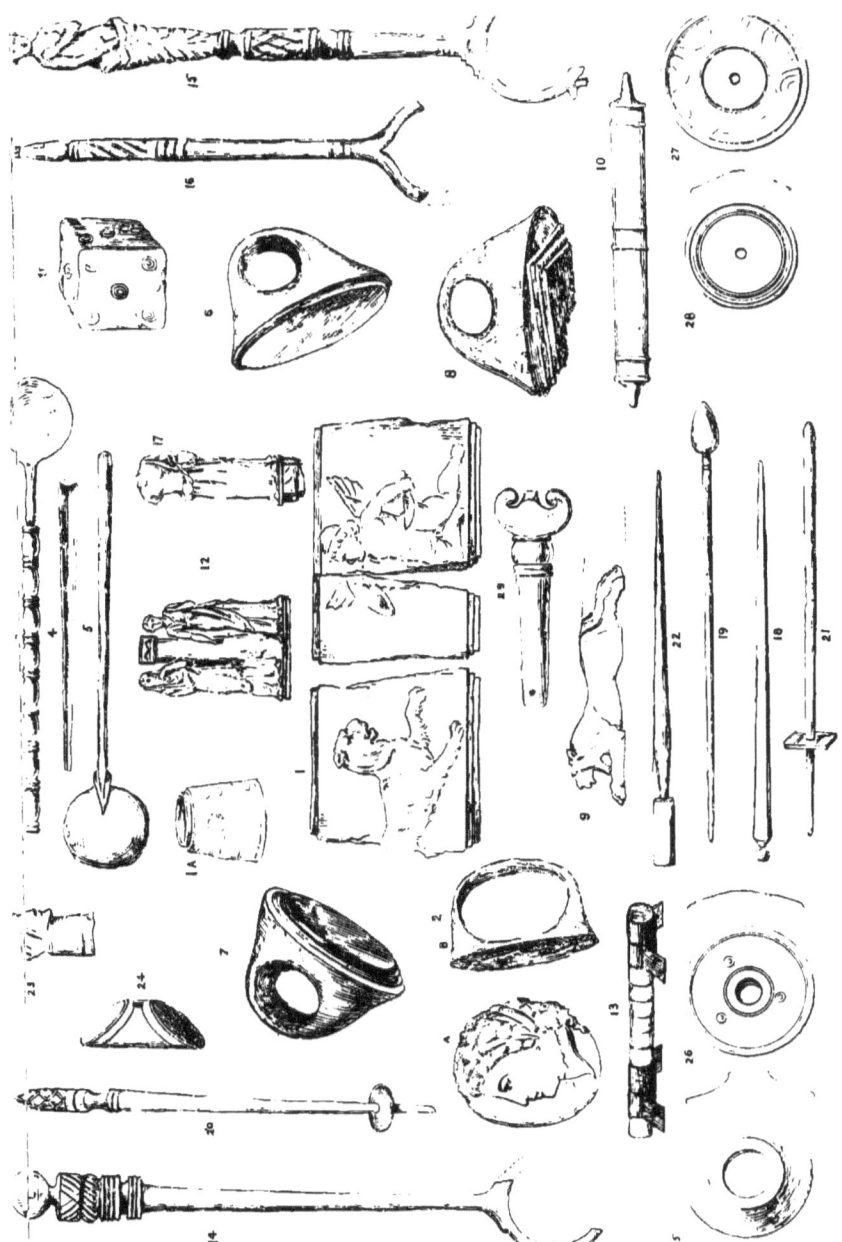

forms and dates, I took great interest. One day, a man, who made it his business to discover stones for building, and who, therefore, might be called a quarryman among the ancient ruins he helped to destroy for the convenience of the living, came to me with the terra-cotta figure of a cock, which still remains in my collection, and, in bearing traces of colour, has an interest of its own, such as is enlarged on in the account below of such relics. On further inquiry, I was taken to the place where this article had been found. Excavations being made there, resulted in recovering from a hole enclosed by rough stones similar terra-cottas, making six in all, being—1, a crouching cat; 2, a ram in a similar position; 3, a goat, likewise crouching; 4, the grotesque figure of a fat man, laughing, and with his hands clasped before his belly, and in the attitude of waddling rather than walking; 5, a head of Hercules, laughing, and with the lion's head drawn over his brows, the claws of the creature being placed against the cheeks of the hero; 6, the figure of a man, supposed to be a priest, squatting on his haunches; both hands are on the knees of the figure, his large beard is trimmed to a heart-shape, the face is laughing, and the nose is turned up in a very quaint manner. These works are still in the numerous body of terra-cottas which are alluded to below.

Close to the spot in question, and evidently deposited there with unusual care, were even more interesting relics, being two paterae of similar form, arranged as a bowl and lid, which cohered so closely at the rims that they could not be separated without fracturing one or both of them (fig. 70A). On breaking into the casket which was formed by the union of these vessels, and satisfying myself that no inscriptions were to be found on either of the paterae, a quantity of earth was removed from between them, and among this earth was a little cylindrical box of lead (fig. 70B), about two inches in diameter and three inches and a half high. The finder now

thought that there was a probability of treasure being
concealed in the little casket, and he cried out for joy.
The box was opened by lifting the lid, and it appeared to
be made of lead, like others which had been found elsewhere; one of which, from Salamis, filled with glass drops,
and the earth which had filtered among them during
many ages, has already engaged our attention.

This leaden casket of Kittium, where this relic was
found, contained a very elegant cylindrical box of ivory
(fig. 70c), sculptured with figures of men or priests adoring
a bull, Apis, and an ibis (fig. 72). Both these creatures
are placed on benches or altars (fig. 73). The lid of the
ivory box is sculptured in relief, with the head in profile,
of a bearded man (fig. 71), whose hair is bound with two

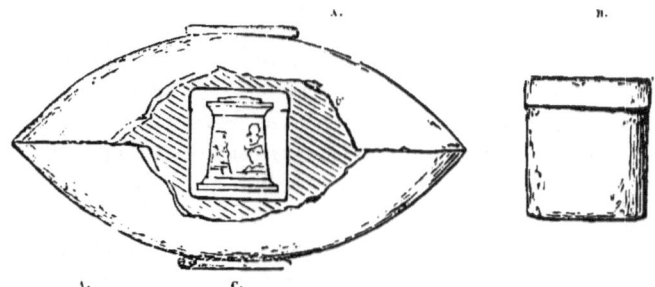

Fig. 70.   Two Paterae (A) enclosing a Leaden Box (B, in which was
found an Ivory Box (c).

fillets. It has been remarked that, not only is this head
of very fine execution, but that critics have not decided
whether it is of Greek or Roman origin; and, above all, that
the style of its execution differs radically from that of the
sculptures on the box itself, which, delicate and elaborate
as they are, show the influence of the somewhat stiff and
jejune mode of Assyrian designs as transmitted through
Phœnicia, and with characteristics which may be due to
the local art of Cyprus itself. Considering these circumstances and conclusions, the latter being based on recon-

dite criticism of the respective and differing styles of the several parts of this curious casket, we are driven to the conclusion that the body of the relic is a copy from some much more ancient piece of sculpture in ivory, embracing that which is, comparatively speaking, an archaic manner of design and treatment, far removed from the elegant

Fig. 71.   Carved Lid of Box.   *Ivory.*

and well-developed style of the medallion on the top, or that the top was made of old, in order to supply the place of the original and far more ancient one, the design

Fig. 72.   Box.   *Ivory.*

of which may, broadly speaking, have been similar to that before us in the medallion in profile.[1] I incline to the second hypothesis, and I do so with regard to the

---

[1] This resembles a *tessera* or ticket for the theatre, of which there are several in the British Museum.

differing types of *style* exhibited by these carvings, and
without ignoring the fact that the subjects represented
on the body of the box may have been in vogue for
gnostic or heretical worship, at a period coëval with the
top itself. The evidence of style is, however, unchallenge-
able.

The finder of this very curious relic of Cypriote antiquity was doomed to disappointment while he fancied
that it might contain treasure. The box, being opened,
enclosed only a small pebble, which has, unfortunately, disappeared. This is the more to be deplored,
because, however trivial the vanished object may have
seemed to the untutored eyes of its discoverer, there

Fig. 73.   Subject carved on Box.   *Ivory.*

cannot be any doubt that a stone which had been so
carefully and, so to say, sumptuously deposited in the
earth many centuries ago, must have had a peculiar
history and characteristics, all hopes for elucidating
which vanished for ever when the pebble was lost.
If, as was probably the case with regard to the glass
drops of diverse colours found in another leaden box, this
little pebble had been piously placed in its casket of
ivory by some relation of the dead in whose grave it was
found a thousand years and more after the last tears
were shed over that grave, how much pathos would have
affected those who had sympathy enough with human

sorrow to enter into the history of the apparently insignificant little stone !

Another ivory group comprises two little figures of women standing side by side, and amply draped in the Greek mode ; the figure on our left is veiled ; her companion is bare-headed. A column, altar, or *term*, is between the figures, and may be taken to indicate the religious purposes of the group.

The ivory rods[1] are conjectured to have been employed on lyres in order to turn the strings of those instruments over the tops of the same ; they are supposed to have served the purpose of a bridge, while other specimens of ivory, already referred to, were undoubtedly used to secure the ends of the strings of the lyre.

[1] Plate vii, fig. 10.

CHAPTER VIII.

BONE AND SHELL ANTIQUITIES.

BONE.

BONE, as a material employed in manufacturing arts, is much more common in the north of Europe, than in the south of that continent and in Asia, where the preferable material ivory could be obtained with comparative ease. The bone antiquities of northern races are numerous and valuable; those of Cyprus are, if not so numerous, at any rate of noteworthy character.

In the course of the extensive excavations which I conducted at Salaminium, I found, among other relics composed of bone, an *étui*, or small case, one foot in height, which takes the form of a statuette of a woman (fig. 74). It was made to open by a socketed joint at the hips of the figure. This little case contained, when found, two or three broken pins of ivory or bone. The art illustrated by the carving of this noteworthy figure is extremely simple, not to say archaic, and indicates the influence of Egyptian modes on the taste of a Greek artist, who disposed the long and severe folds of the drapery with great care, and yet referred to nature for the manner in which they are placed. The eyelids, irides, and eyebrows have been indicated by colour which appears to have been applied in a moist state with a brush; the lips and nostrils are carved in relief.

The hair, which is in large, freely-disposed masses, is tinted and bound in a large knot over the forehead. From the presence of wings on the head, Dr. Birch conjectures that the figure was probably intended for Medusa. The arms of the little carving have been attached to the body by means of pins, one of which I replaced more firmly in order to secure it against loss. The fibrous nature of bone, which distinguishes that material from ivory, may be noticed in several parts of the interior of this extremely rare object. An additional

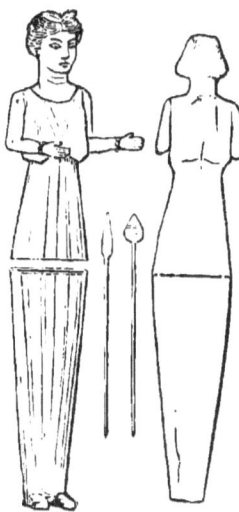

Fig. 74.   Archaic Box and Contents.   Bone.

and irrefragable proof that bone is in question here, is afforded by the unmistakeable cancellated structure of the interior of the relic. The collection of antiquities also contains an elegantly-worked bone carving of a lion, which originally formed the end or top of a pin or small stick, or the handle of a knife;[1] a stop for a hairpin

[1] Plate VII, fig. 9.

carved in the form of a head;[1] bone hairpins of elegant design;[2] and a small but fine carving of two females, full length, with a column between them.[3]

SHELL.

Among the rarest of the materials employed for decorative purposes by the people of antiquity is that of the shells of the sea; but for domestic service shells were largely used, as for spoons, and, above all, as strigils for the bath, and otherwise as scrapers, as well as in some of the modern offices of paper. An exceedingly choice and rare example of the application of shell as a decoration, or rather as a luxury, appears in the beautiful casket, which, with a necklace, three beautiful earrings, and some other miscellaneous objects of interest I found in 1877, while digging in a tomb at Salaminium. It is formed of the shells of a large bivalve, probably of the *Byssus* species, a marine mollusc, the beard of which was prepared and woven into robes of great price, while the preparation of another of its parts furnished the well-known dye. These shells, (fig. 75), measure about five inches in one direction and six and a half inches in the other; the natural hinge which connected them has been broken, and its office supplied by a hinge of bronze attached by two pins to each valve, at one side. When in use, the sides of the casket have been kept together by a hook of bronze, which, turning on a pin outside one valve, catches in a staple which is fixed in the other valve, and passes through a hole in the former. This contrivance is identical with that of innumerable modern instances. On each shell is painted, not, as usual, engraved, in brilliant vermilion, a border of a running pattern; the border on one valve consists of a simple key-fret, or rectangular design, which is marked

[1] Plate vii, fig. 23.   [2] Plate vii, figs. 11, 15.   [3] Plate vii, fig. 12.

in the intervals of the inner side of the border by small indications of a flower and leaves; these are similarly painted in vermilion; the intervals of the outer side of the valve are filled with vermilion dots. The border of the other shell is formed of a running wave-pattern with a dot or spot of colour in each curve; in the centre on this side is an oval mark, also of vermilion, which has been so much obliterated that its character cannot now be explained; perhaps, it was a scarabæus. The first-named, or upper valve is enriched, on part of the border, with a four-armed cross, like that called a Greek cross, placed at the point of the natural hinge. The place of

Fig. 75.   Inscribed Case.   *Shell.*

the bronze hook and staple is distinguished from that of the hinge of the same material by means of a closed hand with extended forefinger, 👉 , which points to the hook. The place of the hinge is marked by the figure of a phallus, surrounded by a row formed of the Cypriote letter ↑. Two other inscriptions of the same language and characters are placed transversely on this valve: they are given in the woodcut.

These inscriptions have been kindly interpreted by Professor Sayce and M. Pierides. They read :—

yi o ta ro po a se te
                           pi   ta

Ταβί τῆς 'Αβροτάοyι

I.e., "Toilet Box of Habrotos".

This word Ταβί is apparently borrowed from the Phœnician ת ֵ ב ָ ה *tēhvāh*.[1] The Cypriote letter which has
been already referred to, corresponds with the Greek
syllables γα, κα, or χα, and is repeated seven times on the
shell.

Infiltrated earth only was found inside this very
remarkable casket.

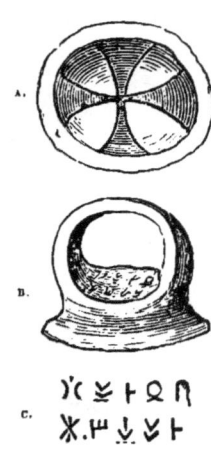

Fig. 76 A, B, C.   Inscribed Ring.   *Glass.*
A. The Device ; B. Position of the Inscription ; c. The Letters.

Curiously enough, I found in the same tomb a ring
formed of glass (fig. 76), which has on the inside surface
of the bezel an inscription in the Cypriote language
identical with that found on the hinged shell box. The
device, which this glass ring bears in a concave depression,
is a rosette or a cross of the shape called *pattée* by the
heralds, in red glass upon a white field, over which a thin

[1] *Gen.* vi, 14, 15, 16, etc., "*ark*".

plate of plain glass is placed, and when the ring was complete and in use, the cross shone through this flat plate of glass.

In a tomb near Famagusta I found no less than eight

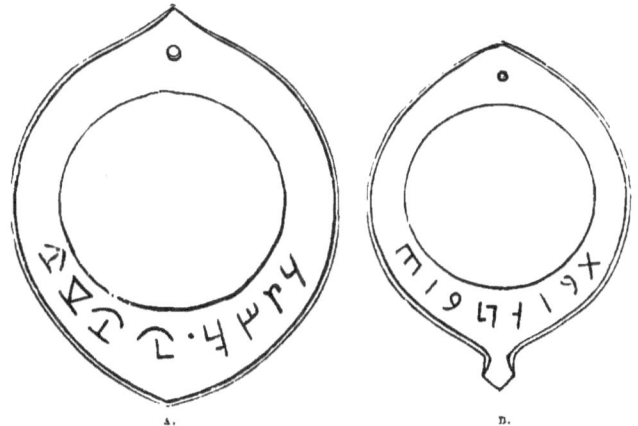

Fig. 77 A, B. Inscribed Ornaments. *Shell.*

remarkable ring-shaped objects of shell, graduating in size from three-fourths of an inch to two inches and a

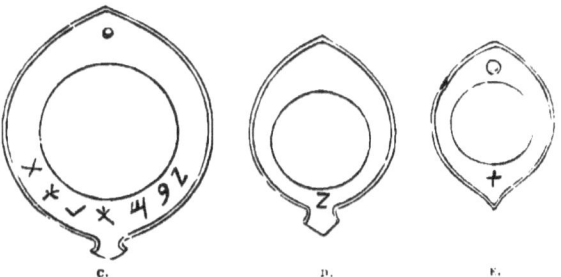

Fig. 77 C, D, E. Inscribed Ornaments. *Shell.*

quarter. They are of oval form, cusped at the upper end and pierced. The lower end is finished off with a pointed spur-like projection. The lower margins of

M

these objects have inscriptions, of which most of the characters are those found in the Cypriote language, and a few on the three largest of the rings appear to belong to the Phœnician language. But from the imperfect number of the relics, no satisfactory interpretation has yet been arrived at (figs. 77, A—H). It has been conjectured

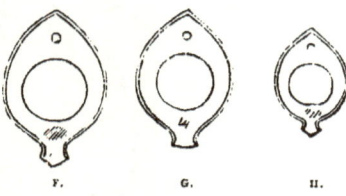

F.　　　　　G.　　　　　H.

Fig. 77 F, G, H.　　　　Inscribed Ornaments.　　　　*Shell.*

that these eight rings of shell formed part of a necklace or breast ornament, to be worn by a priest or other public functionary, upon his breast, the smaller pieces overlapping the larger ones, like tiles, in a vertical row; in which case the inscriptions perhaps run on in grammatical sequence from the less to the greater circles or margins of the relics.

STONE ANTIQUITIES.

HE stone antiquities which rewarded my labours in excavating several prolific sites in the island of Cyprus are not particularly numerous, but in themselves, from the frequency with which they are associated with inscriptions, they possess an enhanced interest. It is a curious fact, that the calcareous stone which is found in the island in great abundance contributes almost always the material for these objects; and from the peculiar nature of its composition, it does not easily discolour from age or exposure: hence, to a casual observer, the stone objects, which undoubtedly range over a period of more than a thousand years, and embrace representations of Egyptian, Phœnician, Assyrian, Greek, Roman, and Early Christian art, appear to have been made within a comparatively recent time—so fresh and clear is the colour of the stone of which they are formed. Next to the objects in calcareous stone, those in marble are most numerous. I have been able to procure several slabs of this material, with Greek inscriptions, and of a fairly early period.

The accompanying woodcut (fig. 77*) represents a fragment of hard stone, two and three-quarter inches in length, which I found at Cerina, or Cyrene, on the

North coast of the Island of Cyprus. M. Pierides considers that the inscription which is scratched upon it is probably part of some Phœnician numeration or calculation. The first sign to the right he believes to repre-

Fig. 77*.   Phœnician Inscription.   *Stone.*

sent 20, and the other strokes, on the first line, 1 each. The numeral 20 is repeated on the second line.

At Cerina, a site worthy of exploration, I found a calcareous stone of rectangular shape, measuring four inches and three-quarters in length, and two inches and a-half in height, with the left hand upper corner roughly rounded off. It is represented by the accompanying illustration (fig. 78), and contains three lines of Cypriote inscriptions, the final *mi* of the first line being broken off.

The reading proposed by Professor Sayce, on the supposition that the stone is perfect on the right hand side, is as follows :—

```
[mi]   e   so   ya   pi   pa   se   ta   o   te
       ke  te   te   ka   mo   ra   ta   mi  a   (?)
                      se   mi   te   to  se  ke
```

. . θεοῦ τᾶς Παφίyας ἤ[μὶ] . . a(?)μιθρὰ με κατέθηκε . .

Κεστόθεμις

"Of the Paphian goddess am I...Amithra set me up....Kestothemis."

M. Pierides, however, considers that a breadth of stone sufficient to contain two characters has been struck from off the right hand side. He would read :—

```
e . se . ja . pi . pa . se . ta . o . te [se . ta]
ke . te . te . ka . mi . ra . ta . u [a . mi]
      se . mi . te . to . se . ri [a]
```

He transliterates the inscription into Greek in this manner :—

Τᾶς Θεῶ τᾶς Παφίας ἠμὶ αὐτάρμι κατέθηκε 'Αριστόθεμις.

We may thus easily arrive at the very satisfactory interpretation of this votive inscription, which that learned *savant* has elicited from the stone :—" I am

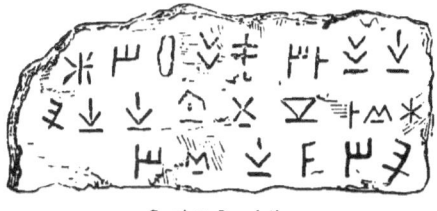

Fig. 78.   Cypriote Inscription.   *Stone.*

the statue of the Paphian goddess, and Aristothemis dedicated me."

The site of Cerina also enabled me to add to the

Fig. 79.   Cypriote Inscription.   *Stone.*

linguistic treasures which I rescued from destruction— a fragment of calcareous stone (fig. 79) of rectangular shape, measuring five inches and a-half in length, and two inches and a-half in height, with the left hand upper corner roughly rounded off, and the right hand corner broken away. Both the fractured corner and the rounded angle appear to have been in their present condition before the stone was selected by the stone-cutter, who has placed on it a distinct inscription, which commences beyond the break, and follows along the curved edge of the stone.

Professor Sayce and M. Pierides agree in their de-
· cipherment of this inscription, in the following lines :—

[se] . a . pi . pa . se . ta . mi . e . o . te . se . ta

Τᾶς θεῶ ἠμὶ τᾶς Παφία(ς)

"I belong to the Paphian goddess"; or, "I am [the statue] of the Paphian goddess".

Paphos, where I spent a considerable portion of my time when in the island of Cyprus, yielded, among other

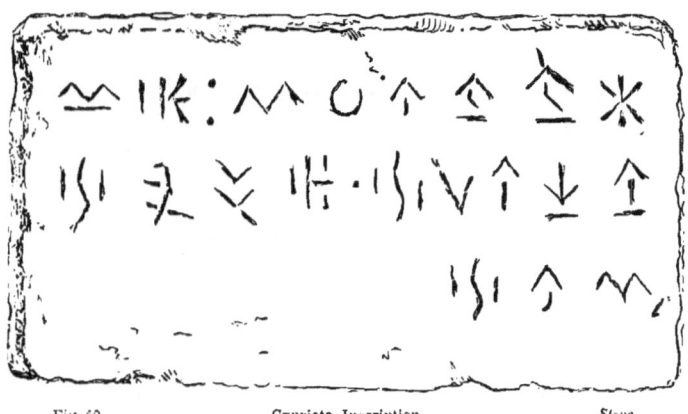

Fig. 80.   Cypriote Inscription.   Stone.

treasures rescued from the oblivion of centuries, several inscribed stones. The inscriptions, and, indeed, all that are given in this work, having been discovered only sub-sequent to Prof. Moriz Schmidt's exhaustive work on the Cypriote syllabary, will be welcome, it is hoped, to philo-logists as new additions to the very considerable *corpus* which is now available for analysis and comparison. It has been my good fortune to be the means of adding, in some degree at least, to this result. Professor Sayce, with his accustomed kindness, reads the inscription which is contained on the rectangular block of calcareous stone, measuring thirteen inches and a-half by seven inches and a-half (fig. 80), in three lines, in the following way :—

mi . e : u . ya . ti . ka . se . a

ne . ke . pi . e . ne . sa . ti . te . ka

ne . vo . u

'Ασικαθίγαυ ἠμὶ . κατέθισαν ἐπὶ κένευ ὂν (or γένευ ὄν ?)

" I am of Asikathiyas : They set (me) up over his Cenotaph (?)"

From Paphos also it was that I obtained for the Lawrence-Cesnola collection of antiquities a fragment of

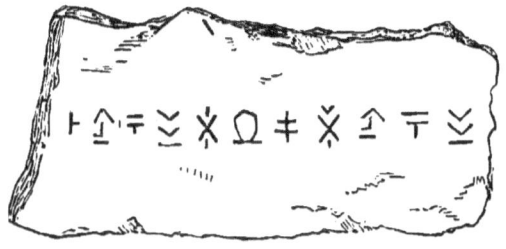

Fig. 81.   Cypriote Inscription.   Stone.

calcareous stone, measuring eight inches in length, by four inches and a quarter in height, on which is an interesting Cypriote inscription (fig. 81). Professor Sayce and M. Pierides, to whom I have submitted this inscription, concur in reading the syllables in the following manner :—

. . . ta . si . na . o . a . ra . pa . ku . si . na . o .

. . . 'Ονασικυπρὰ ἁ 'Ονασιδά[μου] . . . .

If this be so, of which there can be little doubt, we have here a sepulchral inscription recording the name of

" Onasikypra (the daughter or wife) of Onasidamos."

This name is not unknown, from its occurrence among the Cypriote inscriptions.[1]

A third piece of calcareous stone, which measures thirteen inches and a-half in height, and six inches and three quarters in breadth, from Paphos (fig. 82), although in its contour more regular than the two already described, contains portions only of four lines of Cypriote inscriptions; but Professor Sayce, who has fa-

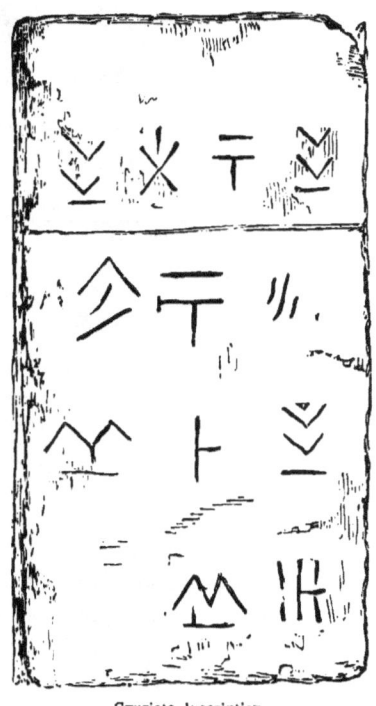

Fig. 82.   Cypriote Inscription.   Stone.

voured me with his conjectural reading, finds that "the fragmentary condition of this inscription makes a translation impossible". The syllables he would read in this manner:—

[1] Transactions of the Society of Biblical Archæology, vol. v. Part I.

o . i . na . o .

---

si . na . pa (?) [*or* to] ne.
mi . ta . o . .   .
. mi . e .   .

In line 3 perhaps we have—ὁ ταμίας, "The Steward", and in the fourth line εμι for ἐιμὶ "I am".

From Salamis also comes a slab of calcareous stone, measuring ten inches and three-quarters in breadth, and

Fig. 83.   Cypriote Inscription.   Stone.

twelve inches in height. On it (fig. 83) are three lines of Cypriote characters.

The third character in line 1 has been erased or tampered with. The inscription is, however, in other respects well cut. The reading :—

. se . ra . pa . ku . mo . ti
mi . e
mo . ta . mo . ti

N

is not yet ascertained; perhaps, "I am of Timokupra;
of Timodamos". The rectangular character with *horizontal* bar, which occurs three times in this inscription
and twice in fig. 85, is a new syllable, not known to
Schmidt, Deecke, or other collectors of Cypriote inscriptions. It is taken here, conjecturally, to be equivalent to the rectangular with a *vertical* bar, of which
the Greek transliteration is μο or μω.

One of the smaller fragments of stone which were
found at Salamis (three inches long) contains (fig. 84)
two Cypriote syllables "*se. a.*" It has been conjectured by those who have a knowledge of the language
that these characters may form the final part of the

Fig. 84.   Fragment of an Inscription.   *Stone.*

word Παφίας. But from the fragmentary condition of this
stone, we cannot advance beyond a mere supposition.

One of the statuettes formed of the native calcareous
stone found at Constanzia, near Salamis, bears a Cypriote inscription (fig. 85). It is ten inches and three-
quarters high, and represents a female figure draped in
a closely-fitting dress without many folds. Round the
neck are marks, which appear to indicate a necklace.
The right hand is laid upon the breast, the left hand
hangs down at the side, coming through a hole of the
drapery. The feet are formal, and placed upon a narrow

plinth or pedestal. The inscription, which is vertical, after the style of the Egyptian sepulchral figures, or *shabti*, commences at the breast, and is continued down the front of the figure to the hem of the robe. The characters, which are in some cases very indistinct, seem to represent the following values :—

. mo . so . te . so . ta . ka . so . mo . to . si . i . mo .

Professor Sayce and Dr. Birch consider the Greek equivalent to be : Μοισίδημος κατάστησέ με—"Moisidemos set me up."

Fig. 85.   Inscribed Statuette.   *Stone.*

Moisidemos, apparently a Cypriote form of the Greek name, Musidemos, or Mousidemos, probably dedicated this as an iconic offering or votive memorial to one of the deities of Cypriote cult, in remembrance of a female relative. This figure was found by an ignorant stone-cutter, who had gone to search for materials. He damaged the statuette, in order to get possession of a small quantity of gold leaf which covered the inscription. I happened to be passing while he was engaged at his work of desecration, and secured the relic for the collection.

A convex piece of calcareous stone exhumed at Soli (fig. 86), measuring five inches by three inches and a-half, evidently the middle part of a statuette of the same conventional form as the previous figure, with the right hand pendent, contains five lines of Cypriote inscription, of which the first line and the last alone are legible, about three intermediary lines apparently having been erased. Professor Sayce, to whose kindness I am deeply indebted

Fig. 86.   Torso of a Statuette with Cypriote Inscription.   *Stone.*

for much help throughout this work, transliterates this inscription thus :—

se to ka se su ? ta i a ne o ne te . . . . .

[Erasures]

se si ka to . . . .

τὴν ὀνείατα . . ἔσχατος
το κάσις

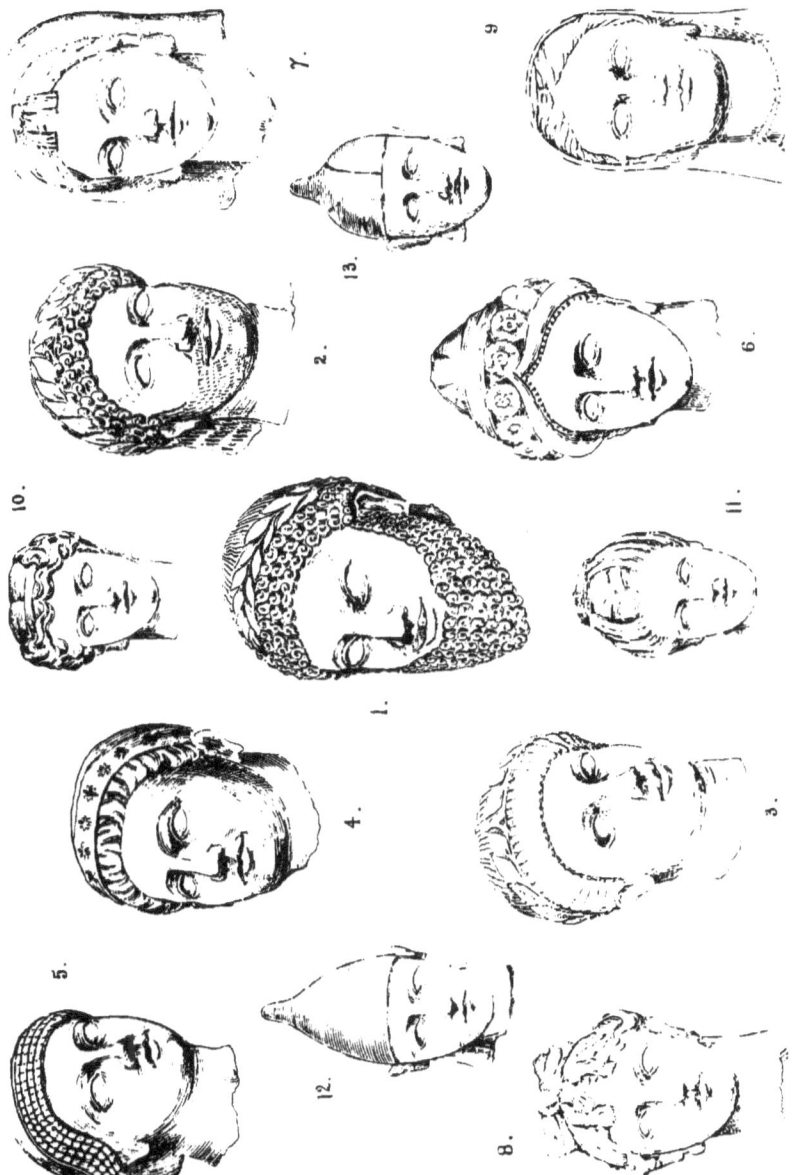

Unfortunately, the mutilated condition of the stone militates against a satisfactory interpretation of the imperfect record which it contained.

There are in this subdivision of the Lawrence-Cesnola collection several stone statuettes of a class which is not unfrequently found, bearing inscriptions in the Cypriote character; but they are not easy of interpretation in the present unsettled state of our knowledge of that language. Besides the perfect statuettes, I found a very large quantity of the heads of similar objects, most of which are Egyptian, Assyrian, Greek, and Roman, in their characters and origin.

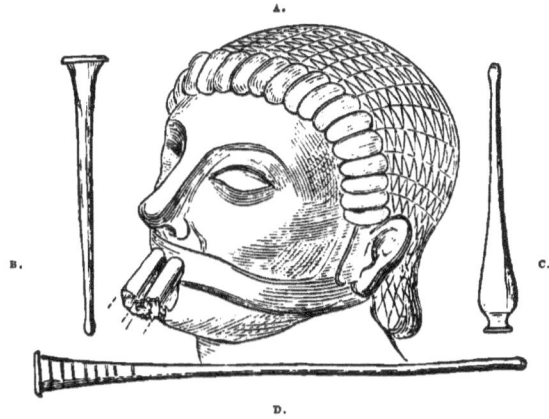

Fig. 87.   A. Head with Mouth-strap and Pipes.   *Stone.*
            B, C, D. Trumpets.   *Terra-cotta.*

The accompanying illustration (fig. 87A) shews a stone head from Salamis in the Lawrence-Cesnola collection, which may be profitably compared with some similar specimens in the British Museum. In this example the treatment is apparently Phœnician, with Assyrian influence. It is the head of a statuette representing a player on the double pipe, which was secured in its proper position at the mouth of the player by a broad fillet or strap passing over the cheeks and fastened at the

back of the head.   Figs. 87 B C D are specimens of the
pipe. trumpet or *lituus*, in terra-cotta, for mortuary purposes, which will be described hereafter in the place
devoted to a consideration of the *fictilia*.

The Phœnician altar, figured on page 99, is worthy of
comparison with several stone models in this collection,

Fig. 85.   Salamis and Constanzia.   *Stone.*

which have the forms of chalices, or, to speak more
strictly, resemble baptismal fonts of very small proportions.

In the year 1877, while I was digging in the land
which lies between the sites of the ancient towns of
Salamis and Constanzia, I found a very remarkable

group carved in stone in the Greek style (fig. 88). It
appears to me to be intended to represent a personification of Salamis, here conceived as Teucer, wearing a
toga, and leaning against a terminal figure of Hermes.
Constanzia, as a female personage, draped in the elegant
folds of the *chiton*, and having her hair bound with a
broad fillet, is leaning in an attitude of ease and grace-
fulness upon the male figure; the left hand and arm
being placed behind her back, and the right arm, from the
elbow to the hand, reposes on the shoulder of the other
figure. This group may have possibly marked the spot
where some territorial boundary between these two sites
existed, or it may perpetuate the memory of some act of
confederation or annexation, so to speak, between the
authorities of these towns. From the introduction of
the terminal Hermes, it is manifest that some question
of boundaries is involved in the conception of this
spirited piece of statuary. The height of the group
is ten inches and a-half.

Dr. Birch considers that this group is apparently that
of a prince and his wife, in the characters of Mars and
Venus. The breeches of the male figure are neither
Greek nor Roman. The man's face somewhat resembles
that of Antoninus Pius, and the portraits of that period;
the woman's is not unlike that of Faustina the elder.[1]

A curious stone carving, unfortunately, imperfect in
the upper part (fig. 89), bears the inscription in Greek
capitals :—

ΑΡΤΕΜΙΔΙ ΠΑΡΑΛΙΑ ΑΠΕΛΛΗC ΑΝΕΘΗΚΕ,

"To Diana Paralia Apelles has offered this."

This is a dedication to Diana "of the Beach" by one
Apelles. The letters, which are well formed, and very

---

[1] This may be compared with Clarac, *Musée de Sculpture*, pl. 835,
No. 2093, Napl. Mus. Borb.; pl. 887, No. 2278A, Boissard: pl. 894,
No. 2287, Rome, Coll. Giustiniani.

nicely cut, seem to belong to the second century after
Christ. Other dedications to this same Diana have been
found before. All these come from the Salines of Larnaca, where probably stood a temple to the goddess,
and where I, and those who worked before me, found

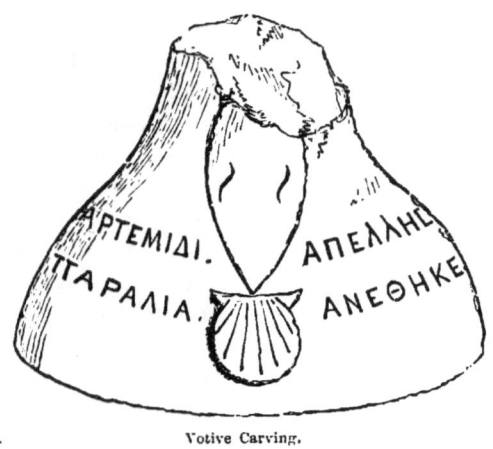

Fig. 89.   Votive Carving.   *Stone.*

many terra-cotta heads, as well as a large number of
gold staters of Alexander and Philip.

On an elegant stone cippus of columnar form, with
plinth and capital of elegant mouldings, two feet high
and nine inches and a half wide, which was found at
Salaminium, is cut the inscription :—

CΩTΠΡA

XΡΠΣTE

XAIΡE

" Farewell, dearest Soteira."

There is a village of the name of Sotera still extant in
the vicinity of Salamis. Here, however, the word is
the name of a female. The sepulchral and conventional formula, embodied in the last two words of this
inscription, is found very commonly throughout the island.

A broken, but still rectangular, slab (fig. 90) of marble, which measures about seven inches long and five inches high, reads :—

Τ Γ Ι Α C N......
C N T H P......
Φ Ι Λ Λ Ε......

Fig. 90. Inscribed Sepulchral Slab. Marble.

" Mayst thou be well, Soter, son of Philalethes."

Another slab (fig. 91) of marble, nine inches and a quarter broad and five inches and three-quarters high, has the usual sepulchral formula ; but the name of a female on the first line has been altered, traces of letters erased being under those that now stand to represent a somewhat unusual name.

Ε Τ Ο Δ Λ
Χ Ρ Η Σ Τ Η
Χ Λ Ι Ρ Ε

Fig. 91. Inscribed Sepulchral Slab. Marble.

" Farewell, excellent Evoda !"

The following sepulchral inscription is on a marble slab (fig. 92) measuring nine inches and three-quarters in breadth and six inches and a quarter in height :—

Ε Τ Φ Ρ Α Ν Ν Ρ
Χ Ρ Η Σ Τ Ε
Χ Λ Ι Ρ Ε

Fig. 92. Inscribed Sepulchral Slab. Marble.

" Farewell, excellent Euphranor !"

On a marble slab (fig. 93) measuring six inches in breadth and twelve inches in height, the following Greek inscription occurs :—

```
ΓΕΜΕΛΛΕ
ΧΡΗΣΤΕ
ΧΑΙΡΕ
ΕΛΑΦΡΑ
COIΓΗ
```

Fig. 93.   Inscribed Sepulchral Slab.   *Marble.*

" Farewell, dearest Gemellus !   Light lie the earth upon thee !"

The latter part of this inscription is the equivalent of the Latin formula, "Sit tibi terra levis", so frequently found on Roman sepulchral slabs.

The following inscription (fig. 94) is cut on a marble slab, broken on the left hand side, measuring six inches and a half in height and three inches and a half in breadth :—

```
... .. ΤΝΗΣ
ΘΑΝΟΝΤΑ
......ΡΑΤΗΝ
....................
......Ν
......ΡΙΤΗΝ
```

Fig. 94.   Inscribed Slab.   *Marble.*

A slab of black marble (fig. 95), broken on both sides, four inches broad and four inches and three-quarters high, contains the following inscription :—

....
......A T.. ...I Σ T Ω......
[A Φ] P O Δ I T H Σ......
......T O N Γ E N O......
......T Θ T Λ O V......
Γ Y N A I K A
....

Fig. 95.   Inscribed Slab.   *Marble.*

The stone remains at Salamis are numerous, but
their size and weight make them valuable prizes to the
local wants of the mason and stone-cutter; hence

Fig. 96.   Carved Altar.   *Stone.*

destruction and mutilation are rife among these lapidary
treasures of the past, and but few carvings of any interest or value can any longer be obtained. Among the

sculptured stones which I recovered is an altar (fig. 96) of Phœnician origin, which measures eleven inches in height and five inches in width at the base, gradually diminishing upwards towards the carved or embattled cornice. On the front is a carving in low relief, and somewhat coarsely executed, representing, as Dr. Birch supposes, a man vested in flowing drapery, and wearing an Egyptian head-dress, in the act of sacrificing at an altar of a very archaic contour.   At the side of this relic another stone represents a man holding a palm-branch, perhaps to indicate that he is the victor in one of the public games or

Fig. 97.   Inscribed Tripod.   *Terra d'Umbra.*

in the circus.   This circumstance perhaps suggests the cause which led to the erection of the altar.

In a village now called Tremitusa, the ancient site of *Tremithus,* near Athieno, the ancient *Golgoi,* I found a stone cippus, which measures three feet in height, four in breadth, and one in thickness.   The pediment, with which it is enriched, has a mythological head in the centre, adorned with ample curls of hair.   Perhaps it is the head of Medusa.   There are three half-length figures upon the panel or entablature.   That in the centre is of a man of middle age; that on the right is of a female;

the third on the left hand is of a man with a head-dress. All these are evidently iconic, and from the strong family likeness shown by the faces, the three persons must be referred to the same family. The execution of this interesting piece of sepulchral sculpture, although in some degree conventional, is spirited, and the expression is pleasing and animated.[1]

Of the stone which has been designated "Terra

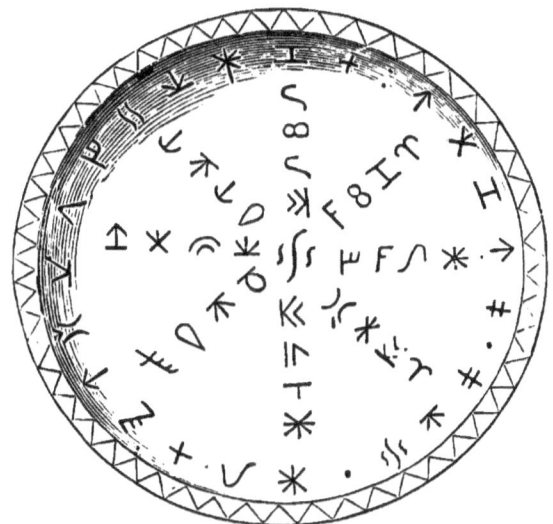

Fig. 98.   Inscribed Bowl of the Tripod.

d'Umbra", I found a sacrificial tripod (fig. 97), which is inscribed with a Cypriote invocation of remarkable length. The height of this object is two inches, and diameter three inches and fifteen sixteenths.

Professor Sayce, to whom I submitted the inscriptions, writes :—" The inscription which runs in a circle round the edge or rim of the bowl reads as follows: commencing at the dot, the lowest character on the accompanying

_____
[1] See Plate ix, fig. 2.

woodcut (fig. 98), and reading along the right hand
side up to the top, and then down the left side of
the figure."

.. pa . ti . ve . i . ti . : lo . ve . i . te . ? . se . ko . la . ma . ti . ni . lo . po . e .
                                                        . ne . te . pa ·

    " This I would translate :—

    Παντὶ γείδ[ε]ι· λόγε ἡδέως(?) κώλα, μάντι, νῖλον πόε βάδην.

    " For every kind : wash pleasantly (?) the limbs, O seer, make a......
walking on foot."

The centre of the bowl is engraved with the character
which corresponds with the syllable *ne*. From this, eight
inscriptions of four characters each are arranged to
radiate out towards the rim in the symmetrical figure of
a star of eight points. " The inscriptions," says the
authority above-mentioned, " are :—

```
        . ti .           . po .              . u .
      . te .           . le .            . ve .
       . ti .          . po.         . le .
         . ya .      . o .     . to .
   . ka . i . re . te . ne . se . to . po . e .
         . ra .      . o .    . ru .
       . te .          . li .          . a .
     . ya .          . da .          . o .
   . ke .              . e .              . u .
```

" This," continues the Professor, " I can only partially
explain. The end of the sentence is marked by χαίρετε,
hail. Ti-te-ti-ya, and po-le-po-o, I do not understand.
Then we have ὑγέλετο, *i.e.*, ἐπιγείλετο, *he chose as a suc-
cessor*. Then ἡ πότος, *verily a drinking bowl*. Then
ὑ ὀάρυ, *i.e.*, ἐπὶ ὀάρυ, *in the time of that*. The last word
I read χεατῆρα, *a libation bowl*. I cannot explain the
signification of the *o* on the bottom of the vessel, and the
letters or characters *i re u*, one on each foot."

In a tomb at Salamis I found an amulet of hard
stone, in the shape of a rectangle, with the corners cut
off obliquely (fig. 99). This has an inscription in five

lines of three letters each upon its face, in irregularly-formed Greek capital letters:—ΙΑΩ . ΜΙΧΑΗΛ . ΡΑΦΑΗΛ. Some of these letters are of peculiar shape, the Ρ and Φ of the latter word particularly so. It has been considered that this object formed part of the necklace of an infant, as an amulet, in accordance with the custom of the Gnostics in the earliest days of primitive Christianity. The three names here recorded are of potency among the votaries of that deluded and degraded mysticism. 1. Jao, or, perhaps, Jehovah; 2. Michael, the Archangel; and 3. Raphael, the Archangel. At a late period of the Byzantine Empire, engraved stones were employed for various pur-

poses as talismans, love philtres, the cure of diseases, the averting of misfortunes, and the neutralising of the effects of the evil eye. Particular properties and virtues were attributed to each variety of hard stone, and the inscriptions contained, in Greek or magical characters, the names of the Æons, and other powers of the Gnostic and Basilidian sects. The god Abraxas, or Jao, here addressed by name, is represented on some stones as a giant armed with a spear and a shield, having his head like a cock, and his legs like snakes.

At Salamis, a rectangular marble tablet, nine inches and a quarter in length, and three inches and a half in height, with a sepulchral inscription of six lines in small irregular Greek capital letters, without division of words, forming three elegiac distichs, was found. This elegant poem is a welcome addition to the Greek anthology, and is evidently the composition of a poet of considerable merit. It reads thus :—

Τὸ πρίν ὃ σύμ Μούσαις στέρξας βίον ἦλθε πρὸ Μοίρας
Ἀσκέπτους νεκύων εἰς θαλάμους Φιλέας,
Τρίσον ἐπ' εἰκοστῶι πλήσας ἔτος· οἱ δ' ὀλέσαντες
Ἐλπίδα τάν μούναν γηραλέοι γενέται,
Μύρονται τὸν ἄνυμφον ἀεὶ γόνον, ἄλλα τὸν ἀγνὸν,
Φερσεφόνη, στείλαις χῶρον ἐς εὐσεβέων.

Fig. 100.   Inscribed Sepulchral Slab.   *Marble.*

We may translate the Greek poem in these lines :—

" Phileas, the Muses' hope and love, hath sped
To the dark chambers of th' untimely dead.
He lived three years and twenty ; now asleep
Their extreme hope his aged parents weep—
Their brideless son. Dread Goddess ! send in rest
This chaste one to the regions of the blest."

This charming elegy will forcibly remind the reader of the almost parallel passages in the unsurpassed poetry of Milton :—

" For Lycidas is dead, dead ere his prime,
Young Lycidas, and hath not left his peer.
Who would not sing for Lycidas ? He knew
Himself to sing, and build the lofty rhyme.
　　　　·　　·　　·
Weep no more, woful shepherds, weep no more ;
For Lycidas, your sorrow, is not dead,
Sunk though he be beneath the watery floor :
So sinks the day-star in the ocean bed,
And yet anon repairs his drooping head,
And tricks his beams, and with new-spangled ore
Flames in the forehead of the morning sky :
So Lycidas sunk low, but mounted high,
Through the dear might of Him that walked the waves ;
Where, other groves and other streams along,
With nectar pure his oozy locks he laves,
And hears the unexpressive nuptial song

ΤΟΓΡΙΝΟΣΥΜΜΟΥΣΑΙΣΣΤΕΡΕΑΣΒΙΟΝΗΛΘΕΠΡΟΜΟΙΡΑΣ
ΑΣΚΕΠΤΟΥΣΝΕΚΥΩΝΕΙΣΘΛΑΜΟΥΣΦΙΛΕΑΣ
ΤΡΙΣΟΝΕΠΕΧΟΣΤΟΙΓΛΗΣΑΣΕΤΟΣΟΙΔΕΟΛΕΣΑΥΤΕΣ
ΕΛΠΙΔΑΤΑΝΜΟΥΝΑΝΕΗΡΑΜΕΘΙΓΕΝΕΤΑΙ
ΜΥΡΟΝΤΑΙΤΟΝΑΝΥΑΦΟΝΑΕΙΓΟΝΟΝΑΛΛΑΤΟΝΑΓΝΟΝ
ΦΕΡΣΕΦΟΝΗΣΤΕΙΛΑΙΣΧΩΡΟΝΕΣΕΥΣΕΒΕΩΝ

In the blest kingdoms meek of joy and love,
There entertain him all the saints above,
In solemn troops and sweet societies,
That sing, and, singing, in their glory move,
And wipe the tears for ever from his eyes."

And, again, we may compare the ἐλπίδα τάν μούναν of line four with the sentiment expressed in the sixth stanza of Shelley's *Adonais*.

" But now thy youngest, dearest one, has perished,
The nursling of thy widowhood, who grew,
Like a pale flower by some sad maiden cherished,
And fed with true love tears instead of dew ;
Most musical of mourners, weep anew !
Thy extreme hope, the loveliest and the last,
The bloom, whose petals, nipt before they blew,
Died on the promise of the fruit, is waste ;
The broken lily lies—the storm is overpast."

When I commenced my excavations in Cyprus, I found that some native workmen, who were employed in extracting from the ruins of Kitium a selection of stones suitable for building purposes, had met with a large fragment, bearing an inscription in fine Greek capital letters. The site where this was found was on the line of the walls of the ancient town, towards the south-east, and not far from a spot which contains a structure retaining the shape of a doorway. The stone itself was calcareous, and of the form of a modern door, with semicircular head (fig. 101). The dimensions were seven feet and three-eights in height, three feet and one-third in length, and four inches and a quarter thick. About three feet and one-third of the stone's height was underground. The inscription was cut on the upper part of the stone. It reads as follows :—

ΑΥΤΟΚΡΑΤΟΡΙ
ΝΕΡΟΤΑ ΤΡΑΙΑΝΩΙ ΚΑΙΣΑΡΙ
ΣΕΒΑΣΤΩΙ ΓΕΡΜΑΝΙΚΩΙ
ΔΑΚΙΚΩΙ.

P

This, in Latin, is equivalent to "Imperatori Nervæ Trajano Cæsari Augusto Germanico Dacico". After taking the exact dimensions of the stone, I gave instructions to have the upper part, containing the inscription, sawn off, and preserved from injury. At a distance of four

Fig. 101.   Inscribed Tablet.   *Stone.*

inches below the last line of the inscription, there were two square holes in a horizontal line, each having the depth of a quarter of an inch, and the diameter of about one inch. In one of these holes, there was a leaf of lead much corroded.

From the position of this stone, and of the inscription upon it, I am led to conjecture that it was originally used for posting up edicts sent from Rome for publication, or the public acts of the Consul of the locality. The small holes probably served for securing a tablet of wood or lead, or other material, upon which were inscribed the sentences which it was desired to promulgate. The date of Nerva's accession to the purple being September 18th, A.D. 96, and of his death, January 27th, A.D. 98, it is not difficult to infer the age of this inscription.

Stone, from the hardness of its nature, would naturally be employed for making stamps. Among this class of

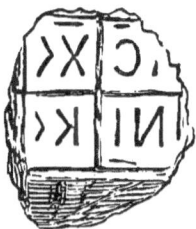

Fig. 102.   Christian Stamp or Mould.   Stone.

objects is a piece of flat stone, carved in intaglio, to serve as a stamp for making ornaments, which are to be placed on the surfaces of terra-cotta vases, lamps, and the like. On one side of this, there are two figures, one of Mercury, the other of a soldier in full armour. It may be that this is a gladiator. On the other side is carved a piece of scroll ornament, a crescent, and a scroll, resembling a portion of a capital of a column. Two clay stamps were found, bearing Egyptian hieroglyphics. Another carved stone stamp (fig. 102) was evidently used for impressing the shew-bread, or, perhaps, the consecrated element in the ritual of the Greek Church. The letters, which are rightly reversed to enable them to be impressed in proper order, are placed in the spaces formed by the four limbs of a thin and plain cross inscribed in a square. Dr. Birch and M. Pierides agree in

I C	X C
N I	K A

reading :—'I[ησοῦ]ς χ[ριστὸ]ς νικᾶ, "Jesus Christ conquers". Some read the last word νικη[τὴρ], "conqueror"; or νι[κητὴρ] κύ[σμου], "conqueror of the world".

The iconic bust of a female (fig. 103), formed of cal-

Fig. 103.   Iconic Bust.   Stone.

careous stone, eighteen inches and a half high, is of interesting art. The hair is in a close and small knot behind, and on the neck a necklace with a crescent, formed probably of a gold ornament, or two teeth of a wild animal, as described above at p. 26. There are traces of colour in the hair and face. This is one of four busts—two male,

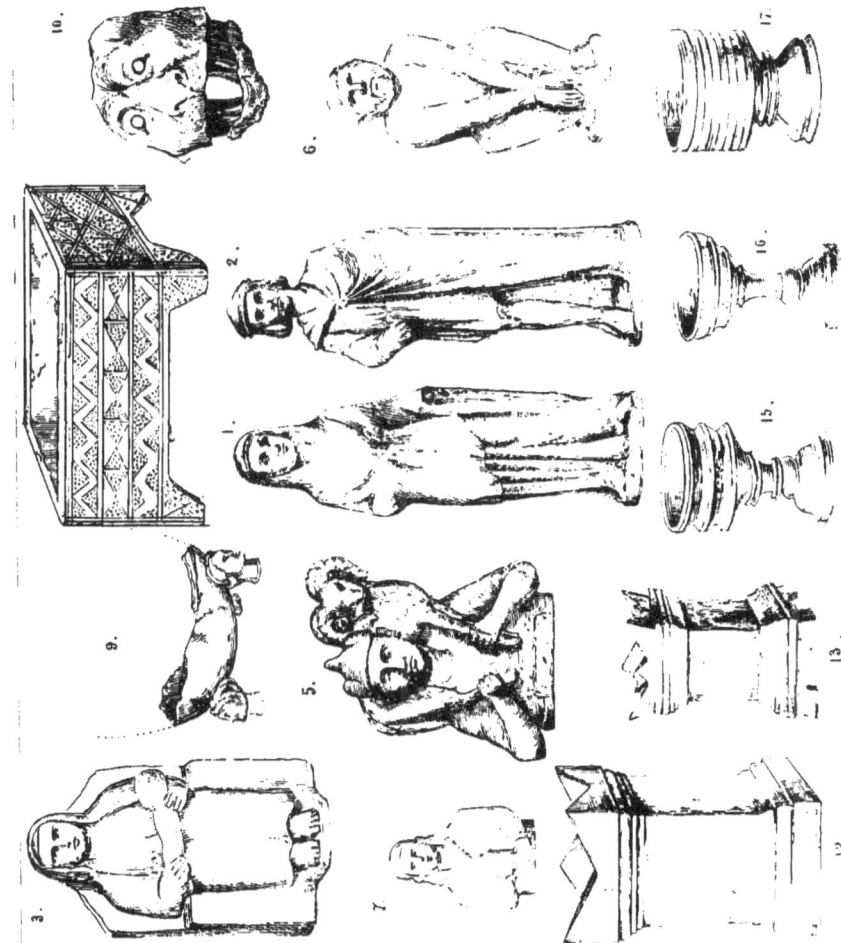

two female—found on the corners of a sarcophagus. The other three were accidentally destroyed.[1] Round the upper surface of the pedestal or plinth, the following inscription is roughly scratched :—

..... T . I . PROCONSVL . P . SERGE......

Of a much later date than either of the above objects is the white marble tympanum of a church door, which comes from a church at Larnaca (*Kitium*), where it was found while men were digging the foundation for a house.[2] It is in perfect preservation, and as sharp as when the sculptor left it. It could not have been exposed to the weather even in Cyprus during any considerable period of time. Jesus Christ is here ascending, seated within a vesica-shaped glory, his nimbus is cruciform. He holds in his left hand a scroll; the other hand is extended in the act of benediction, after the Greek manner, with the first and fourth fingers extended. Four angels are placed at the sides of the glory, with their hands in an attitude of supporting this aureola. At the sides of this central element of the tympanum are represented several subjects, of the kind not unusually found in works of this class, and of much later date than I presume this one to be. On our left is the Crucifixion, with the Blessed Virgin Mary and St. Mary Magdalene weeping. The latter holds her vase, one of the alabastra so well represented by examples in this collection. A skull is at the foot of the cross; the feet of Christ are placed parallel to each other, after the most ancient fashion. Next to this is a smaller panel, showing the Saviour bearing His cross, and accompanied by two soldiers clad in mail, who pull him along. They wear mail hoods. On the right are three panels, representing

---

[1] Serge, or Sergius, was Proconsul of Cyprus in the time of Tiberius. The tomb in which the sarcophagus was found probably belonged to his family.　　　　　　　　　　　　　　　　[2] Plate IX, fig. 2.

the baptism of Christ by St. John the Baptist in the Jordan, in which river appears a fish. Close by is a demon with a tail. The Dove and the Hand of the Lord are seen above. The next panel shows the Annunciation. Between the figures stands a tree, seemingly formed of twisted serpents, on which is perched an eagle or vulture, probably intended for the Evil One. On the ground are two birds like partridges. The Virgin holds her distaff or hank of flax in one hand. The next panel represents the angel seated on the tomb of Our Lord. Below it are carved the figures of the three Maries approaching the sepulchre, at the entrance to which two mail-clad warriors sleep. Below this group of panels is a long frieze, in the centre of which stands the Virgin, in the attitude of an ancient Orante. At her side stands an angel with a sceptre, in the act of calling attention to the Mother of Christ. On one side of this group is a palm; on the other side is an olive tree. The Apostles stand six on each side, with their respective attributes, some in the act of looking up at the ascension of the Lord, as described above.

CHAPTER X

ALABASTER, SERPENTINE, AND CRYSTAL ANTIQUITIES.

ALABASTER.

SALAMINIAN tombs and excavations yielded a very considerable number of antiquities formed of alabaster, about two thousand specimens altogether having been recovered from beneath the soil where I dug. These include numerous forms and shapes, some unusual and unconventional; others, and, of course, the larger, being of types that are not uncommonly to be met with in museums of ancient remains. These alabaster antiquities are in all cases formed for the reception and preservation of precious unguents and perfumes. They comprise *alabastra* proper, *i.e.*, small vases for containing scented unguents or liquids, which, being absorbed by the material, rendered back the odours thus imparted to them, and preserved the aroma for longer or shorter periods of time. The annexed figure (fig. 104) shows an alabastron, with handle in form of a knot, and the foot with three letters carved in relief. Some of these examples retain their covers. With these the large cinerary urns, which are probably of Greek or Roman origin, may be classed, one of which is about eighteen inches high, and contained human bones.

Of the small, but not the smallest, works, are three

112 ALABASTER ANTIQUITIES.

fine scent vases, with fluted sides, one of which, measuring three inches and three-quarters in height (fig. 105) has a winged human figure by way of handle, and is girt about the body, apparently by a fringe or carcanet, with

Fig. 104.　　A. Unguent Vase.　B. Inscribed Foot.　　Alabaster.

pendants, such as the terra-cotta statues wear. The base has three letters in relief. Other vases of extremely elegant forms are comprised in this collection. One of these, of which both handles have been lost, and its foot

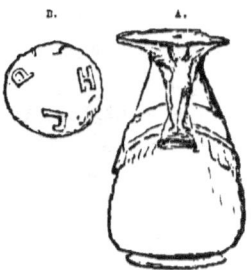

Fig. 105.　　A. Unguent Vase, with Handle in form of a Winged Figure.　Alabaster.
B. Inscribed Foot.

fractured, comprises the original stopper of alabaster. These works are undoubtedly Greek. Fig. 106 is a flat basin, measuring four inches and three-quarters in diameter, like the bowl of a small fountain, having three projections from its sides, besides a spout. Round the rim of this article is a doubtful inscription, which must have been cut long after the making of the object, and has not been read. This comes from Kurium. I am inclined to consider that, although a true piece of antiquity, its value has been sought to be enhanced by the addition of this mysterious inscription, some of the letters of which are of a nondescript character. On a slab of the same material, now forming a mantel-

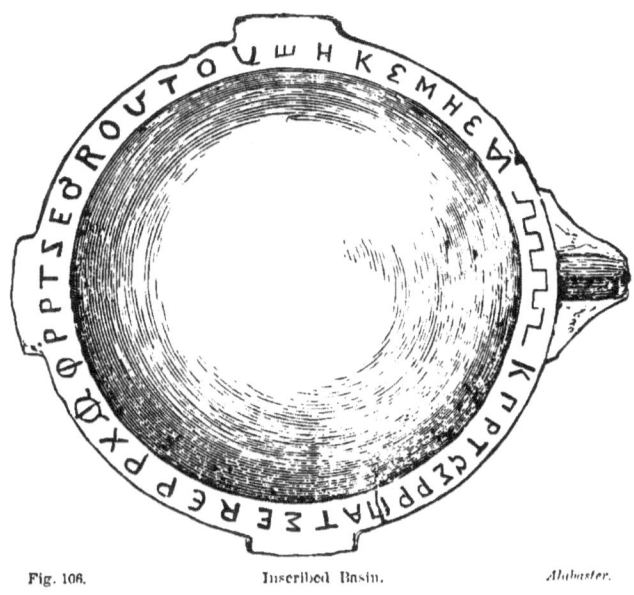

Fig. 106.   Inscribed Basin.   *Alabaster.*

piece in the house of a miller in the same town, I observed an inscription in similar characters. The fireplace which it adorns is of the Lusignan period. There is also among these alabaster antiquities a vase, like a water-cooler, with a wide neck (fig. 107); it bears a band of lancet-shaped leaves, with their points downwards, enclosing the greater part of the body of the relic, but not the whole of it. On a flat space, which has been ground out of one part of the girth, is an illegible inscription in archaic Greek, the form of which, not less than the contour and carved band of this vase, indicates its considerable ancientness. Two other vases have Cypriote letters

Fig. 107. Inscribed Vase. Alabaster.

in relief, being probably the name of the owner or the maker.

The accompanying figure represents an *alabastron* of remarkable form, with three ears, each for a loop to pass through when it was carried. There are in this case

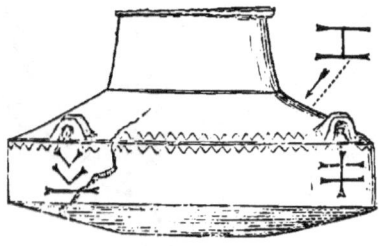

Fig. 108. Inscribed Vase. Alabaster.

also three Cypriote letters, which read " Pa . ve . o ", and may, perhaps, be rendered φαγεο, *i.e.*, " Of Phaveos ". The height of this vase is 4 inches (fig. 108).

The plate here introduced gives figures of several alabaster vases and unguentaria of interesting and noteworthy types.

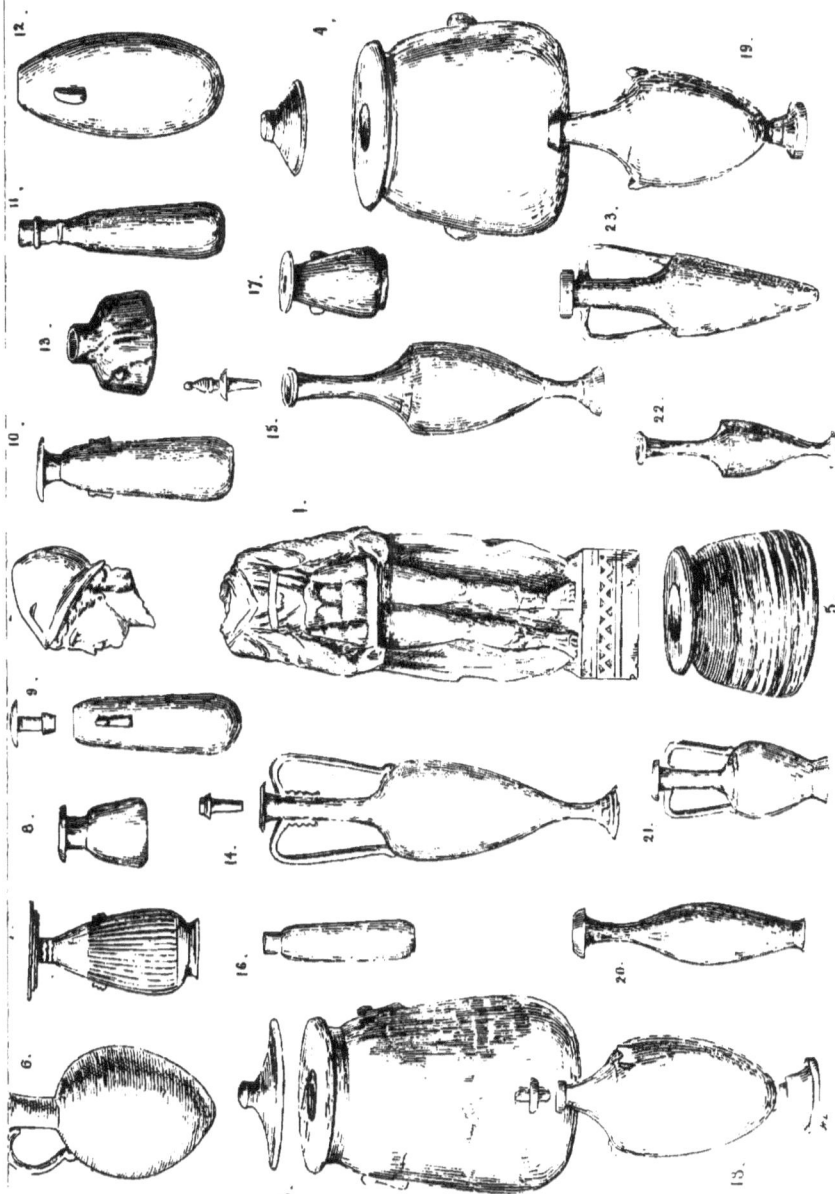

SERPENTINE.

A very elegant vase, measuring five inches in height, and carved out of serpentine stone (fig. 109), comes from Salamina. It is of pear shape, with stripes down the side, which commence from a double circle of a kind of cabled pattern running round the middle of the vase. There

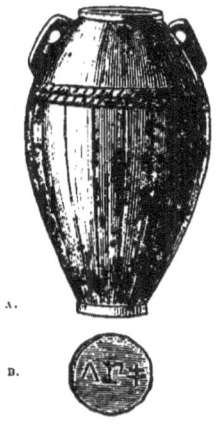

Fig. 109.　　A. Vase.　B. Inscribed Base.　　*Serpentine.*

are two pierced handles for securing a cover with a tie. The circular base of this perfume vase is inscribed with three Cypriote characters—"ko . la . pa", which Professor Sayce reads παλαχοῦ, *i.e.*, "[The vase or bottle] of Palakhos".

CRYSTAL.

Crystal antiquities are excessively rare throughout the island of Cyprus. During the whole of my sojourn there, the number of such relics hardly exceeded ten or twelve; so that I may be considered fortunate in obtaining during the progress of my investigations three crystal objects. Of these, the first (fig. 110) is about an inch

and a half in height, carved or turned in a very elegant
manner, in form of a little vase or pendant.   The base is
square. the body ovoid ; and the top carries a small
silver ring, by which it was, no doubt, attached to a
necklace or chain.

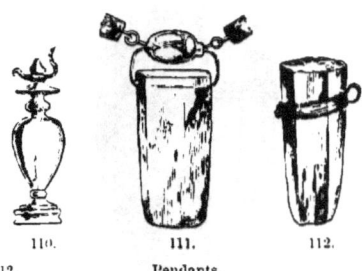

Figs. 110, 111, 112.   Pendants.   *Crystal.*

Another piece of crystal (fig. 111) of somewhat smaller
height is attached by a gold wire ring, upon which is a
small scarabæus in gold-foil, to a necklace (fig. 15),
described at pages 24, 25.   On page 25, I have given
particulars of the third crystal object (fig. 112) in the
Lawrence-Cesnola collection, which, from its form and
general appearance, must also be taken as a pendant
or personal ornament.

CHAPTER XII

CYLINDERS.—CONES.

YLINDERS are, according to Mr. King,[1] the most ancient form of the signet. They are, for the most part, perfectly cylindrical stones, from about one to three inches in length, the respective magnitudes being regulated by the wealth, importance, and social rank of the owner. The diameter of these cylinders is generally less than half their length. In a few examples, the form is varied, by a kind of entasis, into a barrel shape ; in others the converse is found, their sides being like those of a dice-box, slightly concave. A comparatively large hole was pierced longitudinally through the cylinder, to admit a soft woollen cord, by means of which it was tied round the owner's wrist, like a bracelet. This method of use accounts for their never having metal mountings when disinterred amongst Assyrian remains, and my own experience among the tombs of Salamis confirms this fact. These objects have been found in many sites of the Assyrian world in vast abundance. The British Museum possesses a very large series, many with royal names, and composed of a variety of hard stones. The very rare examples extant, mounted on swivel rings in massive gold, prove, by the hieroglyphics engraved upon them, that they were mere adaptations by the

[1] *Antique Gems and Rings.* By C. W. King. 2 vols. 1872.

Egyptians to their national fashion of the swivel-mounted
scarabæus, during the time of the subjugation of Egypt
to the rule of the Persians.

It is not necessary here to examine the different
archæological points of general interest which are exhibited by engraved cylinders. The student who wishes
for information on this subject may with advantage
consult an article by Dr. Birch, entitled "Engraved
Stones", in the *English Cyclopædia, Arts and Sciences
Supplement* (p. 882), where several examples are figured,
and references given to the principal works on this
branch of ancient art. The chapters in Mr. King's book
which are devoted to the consideration of Oriental engraved cylinders may also be perused with beneficial
results. As regards the cylinders which were discovered
by me during my labours in Salamina, these objects of
antiquity consist for the most part of the dark green and
black loadstone or hæmatite, of steatite or of jasper, these
being the materials commonly employed in their manufacture. The mythological and miscellaneous engravings
on their surfaces are usually extremely archaic and rude,
if not rough, in respect to the art which was employed in
their manufacture and execution. The tools were shaped
with an obtusely angular edge, probably fragments of
ἀκόνη or emery stone, a material of great antiquity as to
its use by the lapidary and gem engraver, which, down
to the age of Theophrastus, was imported from Armenia
for the needs of the engraver.

Most of the cylinders in the Lawrence-Cesnola collection are of Assyrian style—the second or Archaic-
Babylonian period of Mr. King's arrangement—after the
seat of government had been removed to Babylon about
B.C. 1675. Several shew Hittite art. I am indebted to
the kindness of Professor Sayce for the greater part of
the following notes, descriptive of the styles and subjects of the most important of these very ancient
remains from Cyprus.

"These intaglios are partly Assyro-Phœnician, partly Greek, partly what I would term Cypriote. The latter are by far the most numerous, and form a peculiar and very interesting class apart, which has already become known to us from the excavations of General di Cesnola. But their number has been largely increased by Major A. P. di Cesnola's discoveries. The art displayed in them is extremely rude, and is modelled after a Babylonian prototype. But I doubt whether they are direct attempts to imitate the products of Babylonian art; they rather presuppose an intermediate stage of art. This is not Phœnician, as is usually supposed, but, as I believe, Hittite. Hittite carved stones found in the neighbourhood of Aleppo display exactly the same style of art, and represent the same subjects as the engraved gems of Cyprus. The latter, however, it must be remembered, are not confined to Cyprus; similar intaglios have been found elsewhere in the Levant; and the art, therefore, which they exhibit, has, I believe, like the so-called Cypriote Syllabary, made its way from the Hittite territory through Asia Minor into Cyprus. The art of the Hittites, so far as we are acquainted with it at present, was based upon that of early Babylonia, not of Assyria.

"Among the numerous intaglios in the Lawrence-Cesnola collection, there are very many which I must pass over in silence, as I have nothing to say about them. Those which I shall specify are remarkable either from their designs or from the presence of inscriptions.

"The large number of objects of Cypriote art gives this collection of engraved stones a special interest, and is of great importance in settling the relation of the art of the early gems found in the Levant to that of the gems of Western Asia, and more particularly Babylonia. Among the symbols which most frequently recur in this class of antiquities of the Lawrence-Cesnola collection, attention should be specially paid to the representation

of the image of the Paphian goddess, the ox-head, the
sun-circle, the figure which may perhaps be intended to
represent the winged solar disk, the serpent, and the
curious spear-like instrument placed in the hand of a
human figure."

In the following list, the paragraphs marked [S.] are
Professor Sayce's notes.

1. A fine cylinder (fig. 113), of which the engraving is
a Cypriote imitation of Babylonian work. Merodach, in
battle with the dragon Tiamat, wears the flounced dress
of the Babylonian priests, and holds the harpê in his
hand. There are perhaps two Cypriote characters on
the gem, *ba-si*, for Βασιλέως. [S.] 7-8ths inch long (see
No. 54).

Fig. 113.   Engraved Cylinder.   *Hæmatite.*

2. This cylinder is manifestly a rude imitation of a
Babylonian gem, representing the battle between the
god Merodach and the demon-birds. [S.] 7-8ths inch
long.

Fig. 114.   Engraved Cylinder.   *Hæmatite.*

3. A cylinder engraved (fig. 115) in the style known to
be Phœnico-Egyptian, but strongly coloured by Assyrian
art. A dove is being presented to Astarte. [S.] A

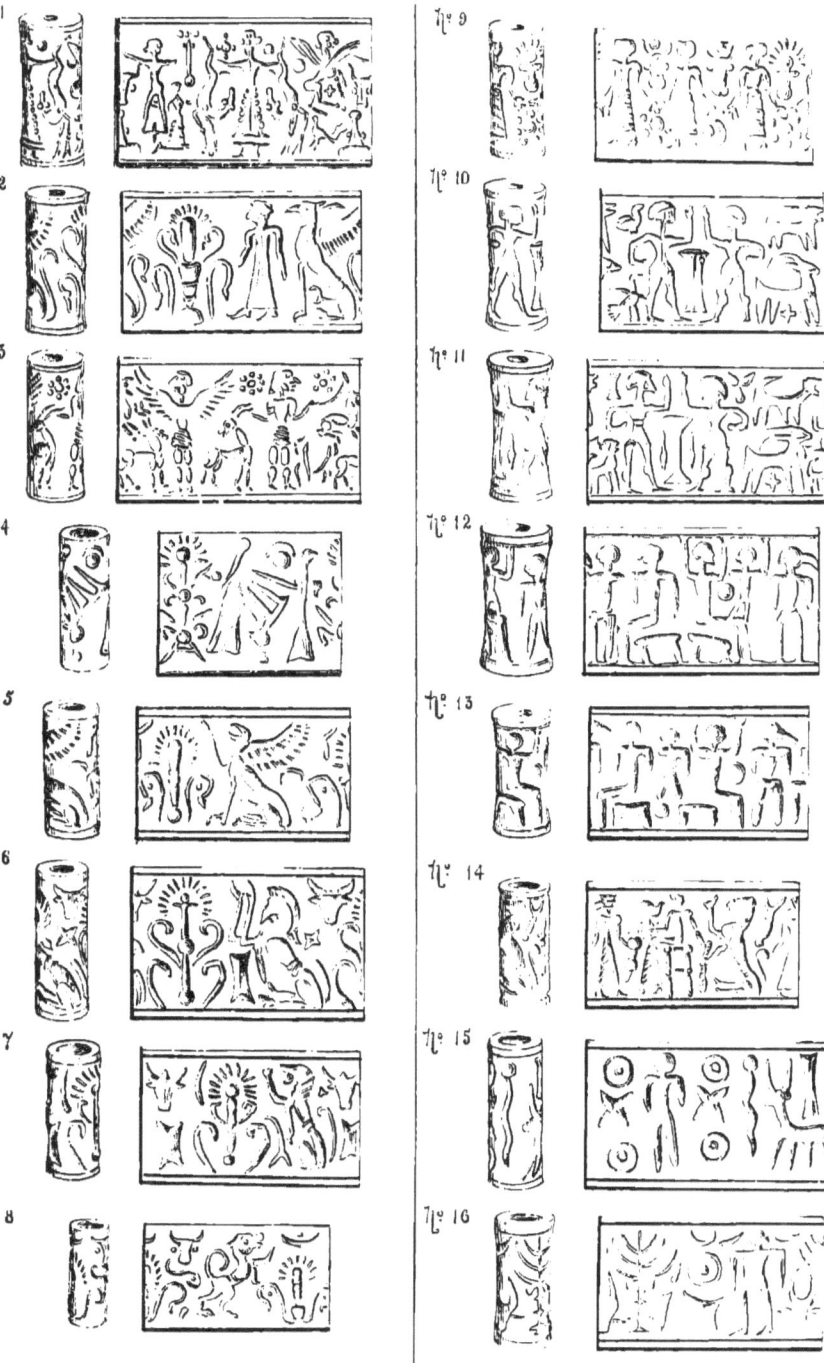

1

2

3

4

5

6

7

8

N° 9

N° 10

N° 11

N° 12

N° 13

N° 14

N° 15

N° 16

griffin winged, and a lion sejant, are also represented, with an emblem like a goat's head, perhaps of Hittite origin. 3-4ths inch long.

Fig. 115.   Engraved Cylinder.   Jasper.

4. This cylinder (fig. 116) is of Babylonian workmanship. Three winged figures, two of which have birds' heads, with crests or crowns, stand side by side, the chief one being the Asiatic goddess, with two animals' heads on her own head. All three figures have boots with turned-up ends, and two hold the sacred tree. [S.] Two of the figures hold gazelles by the hind legs. Fine work. 1 inch long.

Fig. 116.   Engraved Cylinder.   Hæmatite.

5. In the Babylonian style. The Asiatic goddess stands on a pedestal with an animal in either hand. At the side is a winged monster, and two crosses or stars below (see No. 15). A worshipper stands before an altar, with a priest in a flounced dress below. [S.] 1 inch high. *Hæmatite.* (See Plate xii, fig. 1.)

6. The peculiar and rude design of the Paphian goddess occurs on this cylinder as before, a priest with an offering in the hand, and the *shoes with turned-up ends,* which we now know to characterise Hittite art (as may be seen on the monolith lately acquired by Mr.

Rassam for the British Museum), and a winged gryphon behind, which must be carefully distinguished from the Egyptian sphinx. Compare Nos. 10, 11, 19, 25, and 58. [S.] 1 inch long. *Steatite.* (See Plate xii, fig. 2.)

7. This is a curious design. Two animals stand on either side of a pedestal, on the top of which is a human head, with wings (or the canopy which protects the Paphian goddess) on each side. A worshipper stands before the image. [S.] The work is very good. 1 inch long. *Green Jasper.* (See Plate xii, fig. 3.)

8. This is a good example of Cypriote art. The symbol of the Paphian goddess, with four doves on either side, and a canopy overhead, stands by the side of a priest, who presents an offering. Behind him is the head of an ox, a well-known Hittite character. The ox-head occurs on coins of Salamis, as well as on one of the gold rings discovered by Dr. Schliemann at Mykenæ. Compare Gen. di Cesnola's *Cyprus*, pl. xxxiii, 25. The ox-head alone occurs on another specimen in the collection. [S.] 1 inch long.

9. The symbol of the Paphian goddess, accompanied by a flying dove, [S.] is engraved on this cylinder in archaic style. 7-8ths inch long. *Steatite.* (See Plate xii, fig. 4.)

10. This may be compared with No. 58. A winged gryphon, seated in adoration before the Paphian goddess. 3-4ths inch long. *Steatite.* (See Plate xii, fig. 5.)

11. The subject here is a gryphon segreant adoring a figure of the Paphian goddess, the ox-head, cushion, and another symbol. 1 inch long. *Steatite.* (See Plate xii, fig. 6.)

12. On this cylinder occur the figure of the Paphian goddess, ox-head, and seated animal without wings. Compare No. 11. 7-8ths inch long. *Dark Steatite.* (See Plate xii, fig. 7.)

13. Symbol of the Paphian goddess, somewhat curtailed, a lion, or other animal, and ox-head. 5-8ths inch long. *Steatite.* (See Plate xii, fig. 8.)

14. The symbol of the Paphian goddess, with three priests wearing banded or flounced dresses, two ox-heads, and other emblems. 7-8ths inch long. *Steatite.* (See Plate xii, fig. 9.)

15. Professor Sayce describes this cylinder thus :— Two worshippers stand on either side of an altar; behind them are a dog, cock, and gazelle, beneath which is a cross ✛ (Cypriote *lo*). Almost precisely the same design recurs on No. 16. Compare also No. 38. [S.] 15-16ths inch long. *Jasper.* (See Plate xii, fig. 10.)

16. An altar between two worshippers, full-length, lifting up their arms; in the field, three animals, and other symbols. 1 inch long. *Hard Steatite.* (See Plate xii, fig. 11.)

17. A group of five human figures; two seated. Rude archaic work. 1 1-8th inch long. *Jasper.* (See Plate xii, fig. 12.)

18. A figure with a beak-like head between two men seated ; in the field, two disks, and a fourth figure full length. Rude work. 1 inch long. *Jasper.* (See Plate xii, fig. 13.)

19. Full-length figure, seated figure, and animal deity. Curious work. 3-4ths inch long. *Steatite.* (See Plate xii, fig. 14.)

20. Full-length figure and two animals; much obliterated. 7-8ths inch long. *Steatite.*

21. A full-length figure between two combinations of a star with four points, having a sun's disk ⊙ above and below; in the field, a horned animal, snake, and another symbol. 1 inch long. *Steatite.* (See Plate xii, fig. 15.)

22. Two sacred trees, one of which is being grasped

by a human figure, together with an ox-head [S.]; and
other emblems (fig. 117).   1 inch long.

Fig. 117   Engraved Cylinder.   Jasper.

23. Sacred tree, ox-head, human figure full-length,
disk ⊙ of the sun, cushion, or star, and other objects.
7-8ths inch long. *Steatite*. (See Plate xii, fig. 16.)

24. Figure seated before a sacred tree; dirks or
paddles, two circles of the sun ⊙, ox-head, and other
emblems. A good cylinder.   1 inch long. *Steatite*.
(See Plate xiii, fig. 17.)

25. Full-length human figure, sacred tree, disk ⊙, and
ox-head, with three cushions, and other emblems. 1 inch
long. *Steatite*. (See Plate xiii, fig. 18.)

26. Of this cylinder, Professor Sayce relates :—The
sacred tree here stands between two worshippers, behind
whom is an ox-head above a pedestal or altar.   The
three-barred line merely denotes where the scene depicted
begins. [S.] 7-8ths inch long. *Steatite*. (See Plate
xiii, fig. 19.)

27. Of this, Prof. Sayce considers the subject to be:—
A sacred tree, with two circles of the sun on either
side, and two adoring figures, between whom is a dirk,
or rather an instrument like the Egyptian hieroglyphic
sam, which means "to unite".   No. 28 has a similar
design. [S.] 5-8ths inch long. *Steatite*. (See Plate
xiii. fig. 20.)

28. The symbol *sam* (see No. 27), between two worshippers with uplifted hands; the sacred tree, and disk.
5-8ths inch long. *Steatite*. (See Plate xiii, fig. 21.)

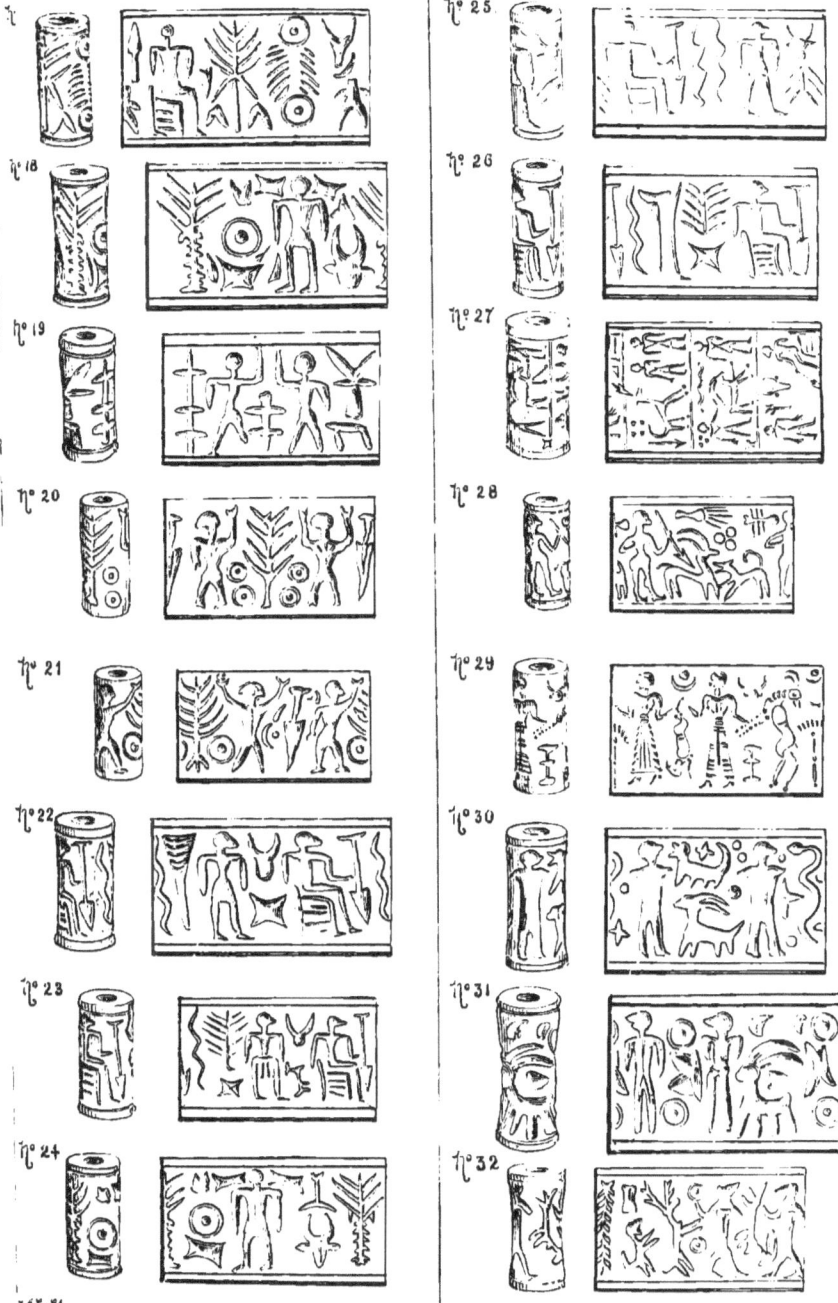

29. The same dirk-like instrument held by two men, one seated with a serpent in front, the other standing with an ox-head and a symbol like the egg-pouch of the skate at the side. This symbol appears in No. 48 as a sun, with three beams or wings at the corners (see also No. 39). I fancy it is a degenerated form of the winged solar disk. It is found on many of the products of Cypriote art.[1] It is also found on No. 21, together with the sun-circle, the stag or gazelle, and the serpent; and on No. 24, along with the sun-circle, the ox-head, and the sacred tree. It is possible that what I have called a star between the horns of the ox-head in No. 45 is really intended for it. In No. 23 its place is taken by a very curious symbol, which looks like two spiral shells. Here we have the ox-head, sun-circle, crescent-moon, and sacred tree, with the fruit hanging down on either side. (See also No. 25.) In No. 72 the sun-circle appears alone among the branches on either side of the sacred tree, in front of which is a seated figure. The design is archaic Babylonian. In No. 53 the place of the sacred tree is occupied by a human figure, with a canopy above, resembling the bar drawn over the human head in the Hittite inscriptions, while the serpent and ox-head are at the side (see also No. 42). The serpent appears along with the gazelle in No. 38, and with a seated figure holding the spear-like instrument in No. 34 and No. 33. In No. 31 we have the same seated figure and instrument; behind is the sacred tree in the form of a palm-branch with the winged sun (?); below and in front are the serpent and an altar (?) (see No. 30).[2] The dirk-like instrument may be an oar. [S.] 3-4ths inch long. *Steatite.* (See Plate xiii, fig. 22.)

[1] See General di Cesnola's *Cyprus*, xxxii, 13, 15, 21; xxxiii, 27, 30.

[2] For the serpent and sacred tree in archaic Babylonian art, see George Smith's *Chaldean Genesis*, p. 91.

30. This closely resembles No. 29. In that cylinder, we have a seated figure holding a dirk or *sam*, snake, *sistrum*, full-length figure, ox-head, and star or cross. In this, the order is modified only by the figure at full-length holding a second dirk or *sam*, instead of the *sistrum*. 3-4ths inch long. *Steatite.*

31. This may be compared with No. 29. Seated figure before a symbol called by Professor Sayce the Egyptian *sam*, a snake, branch, star, full length figure, ox-head, and other emblems. 3-4ths inch long. *Steatite.* (See Plate xiii, fig. 23.)

32. Emblems and figures already described, but differently arranged. 7-8ths inch. *Slatey Stone.* (See Plate xiii, fig. 24.)

33. A seated figure, *sam*, two wavy lines, a full-length figure, and ox-head. 3-4ths inch long. *Steatite.* (See Plate xiii, fig. 25.)

34. Human figure seated on a chair, and holding a paddle or vase in form of the Egyptian hieroglyphic *sam*, or "union"; in the field, a snake or a wavy line, Egyptian *en*; palm-branch, and other symbols. Professor Sayce considers this to be Phœnico-Egyptian, or perhaps Egyptian, with Egyptian hieroglyphics. [S.] Rude work. 7-8ths inch long. *Steatite.* (See Plate xiii, fig. 26.)

35. An interesting intaglio with three compartments, which gives the history of the chase, capture, and sacrifice of the gazelle. In the first compartment are two men, a gazelle, and a tree, which denotes the open country; in the second, one of the men seizes the gazelle by the horn; in the third, he offers the animal to Zeus (?), who is seated on a throne with the head of the gazelle in front. [S.] 1 inch long. *Steatite.* (See Plate xiii, fig. 27.)

36. This is a very interesting intaglio. It represents a huntsman throwing his spear at a gazelle which

is attacked in front by a dog. On one side of the huntsman is a hand, on the other a symbol, which may represent a musical instrument, but is rather, I think, a man's
arm with three reeds in the clenched hand. The symbols on either side of the head of the huntsman may be
Hittite characters; but they may, less probably, be meant
for the Egyptian *sep-khnem*, or perhaps *sep-t*. It must
be noticed that the huntsman is represented as wearing
boots with turned-up ends, that characteristic feature of
Hittite art. [S.]   5-8ths inch long. *Steatite*. (See
Plate xiii, fig. 28.)

37. A cylinder of rude work. Two full-length figures,
one holding a gazelle, the other a goat. The crescent
enclosing a star here is, perhaps, an incomplete disk of the
sun ⊙.   15-16ths inch long. *Hæmatite*. (See Plate xiii,
fig. 29.)

38. Two full-length figures, gazelle, snake, dog, and
other emblems of undetermined value (see No. 29).
7-8ths inch long. *Steatite*. (See Plate xiii, fig. 30.)

39. Two full-length human figures, a gazelle, and the
combination of an unknown character between two dotted
circles ⊙, occurring twice. Rude work. 1 inch long.
Steatite. (See Plate xiii, fig. 31.)

40. Seated figure, gazelle, full-length figure, two dogs,
and a rudely-cut paddle-shaped object or *sam* (see Nos.
28, 29). 7-8ths inch long. *Steatite*.

41. Human figures, gazelles, solar disks ⊙, palm
branch, and other emblems.   7-8ths inch long. *Steatite*.
(See Plate xiii, fig. 32.)

42. A full-length human figure ; a tree with a gazelle
or goat on each side leaping up to the branches. Rude
work.   1 inch long.   *Steatite*. (See Plate xiv, fig.
33.)

43. A cylinder bearing an ornamental frieze or band,
below which are two double ⊙ disks, alternating with a

cross and two bars. 1 1-8th inch long. *Hæmatite.* (See Plate xiv, fig. 34.)

44. This cylinder is of a very interesting character. It is noticeable for the symbols upon it, among which are the ox-head, accompanied by the circle of the sun ⊙ and the head of a goat or horse, like that on the bi-lingual Hittite boss of Tarkondemos,[1] as well as the crescent moon, and a hare. A fracture of the stone makes it uncertain whether the head of the goat or horse is not the first character of a Hittite inscription which gives the name of the accompanying figure. At all events it is followed by another symbol now obliterated, but which looks like a lizard, and then by the crescent which I believe to have been the determinative affix of male persons in the Hittite system of writing (see No. 48). The goat's head was pronounced *Tarku.* [S.] 3-4ths inch long. *Steatite.* (See Plate xiv, fig. 35.)

45. This (fig. 118) is an imitation of an archaic Babylonian cylinder, the cuneiform characters being replaced by an ornamental design in form of two triangles united at

Fig. 118.   Engraved Cylinder.   *Steatite.*

the apices, with a line between them, four times repeated. This symbol may have been assimilated to the Egyptian *crux ansata* on the one side and the Phœnician symbol of Baal and Ashtoreth on the other. Ox-head, with a star between the horns, as on gold objects from Mykenæ, and an animal below. [S.] 3-4ths inch long.

46. A cylinder of coarse work (fig. 119), bearing two

---

[1] Figured in *Trans. Soc. Bibl. Arch.*, vol. vii, p. 298.

HITTITE BOSS OF TARKONDEMOS.

This Woodcut kindly lent by the Society of Biblical Archæology.

priests, ox-head, and other emblems, one of which resembles a *flagellum*. 7-8ths inch long.

Fig. 110. Engraved Cylinder. *Dark Steatite.*

47. Ox-head between two full length human figures,
one holding a sacrificial patera; gazelles, disk ⊙, and
other emblems. 3-4ths inch long. *Light green steatite.*
(See Plate xiv, fig. 36.)

48. The ox-head, crescents, and three full-length
figures, with other emblems. Good work. 3-4ths inch
long. *Steatite.* (See Plate xiv, fig. 37.)

49. A fine cylinder of good and interesting work.
The subject is a stand of offerings, with a lion and

Fig. 120. Engraved Cylinder. *Hæmatite.*

winged disk on one side, and a hog and flying dove
on the other, with other symbols in the field (fig. 120).

50. In this archaic cylinder we may observe animals in

Fig. 121. Engraved Cylinder. *Hæmatite.*

heraldic style on either side of an eagle, which resembles

S

that on a gem in Cen. di Cesnola's *Cyprus*, pl. xxxiv, 24, and has affinities with the double-headed eagle of Hittite art. Compare the eagle of gold found at Hissarlik in Schliemann's *Ilios*, p. 504. Headless figure in front of the animals. [S.] 5-8ths inch long.

51. According to Prof. Sayce this cylinder has two winged gryphons in the Babylonian style and a priest with flounced dress, as on archaic Babylonian gems. [S.] Curious work; 3-4ths inch long. *Steatite.* (See Plate xiv, fig. 38.)

52. Three standing figures, and two sphinxes. A design considered by Professor Sayce to be Phœnico-Egyptian. The winged gryphon has become a sphinx. [S.] Half-inch long. *Jasper.* (See Plate xiv, fig. 39.)

53. Professor Sayce considers this to be worked in the Phœnician style. Winged monsters, ox-head, and figure of a priest (?). (See Nos. 21, 28, and 46.) 3-4ths inch long. *Steatite.* (See Plate xiv, fig. 40.)

54. Lion and sphinx, ox-head, and a full-length figure

Fig. 122.   Engraved Cylinder.   *Steatite.*

of a priest in an ornamental dress, holding a crooked implement (see fig. 122). 7-8ths inch long.

55. A finely engraved cylinder, in a style evidently

Fig. 123.   Engraved Cylinder.   *Jasper.*

Phœnico-Egyptian (fig. 123). Sphinxes and gazelle above,

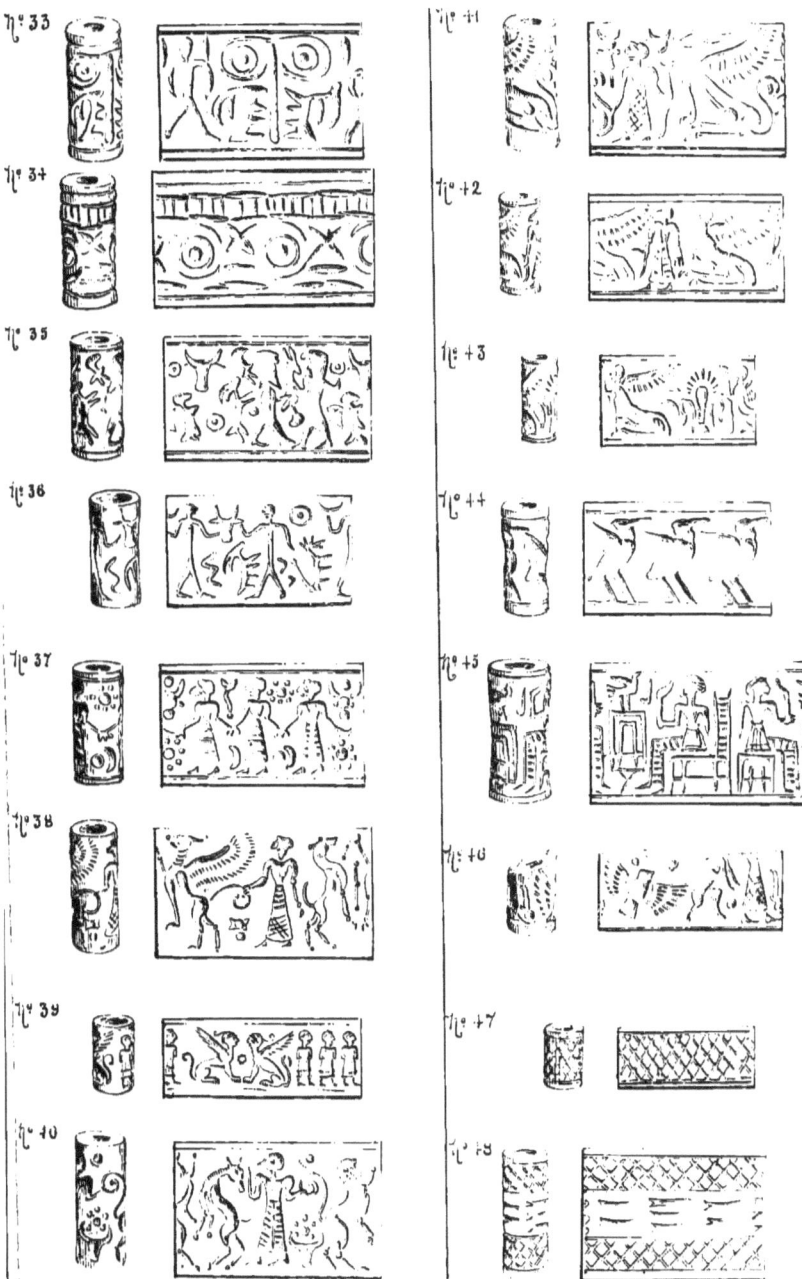

N° 33

N° 34

N° 35

N° 36

N° 37

N° 38

N° 39

N° 40

N° 41

N° 42

N° 43

N° 44

N° 45

N° 46

N° 47

N° 48

on a kind of frieze or heraldic chief, figures in the Egyptian style below the disk of the sun, and the *crux ansata* in the centre, are the designs on this interesting relic. 3-4ths inch long.

56. A priest, seated gryphon, ox-head, and other emblems. 7-8ths inch long. *Steatite.* (See Plate xiv, fig. 41.)

57. A priest holding a crescent-shaped object, and standing beside a seated sphinx or gryphon with up-raised wings. 5-8ths inch long. *Steatite.* (See Plate xiv, fig. 42.)

58. Winged sphinx adoring a tree. Nice work. Half-inch long. *Steatite.* (See Plate xiv, fig. 43.)

59. Sphinx couchant, with long and elaborately-feathered wing, the head regardant, with three feathers for a crest, the beak curved, tail curved, erect; before it a full-length figure of a priest, with the dress represented by horizontal and oblique lines, like coarse hatching. 3-4ths inch long. *Steatite.*

60. Three birds, with long beaks and expanded wings. Rude work. 3-4ths inch long. *Green porcelain.* (See Plate xiv, fig. 44.)

61. This cylinder is fairly well engraved with a curious design of Cypriote (?) workmanship upon which I can throw no light. In the centre is a cock mounted on a pedestal, and two seated figures on either side with wands (?) in their hands. [S.] 1 inch long. *Jasper.* (See Plate xiv, fig. 45.)

62. The lower half only of a broken cylinder. On it are a flying dove, and a man bending before a full-length figure with turned-up boots. Half-inch high. *Hæmatite.* (See Plate xiv, fig. 46.)

63. A kind of fretwork, or fretty pattern. 3-8ths inch long. *Steatite.* (See Plate xiv, fig. 47.)

64. Fretty device, which may be compared with No. 63. The centre has some cuneiform characters arranged

horizontally to form an ornament. 1 inch long. *White
calcined chalcedony.* (See Plate xiv, fig. 48.)

65. A subject of difficult interpretation (fig. 124). It
is in an archaic style, and of good work. 5-8ths inch
long.

Fig. 124.   Engraved Cylinder.   *Hæmatite.*

66. An archaic but uncertain design, which may best
be made out by reference to the drawing. 3-4ths inch
long. *Steatite.* (See Plate xv, fig. 49.)

67. Human figures, disks ⊙, stars or crosses, and other
uncertain emblems. 7-8ths inch long. *Steatite.* (See
Plate xv, fig. 50.)

68. Uncertain forms of human figures; the engraving
very imperfect, or, perhaps, the stone has been exposed
to attrition. 1 inch long. *Hæmatite.*

69. Uncertain device, apparently men and birds.
Coarse archaic work, much worn. 3-4ths inch long.
Steatite.

70. Much work and illegible. 7-8ths inch long.
Jasper.

71. The subject very indistinct. 1 inch long. *Jasper.*

72. Uncertain figures and emblems, perhaps a rude
form of a face. But see No. 29. 1 inch long. *Steatite.*
(See Plate xv, fig. 51.)

73. Unknown and badly-engraved marks and symbols,
not of any value. 3-4ths inch long. *Steatite.*

CONES.

These objects are but little, if at all, later in point of
date than the cylinders. In the collection which I gathered from the tombs of Salamis, among others, are:

1. A spheroidal cone, pierced and ornamented with a series of circular facets (fig. 125A). The subject (B) en-

Fig. 125 A, B. Engraved Cone. *Agate.*

graved on it is a bird, apparently an eagle. Rude work of an early period is shewn in this ancient signet.

2. Rectangular-faced pyramid-shaped cone or seal, pierced, bearing a bird with expanded wings between a crescent and a star. 5-8ths by half-inch. *Steatite.* (See Plate xv, fig. 52.)

3. The Paphian goddess under the canopy of the temple, but without her doves (fig. 126), is engraved upon another of these matrices. This was, naturally, as favourite a device for a seal among the votaries of Venus,

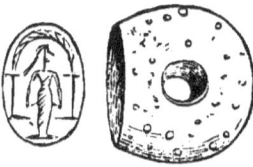

Fig. 126. Engraved Cone. *Hyacinth.*

as the *fleur-de-lis*, the emblem of the B. V. Mary, was in the middle ages in Christian countries. This is a beautifully transparent deep red stone. 1 inch long.

4. A fine cone or seal, not pierced, bearing on the face, which is very convex, according to Professor Sayce, the rude imitation of an Assyrian gem, representing a priest

standing in front of an altar with the crescent moon
above. [S.] 1 inch high. *Calcined agate.* (See Plate
xv, fig. 53.)

5. A pyramidal or bell-shaped cone or seal, with a ring
pierced for suspension. On the face (fig. 127 E) are a
gazelle and tree. This is repeated on the two sides (B, D).

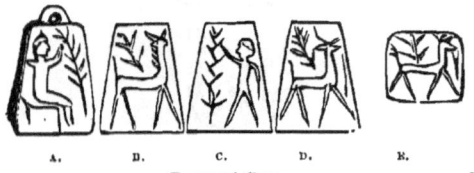

Fig. 127 A, B, C, D, E.   Engraved Cone.   *Steatite.*

The first side (A) has a seated figure holding a tree or
branch; the third (C) a full-length figure holding a tree.
Drawn full size. 1 inch high. *Steatite.*

6. Another fine cone (fig. 128 A) in the collection is of
the style called Phœnico-Assyrian. A warrior in the
Assyrian style is shewn shooting with the bow; before
him an enemy kneels imploring mercy, with a palm-tree

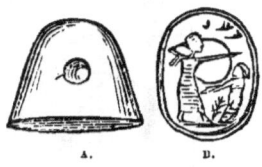

Fig. 128 A, B.   Engraved Cone.   *Hæmatite.*

between. [S.] The face (B) is 7-8ths inch in diameter;
the cone, 3-4ths inch high.

7. A pierced cone of excellent finish, on which a man
is represented holding an animal by the head, and aiming
at it with his spear. [S.] Half-inch long; half-inch
high. *Hæmatite.* (See Plate xv, fig. 54.)

8. A solid seal or cone, in form of a cylinder, but
engraved on one of the circular faces only, with a

rudely-cut figure of an animal. 3-4ths inch long. *Light grey steatite, highly polished.* (See Plate xv, fig. 55.)

9. Small oval seal-cone or seal; a gazelle couchant regardant, beside a tree. 3-8ths inch long. *Steatite.* (See Plate xv, fig. 56.)

10. Cone, pierced. Oval face, bearing a gazelle couchant to the right between two stars. Coarse work. 5-8ths inch high, 5-8ths inch face. *Steatite.*

11. A cone, bearing on its face an object resembling a lizard. Rude work. Half-inch high. *Calcined agate.*

12. Pyramidal conoid, pierced. A star, and some uncertain emblems. 3-8ths inch. *Steatite.*

13. Conoid, pierced in two ways. An uncertain figure. Half-inch high. *Dark stone.*

CHAPTER XIII

SCARABÆI.—BEADS.—INLAYING PIECES, Etc.

SCARABÆI.

ESIDES the cylinders and cones, which point so clearly to the influence of Babylonian, Assyrian, and Hittite domination of art and feeling in Cyprus, the tombs and subterranean chambers of Salamis yielded, during my excavations, a number of engraved gems and stones, used as seals and rings. In this class, I include glass, pastes, crystal, cornelian, agate, jasper, sard, and other precious stones, which bear devices more or less artistically engraved upon them. A considerable number are cut in the form of scarabæi, and scarabæoids. Some of these are obviously of Egyptian origin. From the old civilisation of the Egyptians, it may be taken that these scarabs represent one of the oldest forms of seal. Scarabæi are generally, but not always, pierced through lengthwise for attaching to the wrist, or for setting in a bezel. They are made of talcose schist, or steatite, sometimes glazed by being exposed to the heat of a furnace, or have a blue, green, or red coloured frit placed on them before the firing; agate, cornelian, and other hard materials. On the oval and flat base inscriptions and figures, or representations of deities, men and animals, are en-

graved. These scarabæi, according to Dr. Birch, are often found used as the bezels of signet rings, set either in a small frame of metal round the edge, or with a coiled wire as a spring on each side to hold them. But they are sometimes mixed up with other beads or objects, as pendants for necklaces, or even strung in rows as bracelets. They are to be distinguished from the scarabæi of porcelain, which were used only for the outer beaded work, or decoration of mummies. The scarabæus *cheper*, or *cheperu*, was one of the most common of Egyptian emblems. It represented the self-existent male principle and the Sun, and as such it was introduced into many objects of Egyptian art. According to later authors, the military classes employed it as their device ; but it is found inscribed with the names of priests, and other classes of society. An idea has prevailed amongst recent authors, writes the above authority, that the scarabæus was used for the purposes of money ; but this notion is not well supported, either by the monuments or texts, in which it is never mentioned as an unit of value, and all known Egyptian weights are of totally different form. Although, therefore, it is difficult to determine why it was so much in vogue for articles of attire, its shape on an oval pedestal was remarkably convenient for seals, and well adapted for general use. Among the numerous examples found in Salaminian tombs, I may specify the following scarabæi in the Lawrence-Cesnola collection as being of interest.

1. An important Egyptian pierced scarabæus. On the face, two winged *uræi*, with disks and horns, supporting between them a cartouche, in which is inscribed the name of RA-MEN-KA,[1] or Mycerinus, an Egyptian

---

[1] See *The Egypt of the Past*, by Erasmus Wilson, F.R.S., pp. 65, 87. The third of the series of the great Pyramids of Gizeh was built by him. "Within it were three chambers, in the uppermost of which Colonel Vyse discovered a mummy case, inscribed with the name of 'Menkaura'.

T

monarch of the Fourth Dynasty. Below these are two
seated figures of the Nile river, personified as a Androgy-

Fig. 129.   Scarabæus with the name of Mycerinus.

nous, with a bunch of three papyrus flowers on the head.
These two figures are seated face to face, each one
holding in the interior hand a vase of long and delicate proportions.   3-4ths inch long.   *White glazed
steatite.*   (See fig. 129.)

2. Egyptian pierced scarabæus. The figure of a ruler,
seated, holding a whip or flail, *nexex;* behind him a
crook. *heq.* emblem of rule, power, or dominion, distinctive

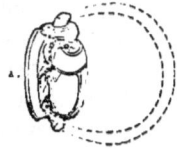

Fig. 130.   A. Scarabæus Ring.   B. Engraved Face.

of Osiris (fig. 130B).   Overhead, in a cartouche, the word
(fig. 131) *Ra-men-cheper*, the prænomen of Thothmes III,
the illustrious monarch of the Eighteenth Dynasty. That

From the floor of this chamber a descending passage led to the second
chamber, in which was found a sarcophagus of basalt, of beautiful workmanship, and representing on its sides the elevation of a temple; while
in the passage between the two chambers was picked up the wooden lid
of the mummy-case. These three objects, together with some bones,
were duly shipped for England; the vessel, however, was wrecked in the
Mediterranean, near to Gibraltar, and the sarcophagus was lost, but the
mummy and mummy case, with its wooden lid, were saved through their
buoyancy, and are now preserved in the British Museum." Col. Howard
Vyse, in his *Pyramids of Gizeh*, says :—" With it were discovered part
of a skeleton, consisting of ribs and vertebræ, and the bones of the legs
and feet, enveloped in coarse woollen cloth of a yellow colour, to which
a small quantity of resinous substance and gum were attached."

the value of this royal scarab was appreciated by the
Cypriote owner from whose grave I obtained it, is shewn
by the fact that it has been set in gold as a ring (fig. 130A),
part of the eye for the swivel and all the bezel being still

Fig. 131.   Praenomen of Thothmes III.

attached to the relic. 3-4ths inch long. *White glazed
steatite*.

3. Egyptian scarabæus, the name of Thothmes III,
Ra-men-cheper, as above, in a cartouche ; and other un-
certain symbols. 3-4ths inch long, set in a gold ring.
Glazed steatite.

4. Egyptian pierced scarabæus. On the face the
hieroglyphics 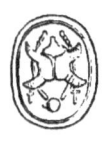 *Amen-Ra Neb*, " The Lord
Amen-Ra". Amen-Ra was the principal deity of the
Theban triad. A large number of scarabæi are extant
with the name of or with reference to the cult of the
god. 3-4ths inch long. *White glazed steatite*.

5. Egyptian pierced scarabæus, engraved with a mythological subject. The sacred beetle, or *cheper*, in his

Fig. 131.   Engraved Scarabæus.   *Agate*.

character as *Creator*, with four wings expanded, and
represented by the artist as deeply barred or striated.
The hind legs of the beetle are rolling forwards the

Sun's Disk. To the lower wings are attached two symbols of life, the cross tau or *ankh*. This is a somewhat rare subject of Egyptian art. It belongs to the fifth century B.C.

6. Egyptian scarabæus of ancient style. On it a crocodile, sacred to, and emblem of, the god *Sebak*, or *Souchis*, one of the principal deities of the Egyptian Pantheon, especially venerated at Arsinoe, or Crocodilopolis. Many names were attached to this reptile, and in the *Ritual of the Dead*,[1] chapter lxxxviii, it is one of the types assumed by the departed soul in the future state. In other chapters (xxxi, xxxii), the deceased turns back the crocodiles,[2] who come to deprive him of his amulets or talismans. On the face of this scarab also is a cartouche, with the Egyptian hieroglyphics *ran ran ran*, words probably mystical—at any rate, not clearly and satisfactorily explained by Egyptologists. 3-4ths inch long. *White glazed steatite.*

7. Fig. 133 is an Egyptian scarabæus, engraved with

Fig. 133.   Engraved Scarabæus.   *Steatite.*

the sacred hawk and feathers of Thmei, or Ma, the Goddess of Truth.[3]

[1] See Bunsen's *Egypt's Place in Universal History*, London, 1867, vol. v, p. 228. "The chapter of making the Transformation into a Crocodile." (Dr. Birch's translation.)

[2] *Ibid.*, pp. 189, 120. "The chapter of stopping those who come to take away the Spells of a Person from him in Hades." "The chapter of stopping the Crocodiles coming to take the Spells of a Spirit from him in Hades."

I may here refer the reader to another scarabæus with an Egyptian goddess. It is a Phœnico-Egyptian scarab, on which is a full-length

8. Egyptian scarabæus. On the face a sphinx, wearing disk and plumes, seated to the right; behind it a vulture; in front of it an uræus. The meaning of this combination of Egyptian symbols is uncertain.[1] 3-4ths inch long. *White glazed steatite.*

9. Egyptian scarabæus. On the face a figure of a man, kneeling, holding a palm-branch, symbol of a (good, or fortunate) year. 5-8ths in. long. *Green glazed steatite.*

10. Scarabæus, pierced. Seated figure, before him two small vases. Good work. Half-inch long. *Steatite.* (See Plate xv, fig. 59.)

11. Egyptian pierced scarabæus. On it a winged figure standing on lion.[2] Rude workmanship. Half-inch long. *White glazed steatite.*

12. Egyptian pierced scarabæus. On the face a lion, with the tail recurved over the back, and walking to the right. In the field, the symbol *neb*, or "lord", and other uncertain characters. 3-4ths in. long. *White glazed steatite.*

13. An oval scarabæoid, engraved with an archaic figure of a lion enraged, walking to the right. Half-inch long. *Cornelian.*

14. Scarabæus, pierced. A lion enraged, regardant. 5-8ths inch long. *Steatite.* (See Plate xv, fig. 58.)

15. Pierced scarabæus. Rude and archaic work. A lion and a bull, back to back, between them a tree. Half-inch long. *Steatite.*

figure of the Goddess Pasht or Sekhet, with four wings expanded. On the head a disk of the sun and uræus snake. It has been already mentioned (see fig. 51, page 49). Half an inch long, set in the revolving bezel of an ancient silver ring of solid substance. *Cornelian.*

[1] Compare another pierced Egyptian scarabæus in the collection, on which occurs a sphinx seated, holding a sceptre; in the field are some uncertain hieroglyphics. 5-8ths inch long. *Glazed steatite.*

[2] Compare with this another scarabæoid, on which is a figure seated on a griffin, as figured and described in an earlier part of the work (see fig. 50, pp. 49, 50). 3-4ths inch long, set on a wire so as to revolve in a plain silver ring. *Striped cornelian.*

16. Egyptian pierced scarabæus. The hieroglyphics of the sentence or motto, " Peace [be] behind you", *i.e.*, " May peace protect you". This motto is not uncommon on Egyptian scarabs. Half-inch long. *White glazed steatite.*

17. Egyptian pierced scarabæus. On the face the symbol of life, *ankh*; a symbolic eye, *uta*; and two crowns, *teshr.* 3-4ths inch long. *White glazed steatite.*

18. Egyptian pierced scarabæus. On it, a triple spiral ornament. and the hieroglyphic word *Tu.* Coarse work. 3-4ths inch long. *Green glazed steatite.*

19. Egyptian pierced scarabæus. On the face the symbols of a hawk, , and leg, , *ba*, or *bu*, between two uræi.[1] This is a mystical combination not yet satisfactorily explained. 5-8ths inch long. *Reddish white glazed steatite.*

20. Egyptian pierced scarabæus. On the face a double *uræus*, scarabæus beetle, *cheper*, a basket, *neb*, and other hieroglyphics of uncertain import. 5-8ths inch. *White glazed steatite.*

21. Egyptian pierced scarabæus, with several uncertain and badly-cut hieroglyphics of uncertain meaning. Half-inch long. *White glazed steatite.*

22. Scarabæus, pierced. Two figures conjoined. 9-16ths inch long. *Steatite.* (See Plate xv, fig. 57.)

23. A finely-carved and pierced scarabæus of Phœnico-

Fig. 131.   Engraved Scarabæus.   *Banded Sardonyx.*

---

[1] The uræus is constantly met with on scarabs; the reader may refer to another pierced Egyptian scarabæus, on which an uræus and star or cross, set in a massy ring on a revolving wire, but without a bezel. It is figured with the gold objects in a former chapter (see fig. 56, page 39). *Milky agate.*

Egyptian style (fig. 134). On the face, a seated figure of the gryphon of Set, with the reed, *a*; water-line, *en*; and other Egyptian hieroglyphic syllables. 3-4ths inch long.

24. A Phœnician scarabæoid (fig. 135). The winged solar disk above the Boat of the Sun and Uræi, or Egyptian asps, is engraved on the base.

Fig. 135.   Engraved Scarabæoid.   *Steatite.*

25. Scarabæus. On the face a star of six points. 3-8ths inch long. *Cornelian.*

26. Pierced scarabæoid. The work very archaic, in the style seen in Plate xv, fig. 53. 3-4ths inch long. *Cornelian.*

27. Pierced scarabæoid. Rude animal or combination of lines. Half-inch long. *Steatite.*

28. Pierced scarabæoid. Rude and arbitrary combination of crossing lines. Half-inch long. *Steatite.*

29. Pierced conoidal scarabæoid of early Cypriote design and workmanship. On the face, in a cartouche, a full-length figure holding a spear or staff. 5-8ths inch long. *Steatite.*

30. Pierced scarabæus. The work in the Cypriote style, and of a good period. Two figures seated in a biga, or two-horsed chariot. The chariot was a favourite subject of the engraver in Cyprus. In the subsequent description of engraved gems, I shall mention two examples. 5-8ths inch long. *Dark steatite.*

31. Pierced scarabæoid. A winged bull statant.

Curious and good work of the Cypriote style. Half-inch long. *Jasper*. (See Plate xv, fig. 64.)

32. This pierced scarabæus is of considerable interest. The work of the beetle is very fine, and is considered by Dr. Birch to be of the fourth century before Christ. The work and design on the face—a lion devouring a

Fig. 136.   Engraved Scarabæus, with Cypriote Inscription.   *Cornelian.*

boar, upon a hatched ground or estrade—is of very beautiful execution. The inscription is read by Professor Sayce to be :—

ⵀ ⵉ ⵔ ⵖ ⵦ ⵥ ⵖ

ko ni to e te mi e.

ἠμὶ Θεητονίκου.

"I belong to Theétonikos."

33. Fig. 137 is a scarabæus of unfinished form, with the under surface engraved with a figure of Mercury,

Fig. 137.   Engraved Scarabæoid.   *Cornelian.*

draped. and holding in his right hand his customary attribute. the caduceus. The style is Greek, and it appears to be of some merit as a work of art.

BEADS AND INLAYING PIECES, ETC.

These objects, from their similar art. will conveniently follow the scarabæi. The list of them is subjoined.

1. Rectangle for inlaying, with a few indistinct characters in the Phœnician or Cypriote language. 3-4ths inch long. *Grey stone.*

2. A rectangular bead, engraved with the Paphian goddess under her canopy, on one side, and the cone

Fig. 138.   Engraved Bead.   *Grey Steatite.*

under its canopy, on the other. Compare the cylinders described on pp. 121-123. 5-8ths inch long.

3. Another, with the cone replaced by an uncertain object. 3-4ths inch long. *Gray steatite.*

4. Rectangular pierced bead. On one side, a Circle of the Sun, with radiations ; on the other, an uncertain emblem of Cypriote design, perhaps the Paphian goddess under the canopy, as already described. 5-8ths by 3-4ths inch. *Dark steatite.*

5. Pierced bead, rectangular. A monogram on each side. 5-8ths by 3-8ths inch. *Steatite.* (See Plate xv, fig. 62.)

6. Rectangular pierced bead. Ornamental devices. 5-8ths and half-inch. *Dark steatite.* (See Plate xv, fig. 61.)

7. Rectangular pierced bead. On each face an uncertain device. Perhaps a lion. Compare No. 51, p. 130. 3-4ths by half-inch. *Dark steatite.*

8. Rectangular pierced bead. On each side a floral

L

ornament of simple and archaic design.   Half by 3-8ths inch.   *Light green steatite.*

9. With these beads may be placed a well-carved object, representing a calf or ox, standing upon a ring or hollow cylinder.   If held with the head downward, this pretty little toy assumes the appearance of a hand grasp-

Fig 139.   Carved Calf and Hand.   *Steatite.*

ing a ring.   The work is of the style characteristic of Cypriote art, and may be attributed to a considerable antiquity.

CHAPTER XIV

ENGRAVED GEMS AND PRECIOUS STONES.

HE ancient graves of the inhabitants of Cyprus, I found, yielded many gems and precious stones engraved with various classical and native subjects. Some of these were set in gold or silver rings, either for use as signets, or as mortuary ornaments. Others, again, were not set in any metal, but found lying loose in the earth of the tomb. Many of the subjects engraved on these stones are of early workmanship; all are beautiful. I append a list of the most important examples :—

1. Oval, with the head of a bearded man in profile to the right, carved in relief. The curling of the beard and hair forcibly reminds us of the treatment of hair in the Assyrian sculptures. There can be little doubt that this is an Assyrian or Hittite gem. Half-inch long. *Deep purple amethyst.* (See Plate xv, fig. 65.)

2. Convex oval intaglio. A figure of Jupiter seated, to the left, in profile, at his feet an eagle. The work of this intaglio appears to be Roman, of the first century B.C. Half-inch long. *Transparent paste.* (See Plate xv, fig. 81.)

3. Convex oval intaglio. A figure of Jupiter seated on a chair or throne, to the left, extending his right hand, in which is an uncertain object. Roman style.

3-8ths inch long.   *Onyx* or *niccolo*. (See Plate xv,
fig. 68.)

4. Circular intaglio. A bust of Jupiter Serapis (fig. 140)
in profile, to the left.   The beard is long and pointed ;
the hair rolled or curled at the ends, and filleted.   The

Fig. 140.   Engraved Gem- Jupiter.   *Sardonyx.*

treatment is manifestly archaic, and the gem may be
considered to be of great age, perhaps the fourth century
before Christ.   Half-inch long.

Ancient gems, resembling the above, with subjects in
intaglio, were especially objects of care and admiration ;
and especially were those sought after which had upon
them subjects such as were fit to be taken with a
religious meaning.   Hence, fine antique portraits of
classical divinities or historical personages are frequently
met with by the seal collector, either in the form of

Fig. 141.   Ancient Gem with Mediæval Setting.   *Cornelian.*

matrices, or as original impressions appended to charters, enriched with a legend of Christian import.
A good example of this use is shown in fig. 141 (kindly
lent by the British Archæological Association),[1] where a

---

[1] From *Journal*, vol. iii, p. 330.

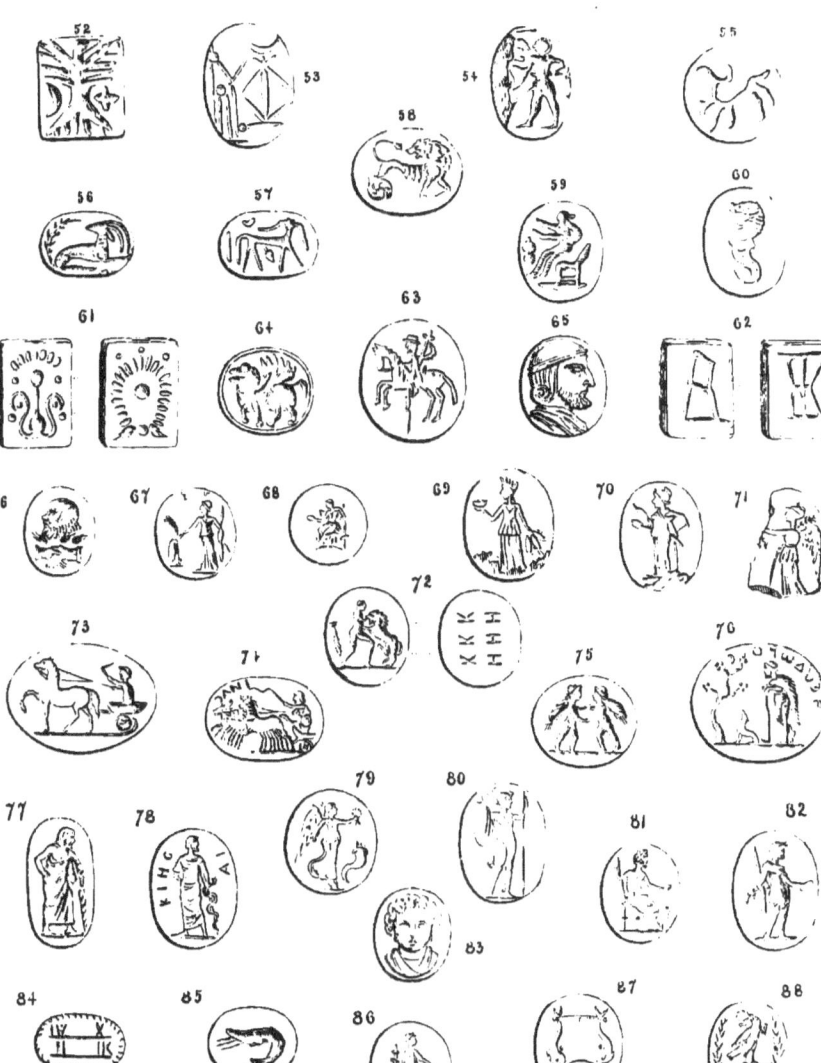

Roman cornelian, engraved in intaglio with a female head, is enclosed in a metal rim, with an inscription shewing that the owner considered the head as a portrait of Jesus Christ, *Christus caput omnium.* Numerous instances of the similar treatment of gems could be adduced, where precisely the same result is obtained, but it is unnecessary here to refer to them. It is sufficient to point out that the collections of charters in the British Museum furnish a large quantity of examples that are well worthy of the notice of writers on ancient gems.

5. Oval intaglio for a ring. A full-length figure of the god Mars, or Ares, without drapery, to the left, helmeted, and holding a spear and shield. Half-inch long. *Cornelian.* (See Plate xv, fig. 80.)

6. Oval intaglio. A full-length figure of the goddess Minerva to the left, draped and helmeted, and holding distaff and lance. Early workmanship. Half-inch long. *Cornelian* or *hyacinth.* (See Plate xv, fig. 70.)

7. Oval intaglio for use as a signet. The subject appears to be the goddess Minerva, full length, with helmet and lance, facing to the right. Before the goddess is a shield resting upon a column. The date of this is about the second century B.C. 5-8ths inch long. *Bloodstone.* (See Plate xv, fig. 67.)

8. Oval for a ring. Finely-executed head of a warrior or the goddess Minerva, to the right, helmeted. The

Fig. 142.   Engraved Gem.   *Sard.*

date may be referred to the first century before Christ (fig. 142). 7-16ths inch long.

9. Convex oval intaglio.   A full-length figure of a

Fig. 143.   Engraved Gem.   *Iridescent and Transparent Paste.*

goddess with a weapon, perhaps Minerva (fig. 143).
Very archaic.   3-4ths inch long.

10. Oval intaglio.   A full-length figure of Minerva,

Fig. 144.   Engraved Gem.   *Cornelian.*

helmeted, to the left, holding up or supporting a warrior
with a spear in his hand (fig. 144).   5-8ths inch long.

11. Convex oval intaglio.   A figure of Athene Nikephoros, holding a spear and shield.   Half-inch long.
Cornelian.

12. Convex oval intaglio gem.   The subject is Athene
Nikephoros, engraved in a good style of art.   3-8ths
inch long, set in an ancient gold finger-ring.   *Deep red
cornelian.*

13. Oval intaglio.   A full-length figure of the goddess
Demeter, or Pomona, holding a basket of fruit and ears
of corn.   The date is the second century A.D.   9-16ths
inch long.   *Cornelian.*   (See Plate xv, fig. 69.)

14. Convex oval intaglio.   A full-length female figure,

Fig. 145.   Engraved object.   *Purple Paste.*

perhaps a goddess, holding a spear, and resting her right hand on a term or altar. 1 inch long. *Purple paste.*

15. Convex oval intaglio. A full-length figure of a goddess with uncertain attributes. The edge is ornamented with a small beading or dotted border. 7-8ths inch long. *Iridescent glass or paste.*

16. Oval intaglio gem. A figure of the god Hermes, or Mercury with a caduceus, engraved in an elegant archaic style. 7-16ths inch long. *Hyacinth.* (See Plate xv, fig. 82.)

17. Oval intaglio. Hermes, or Mercury, with caduceus and wallet, as in *Museo Borbonico*, tom. vi, tav. 2. Figured in Smith's *Class. Dict.* 3-8ths inch long, set in an ancient plain massy gold ring. *Hyacinth.*

18. Oval convex intaglio. Mercury, undraped, to the right, holding a sacred branch as the emblem of peace. This emblem was attributed to Mercury by the Fetiales, who never recognised the identity of Mercury with Hermes of the Greeks, although the Romans of later times transferred all the attributes and myths of Hermes to their own god. Quarter-inch long, set in a plain and massy gold finger-ring of small dimensions and ancient workmanship. *Sard.*

19. Oval, set in gold, with the holes for the insertion of the hoop of a swivel ring. This subject is Hercules

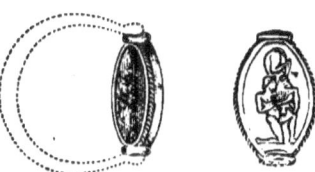

Fig. 14°.   Hercules and the Nemæan Lion.   *Cornelian.*

and the Nemæan lion. The workmanship is Greek, and there is an elegant style of art in the treatment of this beautiful intaglio. The date may be placed at the third century B.C. 3-4ths inch long. *Cornelian*.

20. Oval intaglio, engraved on both sides. The obverse has a representation of Hercules strangling the Nemaean lion, the first[1] of the twelve labours performed at the bidding of Eurystheus. Behind the semi-divine hero is his attribute the club, which he had employed in vain against his foe before he strangles it. The arrangement of this scene is exactly the same as that engraved by Smith[2] from a Roman lamp. On the reverse the letters

Н П Ц

К К К

The ц probably stands for HPAKΛHC. It is difficult to conjecture the signification of the к. 3-8ths inch long. *Jasper*. (See Plate xv, fig. 72.)

21. Oval. On a line, Cupid wrestling with a faun; before them, on a term or column, a figure of Priapus with a palm-branch. Fine Greek work. Half-inch long. I have had this set in a modern gold chased finger-ring. *Hyacinth*.

22. Oval intaglio. On a line, two *Erotes*, winged and helmeted, wrestling. 3-8ths inch long. *Jasper*. (See Plate xv, fig. 75.)

23. Circular and convex intaglio. The chubby head of an infant, Eros, three-quarter face to the left. The field inscribed EPΩTOC. Greek style. 3-8ths inch. *Burnt cornelian*.

24. Oval intaglio in archaic style (fig. 147). Leda reclining on a bank receiving the blandishments of the Swan. In this elegant gem we may indeed behold—

...... " olorinis Ledam recubare sub alis".[3]

The treatment of the subject indicates that the artist was well acquainted with the myth which he had under-

[1] " Prima Cleonaei tolerata aerumna Leonis".
Auson., *Idyll*. xix ; cf. also *Apollodor*. ii, 5, § 1.
Class. Dict., 196. [3] *Ov. Metam.*, vi.

taken to illustrate. 5-8ths inch long, set in a silver finger-ring.

Fig. 147. Engraved Gem—Leda. Heliotrope.

25. Small engraved oval of the style of the second century of our era. The subject is a Fortune, to the left, draped, and holding in the right hand a rudder, an emblem of the government or direction of the affairs of the world; in the left, a cornucopiæ, or Nike. 3-8ths inch long. *Cornelian.* (See Plate xv, fig. 86.)

26. Oval intaglio. A full-length figure of a goddess, to the right, perhaps Fortune, with a cornucopiæ, and other uncertain emblems. Half-inch long. *Cornelian.*

27. Convex oval. A full-length figure of the goddess Fortune, with a cornucopiæ, to the right. 3-8ths inch, set in a bezel in a flat gold ring of ancient workmanship. *Cornelian.*

28. A fine convex oval gem, cut in intaglio, with a full-length figure of Fortune. Of the Roman period. 7-8ths inch long, set in a silver finger-ring. *Sardonyx.*

29. Oval. In the archaic style. Fortune, seated to the right on a tripod, and holding a Nike Apteros, or Wingless Victory, in the right hand. In her left hand, a branch of fruit, which the goddess is placing on an altar. 5-8ths inch long, set in a gold finger-ring. *Yellow jasper.*

30. Oval intaglio. Victory, winged, with a palm-branch over the shoulder, and holding a wreath in the right hand extended before her (fig. 148). The flowing drapery shewn here resembles that sometimes seen on figures of Iris in the Greek gems. 5-8ths inch long, set

X

in an ancient plain gold finger-ring of small proportions.

Fig. 118.   Engraved Gem—Victory.   *Cornelian.*

31. Long oval, chipped at the lower part. The style is of the second century A.D. A winged Victory, turned to the right, draped and crown, holding a rudder palm, or laurel branch, and a chaplet. 5-8ths inch long. *Zoned sardonyx.* (See Plate xv, fig. 71.)

32. Oval convex intaglio. A full-length figure of a winged Nike, or Victory, holding a crown and palm-branch. 3-8ths inch long, set in a fine gold ring. *Garnet.*

33. Convex oval intaglio. A figure of Nike, or Victory, winged, and holding a palm-branch, full-length, to the left. 3-8ths inch long.

34. Small oval. A winged figure of Nike, or Victory, to the left, the drapery flowing in elegant folds. In the field before her a cornucopiæ. Good workmanship. 7-16ths inch long. *Cornelian.* (See Plate xv, fig. 79.)

35. Oval intaglio. A female sphinx with human face, sejant to the left, with the wings extended, elevating the right foot ; on the base line in front of the sphinx a skull is engraved. Half-inch long. *Amethystine coloured paste.*

This curious device closely resembles the subject of a gem ring found about the year 1817 near the ruins of Evesham Abbey, and figured and described in the *Journal of the British Archæological Association*, vol. xxxii, pp. 115-117. In this example, the gem is a dark red cornelian or sard, 7-16ths inch diameter, engraved with the sphinx (fig. 149) sejant, the head bound with a vitta, and the tail elevated and coiled. Immediately in front of the fore feet of the sphinx is a human skull ; and beneath the ground line a headless skeleton is extended, the remains of one of those who had unfortunately failed to guess the riddle of the sphinx, and so fallen a victim

Fig. 149.   Gem Seal—A Sphinx.

to his temerity.[1] The Norman-French inscription on this seal ring is reversed. It reads LI COCATRIX. The engraver probably mistook the subject for a cockatrice, which would be to him, in the thirteenth century, a familiar denizen of the manuscript bestiaries, or natural history books.

36. Oval. A gryllus or nondescript creature, here consisting of a bald head, perhaps of Silenus, an eagle's head, a goat's head and horns, a cock's head crested, in allusion to the Gnostic deity Jao, an elephant's head,

Fig. 160.   Engraved Gem—A Gryllus.   *Sard.*

holding a thyrsus or caduceus in the trunk, and some other emblems, all united with the feet of a bird, and made up into an animal form. Half-inch long.

37. Convex oval intaglio. A gryllus in form of a cock. The head is that of a horse, the body incorporates a head of Silenus, and some other component parts not very distinct. Half-inch long, set in a bezel with a flat strip of gold, forming a finger-ring. *Cornelian.*

[1] I am indebted for the use of this woodcut also, to the kindness of the British Archæological Association.

By this particular name, gryllus, which appears to
derive its origin from a classical word signifying a
cricket, is designated that peculiarly fantastic combination which is found engraved upon gems and precious
stones, and was employed largely in the seal art of the
middle ages. The precise origin of uniting a number of
more or less incongruous devices into one figure, as exhibited by these engravings, cannot be determined with
any degree of accuracy. Conjecture, however, points to
the Gnostic period as the probable era of the rise of this
kind of device. Anticlides is said to have painted similar
devices upon the vases of Greece about the middle of the
fourth century B.C. It may be that the separate symbols each imparted their attributed virtue to the fortunate possessor of the gem, or protected him from ills
not to be otherwise averted. At any rate, the gems of
the Gnostics exhibit many such crude combinations as
these so-called *grylli*. Among the most prevailing combinations is generally found the face of a man in profile,
with a bald head, and nose of that type which is generally referred to Silenus ; and there is little doubt that
the constantly-recurring expression on the face is intended for a portrait of some well-known individual.
Why Silenus should have been chosen to fill a place
in these fantastic riddles is not difficult to solve. In an
impression of an oval gem, in the British Museum, occurs
a gryllus composed of a human head surmounted by that
of a horse holding a *thyrsus* or branch in its mouth, while
a cornucopiæ, and an eagle holding a hare in its grip,
complete an inharmonious whole, which is so grouped as
to make up what at first sight would appear to be a
bird.

Mr. King, in his work already quoted,[1] has engraved
several fine examples of the gryllus. Of the connection

---

[1] *Antique Gems and Rings*, Pl. XXXIX, LVI, LVII, etc.

of Silenus with the gryllus, that author writes :[1]—" As for Silenus, his laughter-stirring visage was, from some reason now lost, esteemed a potent amulet. This is proved from its forming an essential part of almost every gryllus[2] or astrological talisman, perhaps as passing for the emblem of universal knowledge.

Another gryllus shews the same equine and human combination united with legs of a rapacious bird, and a ram's head, holding a caduceus and bunch of grapes in its mouth. Many other varieties could be described. That these ancient objects were valued and sought after in the middle ages is manifested without difficulty by the numerous specimens of impressions of seals appended to charters from the twelfth to the fifteenth century. When selected for use as a seal, the gem or precious stone bearing this potent talisman was set in a matrix or bezel with a rim or border of gold or silver, level with the face of the intaglio, and of a width sufficient to carry a legend. These legends, when not merely personal, display great ingenuity and originality. Mr. W. de G. Birch, in an article upon these relics,[3] has recorded a considerable number of varieties. The only one which I may mention in this place is a pointed oval seal of the fifteenth century, in which is set an antique oval gem of the gryllus kind, engraved in intaglio, with a cock crowing and flapping its wings, the bird itself being composed of a horse's head, a ram's head, and the bald head of Silenus with a pointed beard, because it attempts by the legend to explain some at least of the various significations of the devices. The explanation, certainly, is specious, and,

[1] *Antique Gems and Rings*, pp. 263, 264.

[2] "Especially prominent in that favourite one an elephant's head, carrying in its trunk a palm, a torch, or a caduceus. The elephant belongs to Bacchus as an Indian conqueror, which may explain its adoption as a vehicle for Dionysiac emblems, and the accompanying attributes, all plainly bearing reference to those Mysteries."—[Mr. King's note.]

[3] *Engl. Cyclop., Arts and Sciences, Suppl.*

if correct, affords a clue to the meaning of other combinations. It is an hexameter verse :—

" 'Scriptum signat equus, mittit vir, devehit ales.' "

38. Oval cameo. A figure of Æsculapius, full-length,
to the right, wearing a long dress, leaning upon a staff,
round which a serpent is coiled. 5-8ths inch long.
Green and blackish red cameo onyx. (See Plate xv,
fig. 77.)

39. Oval intaglio. A figure of Æsculapius, full-length,
to the right, holding a staff with a serpent coiled round
it. In the field, the name of the owner or artist KTHCIA.
In the style of the first century A.D. 5-8ths inch long.
Onyx. (See Plate xv, fig. 78.)

40. Oval intaglio. A man in profile to the left,
draped, with a cloak hanging down behind from the
shoulder, offering corn and fruit. Half-inch long, set in
a plain and massy ancient gold finger-ring. This has
been figured in another part of this work.[1] *Niccolo* or
onyx.

41. Oval for setting in a ring. Horseman with spear.
Very early work. 5-8ths inch long. *Jasper.* (See
Plate xv, fig. 63.)

42. Oval intaglio. The favourite subject of a quad-
riga, or chariot of four horses abreast at full speed, to the
right, is here represented. In the field, the inscription
ISAC. Half-inch long. *Jasper.* (See Plate xv, fig.
74.)

43. Oval intaglio gem. A chariot drawn by one
horse, who is pacing to the left, urged on by a
charioteer with a short whip. Greek style and elegant
design. 5-8ths inch long. *Jasper.* (See Plate xv, fig.
73.)

44. Oval intaglio. A bust to the right, not unlike the
portraits of the young Augustus; or, perhaps, a youthful

[1] See fig. 40, pp. 38, 41.

emperor. The cutting of this gem is of first-rate excellence. It may be referred to the first century of our era. Half-inch long. *Sardonyx.*

Fig. 151.   Engraved Gem—A Portrait Bust.   *Sardonyx.*

45. Oval, carved in relief. A bust, full face, of an empress, draped, the hair curled. 3-8ths inch long. *Spinel ruby*, or *coloured paste.*

46. Another oval, of a design precisely similar to the preceding number, and of the same size. *Green paste.* (See Plate xv, fig. 83.)

47. Oval. The Discobolus, resembling closely a gem ring, which has already formed the subject of some remarks in an earlier chapter.[1] 3-8ths inch long, set in a plain and massy ancient gold finger-ring. *Pale green paste.*

48. Round piece for setting as a ring. On a line, an old man leaning upon a staff, turned to the right, and a dog looking up at a tree on the right hand. Over head is the inscription ΘΕΟΔΩΡΟϹ, the name either of the artist or the owner of the ring. Half-inch long. (See Plate xv, fig. 76.)

49. Oval. A male figure with a head-dress, to the left, apparently skipping, or holding a cord in the hands, which passes down to the heels. Half-inch long, set in gold, with rosettes at the sides, and attached to a plain circular gold wire ring. *Green and white mosaic glass.* (The ring is figured in Plate i, fig. 11.)

50. Oval intaglio. A soldier, helmeted, and wearing the usual dress, to the right, with spear and convex shield. Half-inch long. *Calcined agate*, or *cornelian.*

51. Oval. A satyr, full-length, to the left, elevating

[1] See fig. 35, p. 38.

the right leg, and holding a *pedum*, or shepherd's crook, and vase, with globular body and long thin neck. 3-8ths inch, set in a plain massy gold ring of very small calibre, for a youth. *Cornelian.*

52. Oval, for setting in a ring or seal. A head to the left, and an inscription, conjectured by Professor Sayce to read :—IAΩ MIX[AHL], a Gnostic inscription, record-

Fig. 152.   Engraved Gnostic Gem.   *Calcined Agate.*

ing the names of two potent personages in that faith. The reader may refer to a former chapter for some observations on an amulet of Gnostic art.[1]

53. Small circular piece for setting in a ring. A por-

Fig. 153.   Engraved Gem—A Portrait Head.   *Paste.*

trait head in profile to the left, bearded. The work is of the Roman period. 5-16ths inch long.

54. Oval intaglio gem. A *Fides*, or two hands, couped at the wrists, and clasped in saltire; above them three ears of corn. Above these a mask or head of Silenus in profile to the right, similar to the heads found forming parts of *grylli* already described. The hands clasped are the symbols of union, and the ears of corn represent increase; but the relation of the head of Silenus to this emblematic device is difficult to interpret. 5-8ths inch long. *Jasper.* (See Plate xv, fig. 66.)

55. Oval intaglio, perhaps Gnostic, carved on both sides. On the obverse, within an engrailed border, a

[1] See p. 103.

kind of platform or *estrade*, on which is an altar, between two worshippers on one side, and a priest sacrificing an animal on the other. Very archaic and indistinct. On the reverse, an uncertain inscription in four lines, of

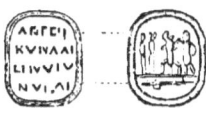

Fig. 154.

Cornelian.

a character which resembles Greek. Half-inch long. *Cornelian*.

56. Oval. A bull and star, as described in the account of gold rings in a previous chapter.[1] 3-8ths inch long, set in a small but ancient gold ring, for a child. *Red jasper*.

57. Oval intaglio. A tree, with a goat on each side of it, leaping up and browsing on the foliage. 3-8ths inch long. *Cornelian*.

58. Oval intaglio. An eagle, close, regardant, holding in its beak a chaplet or crown. 3-8ths inch long, set in a plain and massy ancient gold finger-ring of somewhat small dimensions. *Cornelian*.

59. Oval intaglio. An eagle, close, regardant, to the right, holding a garland or chaplet, at its feet an uncertain object. In the field, the inscription EAET. 5-8ths inch long. *Cornelian*.

60. Oval intaglio gem, from a finger-ring. An eagle, regardant, to the right, holding a garland or crown, and perched upon a rock between two palm-branches. 3-8ths inch long. *Jasper*. (See Plate xv, fig. 88.)

61. Oval scarabæoid, not pierced, probably for setting in a ring or fleurette. The subject is a hippocamp. 3-4ths inch long. *Calcined steatite*. (See Plate xv, fig. 60.)

[1] See fig. 41, page 11.

V

62. Oval gem. The subject appears to be a lobster or shrimp. This is of fairly early Greek workmanship, and may be referred to about the second century before the Christian era. 3-8ths inch long. *Cornelian*. (See Plate xv, fig. 85.)

63. Oval for setting. A seven-stringed lyre. The sounding board carved in the form of a small animal, probably a dog, lying curled up. Half-inch long. *Amethyst*. (See Plate xv, fig. 87.)

64. Oval intaglio, engraved on both sides with uncertain figures or letters of mystical value, some of which are not unlike Cypriote syllables, but they cannot be deciphered. 5-8ths inch, the edge bevelled. *Cornelian*.

65. Oval engraved gem. Two lines of Roman numerals, perhaps of mystic or magical import. The numbers are—x, vi, iii, ii. This edge of the engraved stone is frilled or engrailed. Half-inch long. *Agate*. (See Plate xv, fig. 84.)

66. Oval. The Temple of Paphos, as figured and described in a former part of the work.[1] 3-8ths inch long, set in a gold ring. *Cornelian*.

[1] See fig. 39, pp. 40, 41.

CHAPTER XV

CHALCEDONY, ETC.

HE number of objects which I discovered at Salamis and other sites composed of chalcedony and other hard stones is not very large, but, considering the rarity of such antiquities, my collection is fairly well supplied with them. The use of chalcedony is, we are told, very ancient. The oldest dynasties of the Egyptian Empire have contributed many objects formed of it to the museums of Europe. The name of this substance is believed to be derived from Chalcedon, in Bithynia, where the first specimens of the material were procured. According to some writers, it is a kind of agate, with milky veins and cloudy spots in it. Others describe it as a stalactite of the quartz species, of a dull grey tint, with blue and purple veins and blotches. Another class of writers consider that chalcedony is a species of quartz, semi-pellucid, of a whitish, bluish, smokey-grey, or yellow and red colour. It is two and a half times heavier than water.

A modern author on precious stones states that chalcedony is a kind of quartz: according to Fuchs, pure quartz with opal disseminated through it. This stone is usually of a greyish colour, but sometimes occurs milky white, pinkish, or of a smalt blue; in the latter case it is called sapphirine. It is never found crystallised. Some Indian varieties are yellowish, which is owing to the presence of

oxide of iron. It is often found lining agate geodes, in
trap rocks, and sometimes stratified, various tints alternating. It is semi-transparent, translucent (to nearly
opaque), and as hard as quartz, but much less fragile,
being very tough, and breaking with an even fracture,
exhibiting little or no lustre. It is found in flints.
From its hardness and toughness, this stone is well
adapted for engraving, and has been used for this purpose from the most ancient period.[1]

That the chalcedony was esteemed by the ancients to
be one of the most precious stones is sufficiently shewn
by St. John the Divine, who, in his account of the foundations of " that great city, the holy Jerusalem", writes:
" And[2] the foundations of the wall of the city were gar-
nished with all manner of precious stones. The first
foundation was jasper ; the second, sapphire ; the third,
a chalcedony."

Fig. 155 represents a small chalcedony vase found in
a tomb at Salamina in 1867. The vase is of late Egyptian style, and of the shape of the Egyptian *situla*, or

Fig. 155.   Inscribed Situla.   Chalcedony.

bucket. Around the upper part of this small vase is
an ornament like a Phœnician inscription, but the letters

---

[1] H. Emanuel, *Diamonds and Precious Stones*, 1867.

[2] Rev. xxi, 19.

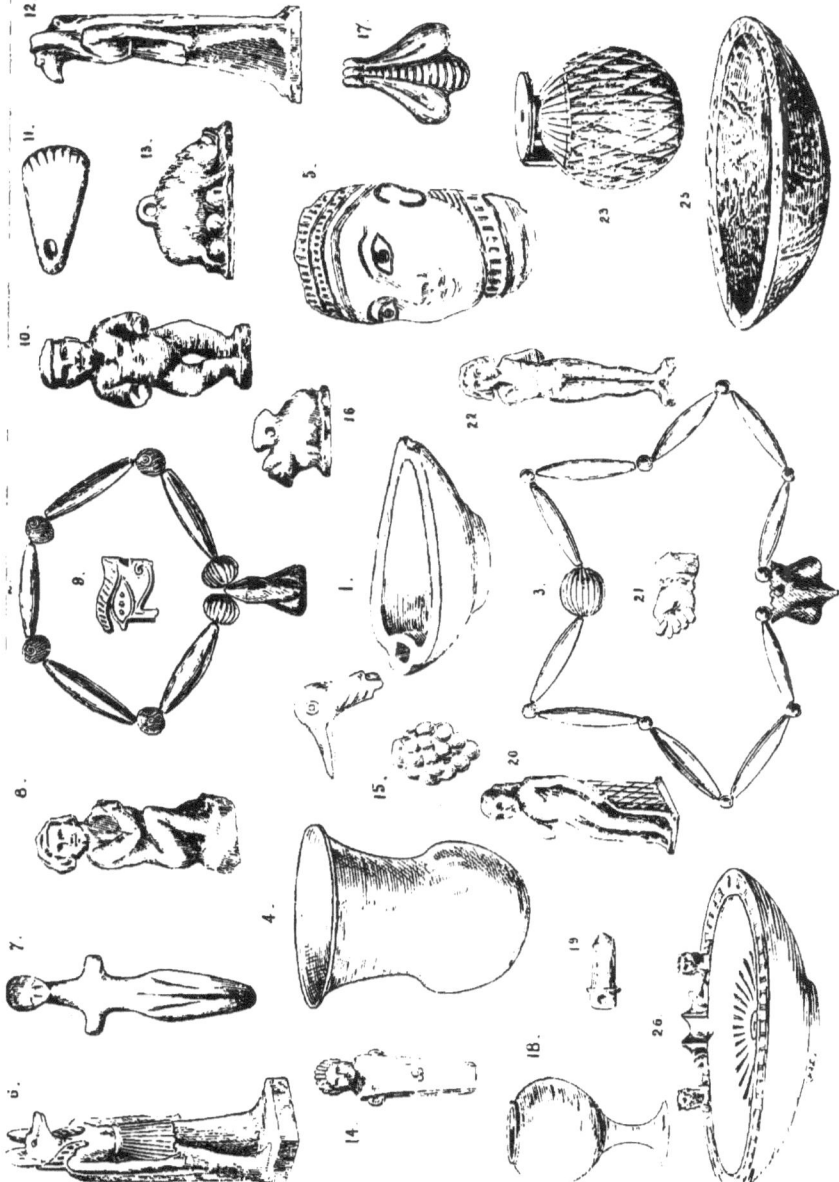

are so indistinct, that it is impossible to conjecture the
signification of the writing. Inside, suspended by a gold
wire from two small handles and the top of the vase, is a
little amulet of uncertain shape.

The accompanying figure (156) represents an amulet,
or toy, carved in form of the cuttle fish, or sepia. The
shield-shaped body is adorned with an inscription in

Fig. 156.   A. Inscribed Amulet, in form of 'the Cuttle Fish.
                  B. The Shield Enlarged.   *Chalcedony.*

Phœnician letters, but they are unfortunately so indistinct from age, and so nearly obliterated, that it would
be rash to hazard a conjecture as to their meaning.

An inscribed roundle, or plaque, perhaps an amulet or
inlaying piece (fig. 157), which I found in the ground at
Salamis, has upon it an eagle or other bird displayed, sur-

Fig. 157.   Ornament.   *Chalcedony.*

rounded by an illegible and nearly obliterated inscription
in characters which may be Phœnician or old Greek.

Among the more interesting objects belonging to this
class, Plate xvi, fig. 1 represents a toy-duck, fitted with
a moveable head, and a lid of the back and wings, now
wanting. This is formed of a bluish-white chalcedony.

There are two necklaces or bracelets in the collection,[1] composed of bugles of ovoid, cylindrical shapes, alternating with carved or striated spherical beads, some of which are painted with circles or amulets of blue, pink, and yellow colours. Each of these bracelets has a pendant, undoubtedly in form of a phallus, one of which shews traces of gilding, and is painted with bands of red, and other colour ; and it is so formed as to represent on one side that object in a quiescent state, and on the other as the emblem of the god of gardens. Of chalcedony, I found also a handsomely-shaped bowl or drinking-cup of a yellowish tinge,[2] with fluted body, and wide swelling lip ; the whole in some respect resembling the bowl of a modern goblet. In the same plate, I have figured an enamelled female head of great beauty.[3]

Plate xvi, fig. 6, represents an Egyptian amulet in form of Anepu, or Anubis, the jackal-headed god, who, according to Greek legends, was the son of the goddess Nebta, or, according to other and, perhaps, more orthodox traditions, the son of Osiris and Isis. The jackal, a common Egyptian animal, was exclusively the emblem of Anubis, who is almost always represented—as, indeed, in the present specimen—with the head of the jackal instead of the human head. In the system of the Egyptian Pantheon, Anubis was the divinity who presided over the processes of embalmment and sanctification of the dead, and guarded the " Roads of the South and North of Heaven and Earth". In this example, he is walking, with the left foot advanced in the Egyptian manner, wearing the head-dress, called *namms*, and the tunic, called *shenti*, around the loins. The next object represented in the same plate is an amulet, or toy, perhaps a doll, of light blue colour, almost white. It appears to be a rude and uncompleted figure of a female.[4] A kneeling figure of uncertain period and style is placed

[1] Pl. xvi, figs. 2, 3.   [2] Fig. 4.   [3] Fig. 5.   [4] Fig. 7.

next in order.[1] A symbolic eye, called *utu* by the Egyptians, to whose workmanship this little amulet must be assigned,[2] is of interest, coming, as it does, from Cypriote tombs. These symbolic eyes are attributed to the " Sun and Moon"; or they may be taken as the " Eyes of the Hawk of Ra", the Sun God, by the opening of which that deity illuminated the universe. To the pointed oval opening of the eyelids were attached two appendages,—the drop, and the spiral line like a lituus. The Egyptian name of the eye is apparently derived from the word *sound*, or *whole*, and the appendages, according to Dr. Birch, may represent a tear dropping from the eye, or the cheek-bone of the " Cow of Athor", the " Mystical Mother of the Sun". The right eye represented the Sun, and the left, as in the object before us, the Moon. It is a not uncommon ornament in Egyptian collections of antiquity, and is found adapted to various purposes, such as pendants, or beads of necklaces and bracelets, in which cases it is generally perforated, or provided with a ring carved out of the same substance, for suspension. There can be no doubt that the symbolic eye was used as a kind of charm or amulet, not only of sepulchral, but of domestic use ; and it is known that those made of hard stone were worn round the neck. They are formed of many and various substances, such as lapis-lazuli, serpentine, hæmatite, obsidian, red jasper, green felspar, cornelian, and even porcelain. There are several very fine specimens of symbolic eyes in the British Museum and the museum of the Duke of Northumberland at Alnwick Castle.

A little figure of the god Ptah-Socharis-Osiris,[3] shewing that god, formed of a light blue chalcedony, in the shape of a naked dwarf, wearing a skull cap, with his legs bowed, and the hands, now broken off, on the hips, is given in the same plate. Another object is a figure of

[1] Pl. xvi, fig. 8.　　　[2] Fig. 9.　　　[3] Fig. 10.

the god Chons, or Chonsu,[1] the divine son of Amon and Mut, the third element in the *Triad of Theban Divinities*, and a lunar god, apparently the oracular enemy of the revolters or enemies of the gods and the expeller of demons. The lunar disk, with which he is always properly represented, is broken from the head of this ancient carving, wherein the god is represented with a hawk's head, walking, the hands clenched, and the arms pendent.

Among small miscellaneous objects of chalcedony or other allied stones, I may refer to an object resembling a human foot;[2] a sow giving suck to her litter, with a carved ring on the back for suspension as a pendent amulet;[3] a pendant, in form of a ram or goat, also with a pierced ring;[4] a terminal figure of Hermes;[5] a bunch of grapes;[6] a bee, or wasp, the head wanting;[7] a stud, or pin, with a hole pierced in the head;[8] and a clenched hand,[9] with the thumb protruded between the index and middle fingers, similar to that described among the gold objects in Plate I, fig. 15.

A very beautiful bright blue-coloured *unguentarium*,[10] carved out of chalcedony, is in form of a globe upon a circular foot, not unlike a modern goblet or wine-cup. It measures an inch and a half in height, and was probably used to contain a small quantity of precious ointment or perfume to be placed near to the body of a departed relative in the Salaminian tomb from which I obtained it. Plate xvi, fig. 20, is a figure of Harpocrates treated in the Egyptian style. He is called Harpaxrat, or Harpocrates, " Horus, the Child of Isis", and is seated, naked, in the attitude of being in his mother's lap, with the symbolical lock of hair, called *rut*, at the side of his head; the index finger of the right hand is raised to the mouth. Another chalcedony relic[11] shews a standing

[1] Pl. xvi, f. 12.   [2] Fig. 11.   [3] Fig. 13.   [4] Fig. 16.
[5] Fig. 14.   [6] Fig. 15.   [7] Fig. 17.   [8] Fig. 19.
[9] Fig. 21.   [10] Fig. 18.   [11] Fig. 22.

figure of the same Horus, also with the finger in the mouth. An elegant *aryballos* in sapphirine chalcedony, with a body imitating the markings of a fir-cone;[1] a bowl with a radiated star-like ornament at the bottom inside, and having the rim adorned with a coloured band marked out in small squares, and carved with two lions sejant gardant, back to back;[2] and a plain bowl of somewhat thick substance, marbled with dark blue veins,[3] complete the description of the most important chalcedony relics which the tombs of Cyprus yielded to my diggings.

[1] Plate xvi, fig. 23.   [2] Fig. 26.   [3] Fig. 25.

CHAPTER XVI.

GLASS.

IT is unnecessary here for me to enter upon a dissertation concerning ancient glass. Many works and treatises upon this fertile subject will recur to the minds of most readers; and there are, indeed, few antiquaries who do not know where to turn for information as to the various characteristics which ancient glass exhibits, the shapes and peculiarities which the vessels themselves affect, their sizes and colours, and even the successive steps in the manufacture of the material. Exquisitely beautiful examples of ancient glass are preserved in many museums, and to them the Island of Cyprus, where the arts which ministered to taste and refinement pre-eminently flourished, has not been found slow to contribute.

The total number of these remains in the Lawrence-Cesnola collection is very considerable, probably not fewer than four thousand in all. There can be no reasonable doubt that some of these examples were made at Tyre by Phœnician workmen, who were for a long time the sole possessors of the craft of producing and

shaping the material. Others, again, are Greek, and
many belong to the Roman period. It is difficult in
many instances, so closely do the styles approach each
other, to distinguish the one class from the other. These
articles are of various sizes, from the tiny *unguentarium*,
lachrymatory, or "tear-bottle", which was doubtless used
to contain scented fluids or essences of unusual precious-
ness, to vases which are capable of holding as much as
half a gallon of costly liquids. Besides these, there is a
certain number of *phialai* or *paterœ* of differing diameters,
none of which exceed a foot.

A *patera* of pale clear citron colour has two handles in
the form of serpents crawling on its edge. Several paterœ comprise cords of cotton, a material which appears
to have been coloured before it was incorporated into the
edges of the vessels, which have been turned over for the
purpose. Bowls exist in the collection, some of which
have been moulded in radially-disposed flutings, and
some are impressed with patterns. These, like many
other examples, reproduce patterns of metal ware.
Many *acetabula* also occur, including a few which are
sumptuously coloured in purple lines. Of these, some
have their sides pressed inwards, in order to afford a safe
holding for the fingers. One or two bear devices moulded
in relief. Of these, one bears three of the so-called
"Amazonian" shields, with satyric masks, tears, a laurel
wreath, and archaic trees. The bottles are, for the most
part, tall and thin, some having short and others long
necks, short and bulbous forms, with narrow or wide
mouths, lipped and lipless. Others are with and some
are without handles, some are ovoid, others are square,
globular, fluted, depressed, or oblong. Many of them
exactly reproduce the forms of metal, and not a few exhibit the shapes of ceramic types. Two oblong plates of
glass occur among the remains of that material, measuring
eight inches by six. The very nature and form of these

articles suggest their employment as window-panes.
These were found in Salamis, and connected with terra-
cotta sarcophagi of the Roman period, which were generally made with covers, while few of them consist of one
piece. Usually, they are composed of two or more square
tiles cemented together. The glass was intended to
allow the faces of the dead to be seen within the coffins.
The bodies of these sarcophagi are enriched with rude
reliefs of bulls, birds, and festoons of flowers bearing
traces of colour. On a single tile of this kind, I found a
long Greek inscription, giving an account of the family
of the deceased and his quality. Among the greatest
varieties of this class are two beautiful amphoræ, i.e.,
" lachrymatories", of a pale and delicate green colour,
and four inches long, both of which were fitted with
funnel-shaped neck linings of pure gold, which are now
detached from the glass. They are probably used to
strengthen the glass. In the New York Collection of
Cypriote Antiquities is a similar object, attached to an
alabastron-shaped vase of crystal. The greatest variety
of the kind before us is a small lachrymatory (fig. 158)
of very dark colour, and richly painted with flowers and
birds in a spirited and entirely realistic manner, and of
the most unusual style. It may be of Greek origin. The
figure is the full size of the relic.

There is a figure of a peacock in the centre of the
bottle (fig. 158 A), perched upon flowering foliage,
elegantly depicted, and on the other side (fig. 158 c)
a flock of singing birds appear to be disporting among
the flowering branches, which the artist who decorated
this beautiful, indeed unique, vase, has represented in
a charmingly natural manner. The lining of the stopper
(fig. 158 B) is worthy of attention on account of the
comparative rarity of such adjuncts to ancient bottles.

Equally interesting is a circular lid of hand-painted
glass (fig. 159), on which is a figure of Venus, undraped,

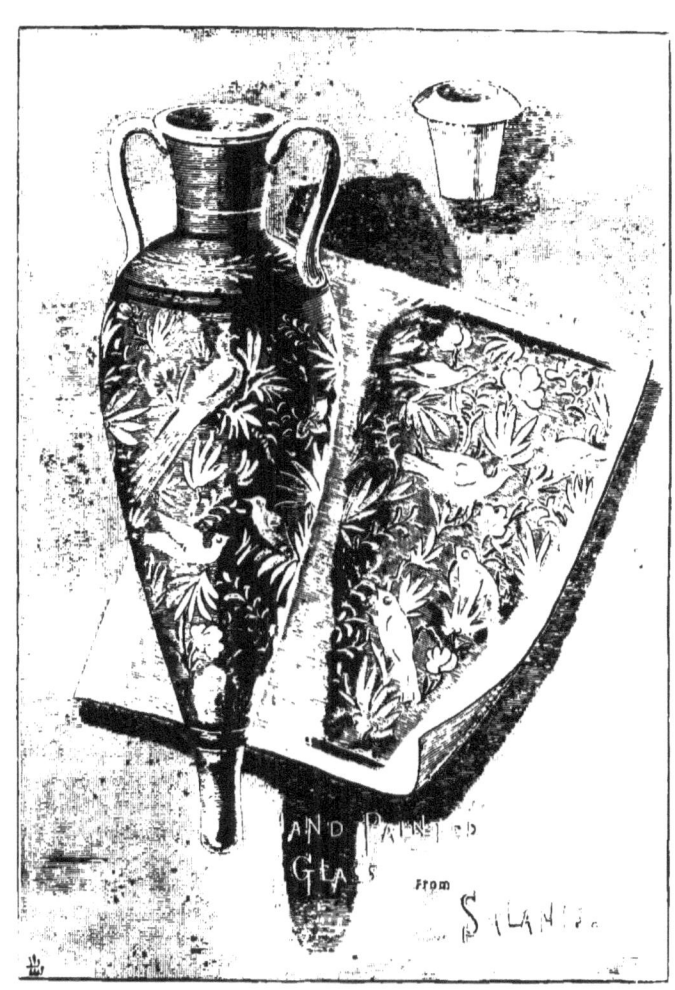

HAND-PAINTED PHŒNICIAN GLASS VASE.

with an ample robe, arranged in elegant folds, falling
down behind and at her side. The flowers and foliage in
this case also are mostly freely treated, and it is evident
that both the vase and the plate of glass are works
of artists of the first class. The high standard to which
the decorative arts of Cyprus attained during the early
Greek period is shewn in these two relics in a very clear
and forcible manner. We may indeed picture to ourselves without difficulty the great variety of subjects and

Fig. 159.   Painted Lid—Venus.   Glass.

styles which the ancient Cypriotes adorned, when examples so beautiful as those at present before us, although
they are but few in comparison to the hundreds which
must have paid the penalty of their fragility, have survived to point to the refined civilisation of five-and-
twenty buried centuries.

Among other forms and uses to which glass appears to

have been applied in ancient times in the island of Cyprus are finger-rings[1] of exactly the shape which occurs in ivory. One or two instances of this category exhibit hollows, in which engraved gems of glass or other material have been inserted and attached by cement. One of these rings bears an inscription in a Cypriote character. These rings were used for the same purpose as

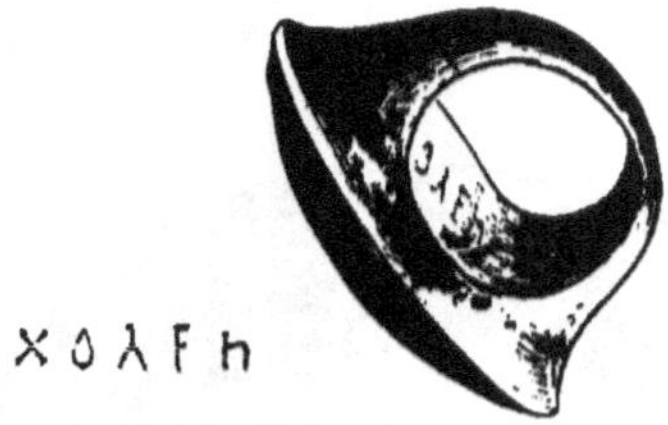

Fig. 160. Ring with Inscription. *Glass.*

those in ivory. Hairpins of glass (fig. 161), furnished with disks at one extremity of each and a ring-handle at the other end of each example, occur with frequency. They show the spiral lines of coloured glass, which we associate, perhaps too strictly, with Phœnician workmanship.

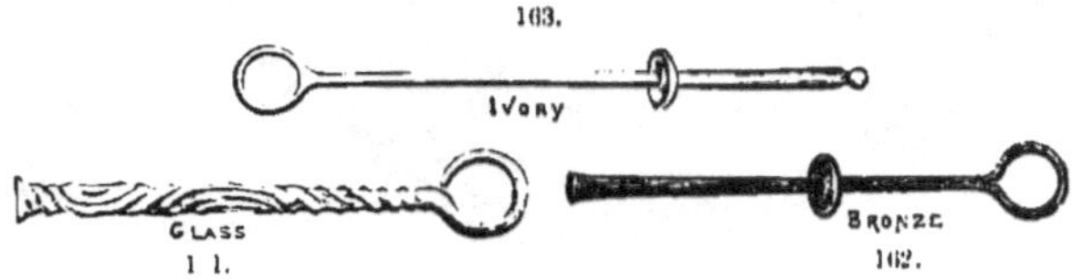

Figs. 161-163. Hairpins.

ship. They may be compared with the shapes of bronze (fig. 162), and ivory (fig. 163) hairpins which I have placed here in juxta-position to them.

Some of the vases and small bottles having dark violet, or blue, bodies are enriched with fine lines of white opaque glass wound spirally about them in a very elegant

[1] See fig. 76, p. 80.

manner, and ending in heads of serpents of the same material. Others of the bottles of smaller sizes are moulded like the fruit of the date tree, and their colour is of dark maroon, as if to indicate the natural colour of the fruit.

A numerous and very interesting group of these relics consists of small amphoræ of dark bodies enriched with pale orange and other coloured chevrons, and rings of semi-opaque glass.

There can be no doubt, says Dr. Birch, that the Phœnicians exercised, if they did not discover, the art of glass-making at a very early period. According to the legends, Phœnician traders, on their return from Egypt to their Syrian homes with a cargo of natron or soda, while cooking on the sand under the shadow of Mount Carmel, accidentally produced glass, and thus

Fig. 164.　　　Phœnician Unguentarium.　　　Glass.

discovered the art. The district of Tyre, and, at a later period, that of Sidon, subsequently become central sites of glass manufacture, and, indeed, specimens of Phœnician glass, both transparent and opaque, have been discovered on those ancient sites. This material became a staple product of their commerce, and small glass vases, of which fig. 164 in this collection is a good example,

resembling Egyptian types, of a pale or dark blue, or
white colours with undulating or zigzag lines white,
yellow, or light blue, which do not pass entirely through
the substance, moulded in sand matrices, were exported
by the makers to Asia Minor, Cyprus, Greece, the Isles
of the Ægean and Adriatic Seas, and even to Etruria, the
Mediterranean shores, and, in fact, wherever these enter-
prising traders penetrated in the ancient world. They
were highly valued, sometimes mounted on gold stands.
Their use appears to date from the fourth century B.C. to
the commencement of our era. The above figure represents in half-size a bottle of dark blue ground with
yellow *dancettée* bands and lines. I found these, and
many similar vases, always in tombs containing alabaster
vases of closely-allied forms, but never in connection with
terra-cottas, coins, or other glass vessels. The same re-

mark applies to these primitive glass vessels,
which Dr. Birch[1] has stated with respect to the
archaic *fictilia*, that many of the vases found in
Cyprus are probably Phœnician, but the early
population of that island was so mixed in its
Semitic and Hellenic elements that it is difficult to determine, in the absence of inscriptions,
to which race they belong.

Another form of *alabastron*, also of Phœnician manufacture, is that shewn in fig. 165.
For the loan of the woodcut representing it,
I am indebted to the kindness of the Council
of the British Archæological Association. It
is a long and thin body, without any neck
or lip, the base rounded off in form of a
bluntly-pointed oval, the shaft tapering gradu-

Alabastron.
Fig. 165.
Glass.

ally to the mouth. The colours of this beautiful vase are beyond description. Pink, opal,
blue, and pearly colours flash from it when turned round

[1] *History of Ancient Pottery*, new edit., p. 110.

slowly before the eyes, and beneath the iridescent granular surface, deeper and darker shades of colour appear to lie. The capacity of these vessels is not very great, but they could no doubt contain an appreciable quantity of perfume or precious unguent.

Fig. 166 represents one of those beautiful amphoræ of the style called Phœnician. It is of elegant form and proportion. The handles are very delicately made. Al-

Fig. 166.   Amphora.   Glass.

though in form of a wine jar, there can be no doubt that this little vessel was intended for the safe keeping of balsams, or costly unguents for the toilet.

Another small amphora (fig. 167) of proportions not quite so delicate as the preceding example, has a broad band of light colour round the neck in an oblique direction. The handles are broader and flatter in this specimen, for the woodcut of which I am indebted to the kindness of the British Archæological Association, before whom the vase, with several others, was exhibited by me lately. The contrast of the colours—deep blues and

A A

pale yellows—is very beautifully arranged in this elegant
relic.

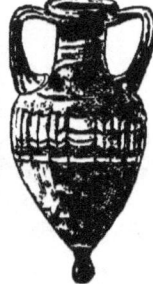

Fig. 167.   Amphora.   Glass.

Of the same style and manufacture, but of somewhat
different form, are the two-handled vases, of which a
specimen (fig. 168) is here given. Resembling the amphora as to its body and neck, the foot is enriched with
a small thick round base, hardly sufficient to enable the

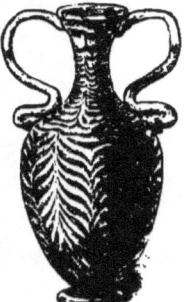

Fig. 168.   Two-handled Vase.   Glass.

vase to stand upright securely, and the handles are more
elaborately designed. The colours of these vessels are
exceedingly beautiful, but they are blended so intricately,
that it is difficult to describe them.

Another form not uncommonly affected by Phœnician
manufacturers of unguent vases is that known as the

diota, or vessel furnished with two handles, in form of
the human ear. These little vessels, like the amphoræ
already described and figured, derive their form from the
large ceramic jars destined to contain wine, but, from

Fig. 169.   Phœnician Diota.   Glass.

their small size and very moderate capacity, can only
have been employed to store liquid perfumes of great
price, and cosmetic preparations for the bath or the toilet.
Fig. 169 represents a diota of this sort, with dark opaque
body-colour traversed spirally by bands of creamy yellow,

Fig. 170.   Phœnician Diota.   Glass.

the body well proportioned, the neck short, and the foot
and lipped mouth small in proportion to the bulk of the
body. For this illustration and the following three I am
indebted to the British Archæological Association.

A closely allied form of diota, but of very different proportions to the foregoing example, is shewn in fig. 170, where the relative size of the body is reduced, and the neck, lip, ears, and foot are enlarged. In this instance, the light-coloured portions seem to develop more symmetry in their application, and partake of a more defined pattern, evidently an advance upon the simple undulations of the examples already described.

Fig. 171.   Hydria.   Glass.

The elegant form of the Greek hydria, or water vessel, no doubt recommended itself to the Phœnician makers of *unguentaria*, for we find the form seen in fig. 171 extensively used by them for these objects. In the example

Fig. 172.   Hydria.   Glass.

sively used by them for these objects. In the example before us, the method of laying on the light-coloured pattern is clearly shewn. Beginning at the lowest part of the body, the operator appears to have laid on a liquid

or viscid slip from a receptacle with an orifice, or, perhaps, a fine rod of glass. Taking a rapid spiral turn, he
reached the wide part of the body, and there commenced
a zigzag, which at the first was irregular, but gradually
attained accuracy of measure. On reaching the upper
limit of the body, the zigzag melts away into a few
circular lines, and a rapid spiral brought the embellish-
ment to a close near the lip. Perhaps the coloured surfaces were rolled afterwards while still hot, so as to
impress the pattern into the dark body-ground of the
glass. Fig. 172 is another hydria, not so upright in its
contour, but equally remarkable as a work of art, and
equally representative of the Phœnician art-manufacture.

One of the most curious discoveries which I made in the
tombs of Salaminia was that of an egg-cup of Phœnician

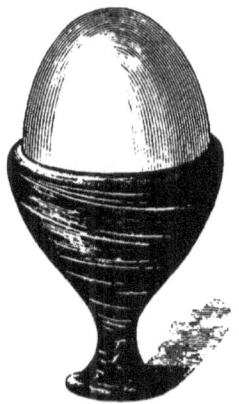

Fig. 173.   Egg-cup with an Egg in it.   Glass.

glass of dark blue ground, with pale, whitish-yellow
bands (fig. 173), containing still within its bowl the
shell of an egg placed with the cup as a votive offering
to the departed friend of the giver, in the grave.[1]   In

[1] A *cothon*, or small two-handled cup of black ware, has recently been
found at Cameiros in Rhodes, containing the remains of a sepulchral offering of five eggs and two knuckle-bones. It is now in the British Museum.

shape, this ancient relic of more than two thousand
years' antiquity differs but little, if at all, from a modern
egg-cup, but the manufacture is totally different, as
this has been made hollow, in ovoid form, and then
pressed inwards, so as to form two hollow cups one
within the other. This method of blowing glass vases
has of late years been resuscitated, and the application of
quicksilver to the inner surfaces produces in some of
these modern glass vases a peculiar and fictitious effect.

The Phœnician vase, or bottle, which forms the subject
of the accompanying illustration (fig. 174), half-size of

Fig. 174.   Painted Phœnician Vase.   Glass.

the original, is painted by hand, to imitate marbling, with
black, white, blue, and yellow pigment upon the natural
translucent glass which constitutes the substance of the
relic. This specimen, and, indeed, all the others of the
Lawrence-Cesnola collection, which antiquaries have
agreed—in my opinion, somewhat arbitrarily—to call
Phœnician, were found associated in tombs of Salamina,
and other ancient Cypriote cemeteries, with ancient
Greek coins and statuary, or terra-cotta, which I consider to belong to an archaic Greek period.

With regard to the causes of that superbly brilliant
iridescence and gorgeous colouring which have supplied

some of the greatest attractions to the Greek and Roman classes of glass antiquities, I may state the results of my experience and very careful investigations of the subject. Very many examples yet remain, which are as clear and unchanged as they were left by the ancient workman. They have undergone no alteration except a considerable loss of weight. No traces of iridescence appear on their surfaces, and yet their antiquity cannot be questioned; for I found some of them in situations where they were not in contact with earth, that is, standing on stones, or in amphoræ, and thus entirely protected from the effects of the air. Some of these relics, on being touched, fell to small pieces, that is, they thus returned to their elements. Other articles have been in contact with the earth over parts only of their surfaces. Wherever this has been the case, iridescence occurs on those portions which have been subject to the influence of the earth. Many more relics are entirely iridescent, and exhibit flashings of the most lovely colours. These have been in close contact with earth, and experienced its effects. It is to be added that the character of the decomposition in question varies according to the nature of the earth which surrounded the relics. Diggers who were experienced in seeking them were able to decide in what kind of earth any given relic has been discovered. Some of these examples have been subject to diverse influences, e.g., the inside of a vase has contained a liquid, or other substance, which produced one kind of iridescence, and the surface of that part of the example is granulous, while the outside of the same has been affected by other causes, or affected by the earth itself, which has produced another kind of iridescence, and the substance of this glass has become flaky. I have reason to believe that these facts have not been recorded until now. They are at once curious and instructive.

Of the numberless varieties of iridescent glass bottles

and vases, I have selected a few for illustrating this part
of my work. The accompanying woodcut (fig. 175)
shews an elegant shape of the Greek period, fifteen
inches in height, richly coloured now by the effects

Fig. 175.   Iridescent Bottle or Vase.   *Glass.*

of time, which has enhanced its beauty with an iridescent lustre of opalesque and golden flashes of light
and colour. The depressions are made round the body
in two rows, probably for ornament, rather than for
rendering the grip of the vessel in the hand more secure.

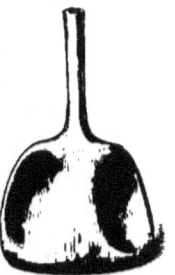

Fig. 176.   Iridescent Bottle.   *Glass.*

Another (fig. 176), of equal height to that which has
been already mentioned, comes also from Salamis, and in
form may be considered somewhat rare. The depressions

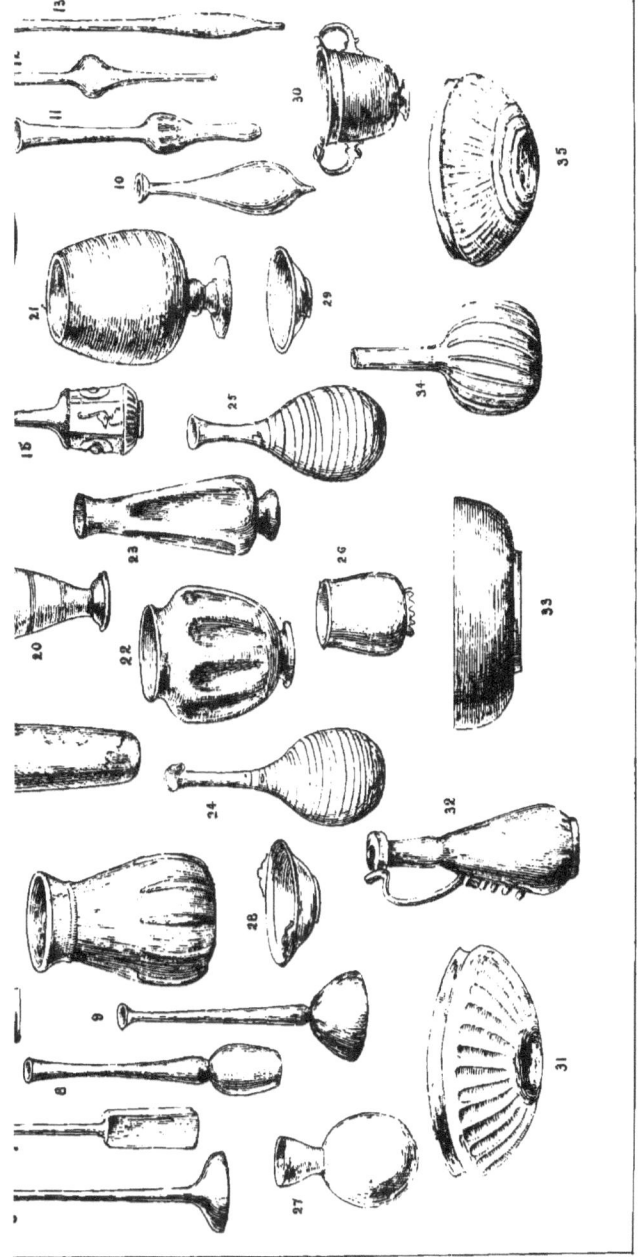

in this example are in size larger, and smaller in number. The depth to which they are pressed into the body reduces the capacity of the vessel very much.

Closely resembling these bottles, and of the same date, is a flat bowl (fig. 177),with a circular lip, widening out-

Fig. 177.   Bowl.   *Glass.*

wards all round, and having four well-marked depressions on the side.

There are twelve small and very heavy archaic *unguentaria* of bluish-green colour, with a small orifice, all of which come from Phœnician tombs. Vessels of the kind shewn in the annexed illustrations (figs. 178, 179) are also of considerable rarity. The tall cup is eighteen

Fig. 178, 179.   Vases ornamented with Studs or Teardrops.   *Glass.*

inches high, and has a small foot and banded lip or mouth The bowl is five inches high, and nine inches in diameter. Both these, as well as others in the collection, are studded with little tears or drops of glass, and produce a *bizarre* effect. The iridescence upon them is of a magnificent nature. These also come from Salaminian tombs.

B B

The elegant drinking vessel which forms the subject of the accompanying woodcut (fig. 180), from a friend's collection, I introduce here for comparison with the moulded glass in the Lawrence-Cesnola collection. But it so closely resembles the form and style of glass vessels

Fig. 180.   Inscribed Drinking Cup.   *Glass.*

found in the island of Cyprus, that it may well have been found in the island. On this is moulded, or impressed in relief, the Greek inscription in capital letters :—

KAI ETΦPAINOT.

The entire legend on a few other specimens of the same kind of drinking cup, found in Cyprus, is κατάχαιρε καὶ εὐφραίνου, signifying, " Rejoice, and be merry". There is a very similar glass in the British Museum.

Fig. 181 represents a drinking vessel (of which the British Museum also possesses an example), moulded with

Fig. 181.   Drinking Vessel with Moulded Inscription.   *Glass.*

an ornament, consisting of palm branches and chaplets for a victor's brow, appropriately enriched with a Greek inscription on a band in the centre of its height, which seems to point to the fact that the cup itself was a prize or a gift to one who had conquered in a public game or competitive contest. The inscription reads, in elegant Greek capital letters :—

ΛΑΒΕ ΤΗΝ ΝΕΙΚΗΝ.

I.e., "Take the Victory".

Among other specimens of this moulded glass, I have found a deep cup, or drinking vessel (fig. 182), on which are embossed or moulded in relief the heads of Gorgons and the *pelta*, or shield used by and attributed to the Amazons, combined with floral and other ornaments.

Fig. 182.   Moulded Drinking Vessel.   *Glass.*

This vessel is of the late Greek or Roman period. It is covered with a finely iridescent colour, which varies from gold and opal to blue and purple tints as the light is allowed to fall upon it.

One of the most interesting of the smaller objects of

Fig. 183.   Head of a Goddess.   *Glass.*
A. Front view. B. Side view.

glass is that represented by fig. 183 (A, B), a flat piece of glass moulded with the full face of a goddess upon both sides. The expression, which is evidently the work of a good artist, appears to be that usually found upon portraits of Venus; and from the universal cultus of the Goddess of Love in the Island of Cyprus, it may be justly conjectured to be a representation of that divinity.

A small object in blue moulded glass represents a seated female figure, with a high head-dress and ample robe

Fig. 184.   Moulded Figure.   *Glass.*

(fig. 184). It is difficult to decide to what divinity this talisman or toy is to be attributed.

In addition to the vases and other objects of glass which I have already mentioned, I found a considerable number of coloured pendants for bracelets and necklaces,

185.   186.   187.   188.

Figs. 185-188.   Pendants in form of Human Heads.   *Glass.*

composed of quaintly curious heads of men (fig. 185), some of very archaic proportions (fig. 186), and others, perhaps,

189.   190.   191.

Figs. 187-189.   Pendants of Animal Forms.   *Glass.*

intended to represent tragic and comic masks (figs. 187, 188). One of these pendants is in form of a bull's head (fig. 189) of very fine workmanship and excellent proportion; another (fig. 190) is in form of a crescent, composed of two teeth or tusks of a wild animal, a favourite design for a necklace, as I have already pointed out in the description of the gold objects,[1] and in the notice of the

192.   193.   194.

Figs. 192-194.   Vase-shaped Pendants.   *Glass.*

stone iconic bust of a lady of rank.[2] The head of a pig, or boar, forms the subject of another of these objects (fig. 191), and there are others in form of jugs (fig. 192) and vases (fig. 193). They are all of an early date, beautifully iridescent from their contact with terraqueous substances in their places of deposit.

A circular pendant of a similar nature (fig. 194) is inscribed with the Greek letters ΤΕΙΟ or ΤΕΙΟΤ.

[1] Page 26.   [2] Page 108.

CHAPTER XVII.

TERRA-COTTA.

THE ancient terra-cotta remains which I obtained from Salamis, and other Cypriote sites, are exceedingly numerous. They may be divided into several classes for the sake of description and illustration. I begin with the

I.—STATUES AND STATUETTES.

The greater number of these objects were discovered in tombs, and they consist of effigies of the gods and goddesses ; portraits or iconic figures, which are gracefully draped in toga and tunic ; effigies, about one hundred in all, of females, some of whom carry instruments of music, including lyres and a flute. One of this class bears a tambourine in one hand and a dove in the other.

Terra-cotta figures conceived in the Assyrian style are naturally not so frequently found as those in the Greek or native Cypriote styles ; but there is in the collection the upper part of a figure of a man in the Assyrian style, wearing a conical head-dress, or helmet, with

TERRA-COTTA STATUETTE OF VENUS

tasselled ear-flaps, a reeded gorget round the throat, and a fringed cape of peculiar shape.

Fig. 195.   Male Figure of Assyrian Style.   *Terra-cotta.*

Another specimen of this Assyrian or Egyptian style is the upper part of a female, with closely-curled hair

Fig. 196.   Female of Assyrian Style.   *Terra-cotta.*

hanging down in a stiff and formal manner on either side of the neck (fig. 195). The two necklaces with which the figure is ornamented have been already alluded to in an earlier chapter.[1]

Fig. 196 represents a terra-cotta statuette of the

[1] See p. 23, fig. 14.

Youthful Hercules, standing upon a narrow plinth, and holding in the right hand a club, his usual and well-known attribute ; in the left hand, the wonder-working

cornucopia of Amalthea. Over the right shoulder of this figure, a belt or fillet passes, holding up at the back of the hero the lion skin with which he is usually depicted.

The annexed illustration represents (fig. 197) a figure, in the Phœnician style, with Assyrian influence, apparently of Hera (Juno), or Demeter (Ceres), draped in a *chiton poderes*, or tunic, to the feet ; the hands, with bracelets, at the side, and collar round the neck. A long shawl, or *peplos*, forming a kind of *kalyptron*, passes over the head like that over the figures of Hera or Juno, and Demeter, indicating a married goddess, possibly Aphrodité. The inscription at the back (fig.

199) is obscure ; possibly, Dr. Birch tells me, Cypriote ;
with vertical lines introduced at intervals. The second

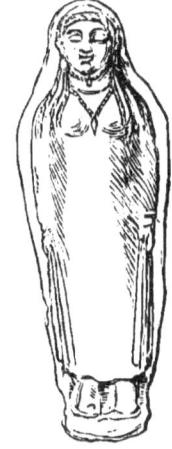

Fig. 198.   Inscribed Figure.   *Terra-cotta.*

Fig. 199.   Inscription at back of Fig. 198.

and seventh characters are not in the usual Cypriote
alphabet. It may read :—

Ta . xe . lo . le . li . po . e .mo.

Ταξίλλη ἐποίησέ με ;

but the reading of this archaic inscription is very uncertain.

C C

A very pretty example represents a lady seated and suckling her infant; a second stands with the child in her arms; another stands, half draped, in the manner of the Venus of Milo, and in an attitude not unlike that of this famous statue.   One of the statuettes

Fig. 200.   Statuette.   Terra-cotta.

of this class is of a very elegant design (fig. 200). It represents a female with the flowing drapery of the best Greek period, falling down over the back and lower parts of the statuette, the body reclining in a graceful curve against a small term or altar, with a carved capital and moulded base. The arms are wanting, but, notwithstanding this defect, the great beauty of the object is readily apparent to the most superficial examination.   I owe the use of this block to the kindness of the British Archaeological Association.

A similar work resembles the " Pudicitia". A female female figure stands erect, with large wings displayed and rising above her head, and holding in her right hand a fir-cone, which is the frequent emblem of Venus, and in the left hand objects like apples, which cannot now be recognised. An ancient figure of a charming young girl is in the attitude of a Muse playing on a large lyre, which is placed at her side. Her elegantly-disposed draperies bear traces of colour, the toga is still of a pale pink, the tunic is of a redder hue, the sandals are scarlet. It probably represents the Muse Erato, or Polyhymnia (fig. 201). The head of this figure is adorned with a

Fig. 201.   The Muse Erato or Polyhymnia.   *Terra-cotta.*

coronal of flower-shaped ornaments, and a cap-like head-gear surmounted the coronet. A tall and graceful sta-tuette of this class which shows a peculiar style of sculpture, being of a somewhat finer, if not more laboured, order of treatment, seems to be in the act of walking

towards the temple, because she holds on her left shoulder
a large tray, bearing an offering of a cake, and, in her
right hand, carries a small hare, or rabbit. The drapery
of this figure is extremely beautiful, and has been studied
by a very accomplished artist. Two seated statuettes of
draped women occur. At the side of each is the figure
of a winged youth, very closely resembling that which is
described above. It is probable that these figures, although those of the females are fully draped, represent
Venus and her son. In the lap of one of the seated
figures are what look like flowers. A statuette of a
draped female wears a helmet, or cap, with a high crest,
like a Phrygian cap. At the side of two women figures,
each of which holds a bowl, is a pig. The animal looks
up, as if it expected to be fed. Both these females have
their hair flowing over their shoulders in long tresses,
and trained in large coronets above their heads. The
one looks slightly downwards, the other has raised her
face, and gazes forwards.

In another statuette, the hair of a lovely and slender
young female is covered with a conical hat. An erect
and nearly naked female figure, probably that of Venus,
shows strong traces of deep blue on the drapery, a
ruddy tint on her flesh. The robe which lies over
her shoulder falls behind, and, returning to the front,
is thrust between the legs, from whence it issues in
full folds. One of her arms is placed akimbo on her
left hip, the other hand is on an altar at her side, the
left leg is crossed before its fellow. There is a pretty
figure of a tall woman draped in a tunic, and walking
with a vase upon her head. A garland which is under it
is distinctly pink. A lady, the contour of whose figure
is very robust, stands erect, her drapery being closely
held about her form. She is wearing above her hair
a large garland, which is coloured of a deep reddish
tint. The face and general style of this statuette are

TERRA-COTTA ROUND STATUETTE OF A DRAPED FEMALE.

of peculiarly lovely Greek type, and of a noble and pure
kind of art. Another charming statuette stands fully
draped, the toga being held at each shoulder by a fibula
at the side of a tall pedestal, on which her left hand
is placed. As this hand is, unfortunately, broken, we
cannot say if it originally held anything, or if it is only
drapery which seems to fall from over the wrist. On
her head is a lofty lunette-shaped coronet. A larger
figure is standing fully draped, the ample toga being
thrown over the head so as to form a veil. Her mature
form suggests that she is a widow; or this may be the
winter costume of a noble Cypriote lady. This example
seems to have been painted pure white over the flesh, as
well as the garments. There are two other similarly
clad figures, one of which is enveloped over the head and
its lofty coronet, while her hands are covered by the
toga; the other, the matronly proportions of which have
perfect dignity, while the attitude has the freest and
most graceful movement, is bareheaded. Over the forehead rises a tall coronet. The face of this work has been
finished with unusual care, and possesses great sweetness
of expression, with suavity and beauty of features.

Among these effigies of draped females, none is more
interesting than that of the young woman who stands
almost entirely wrapped in her toga, having drawn part
of its edge over her mouth and nostrils, as if to keep out
cold air. There is an almost exactly similar figure of a
girl, who has thus, but not quite so closely, wrapped her-
self up. Another figure wears a toga folded about her
head, and falling closely over both her loins. The iconic
statuette of a lady (fig. 202), whose toga is gracefully disposed in a loop under her right arm, while part of that
garment is wrapped about her left arm, wears a kerchief
on her head, in which she has bound the masses of her
hair. The costume is finely treated.[1]

[1] This illustration also is kindly lent to me by the British Archæological Association.

Besides the above-mentioned figures of ladies, there are two statuettes of women bearing offerings. Each of them carries a dove held before her body in a highly characteristic fashion. These are probably peasant women, who are bearing offerings to the Temple of Venus. The female who carries the bird, whose tail is spread out, has

Fig. 202.   Iconic Statuette.   *Terra-cotta.*

hair coloured of a deep red. A statuette of a portly matron seems to convey a touch of satire such as is of no uncommon occurrence in these works. She sits and holds a partly unrolled scroll on her knees, and, altogether, as if she were one of those "thirsty plants imbibing", whom the Laureate satirised in his account of the pupils of the "Princess".

Two associated examples, seated side by side, are, unfortunately, broken; but enough exists to shew that one has extended on her knees a half-unrolled scroll, coloured blue, from which, as her action unmistakably declares, she is in the act of singing. In one hand, she holds a spherical object, probably a ball. The companion member of this group is broken. It is believed to have originally carried a musical instrument. A tall damsel bears offerings of grapes in one hand, and fruit of different kinds, or flowers, in a dish in the other. The

Fig. 203.   The Goddess of Rain.   *Terra-cotta.*

collection contains also the representation in terra-cotta of a young woman advancing against the wind, as the positions of her legs and hands and the disposition of her draperies suggest. A torch is in her left hand, the flame of which is drawn backwards. On the head is a wreath; the hair is tied in a long knot. This is probably a Bacchante, or a Maenad, under the influence of Bacchanalian inspiration.

A demi-figure, the lower half of which is lost, carries
an infant rolled in her voluminous toga, exactly in the
same manner as that of innumerable groups of the
" Virgin and Child". A tall female figure stands by a
lofty pedestal, or column, and, holding upwards her
coronetted head, rests her right arm on it, while her
drapery drops freely from her fingers. A naked female
reclines against a rock with a vase on her shoulder, and
is the nymph of a spring ; water pours from a lion's head
at her side. The inscription, in Greek capital letters on
the base, " ΘΕΑ ΙΙ ΟΜΒΡΙΟΣ", attests that this is the
Goddess or Nymph of Rain (fig. 203). Green colour is
still distinctly shewn upon the pouring water. In another
example, a woman carries on her shoulder a draped child,

Fig. 204.   Inscribed Statuette.   *Terra-cotta.*

who sits at ease in the most natural manner. A fully-
draped lady (fig. 204), whose tunic is drawn over her
her head, stands erect, and carries a draped infant upon
her left shoulder. On the front of the stand, or plinth,

TERRA-COTTA ICONIC STATUETTE OF A YOUNG GIRL.

at the foot of this statuette, perhaps Demeter Kourotrophos, which I obtained from excavations at Dali, is the Cypriote inscription :—

. se . o . ve . le . ke . mo . ti .

which may be read—*Τιμοκλέους*, perhaps a Cypriote name in the genitive case, to be referred to Timocles, who was in all probability the artist who made the statuette.

The standing figure of another lady (fig. 205), whose hand is wrapped in her toga, and on whose head is a coronet, retains a complete coat of brilliant white. The plinth, or base, also bears upon it an impressed inscrip-

Fig. 205. Inscribed Statuette. *Terra-cotta.*

tion in Cypriote characters, which appears to have been scribbled over with black lines, as if it had been intended to cancel the inscription. The Cypriote inscription is as follows :—

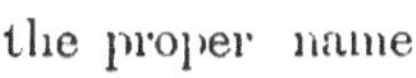

. va . bi . na . li . zo .

This is probably the proper name of the female personage, as Zolinabia or Zenobia, who is represented by the object, or the name of the artist to whose conception the statuette owes its origin.

The accompanying illustration (fig. 206) shews an interesting statuette of a female, at full length, which may be ascribed to Aphrodite, the Goddess, who, as I have shewn before, was so universally and so pre-eminently a subject of the Cypriote cult. This figure is in the Phœnician or Assyrian style, resembling the goddess Ishtar.

Fig. 206.					Statuette.					*Terra-cotta.*

The hands appear to be holding the breasts, and the hair is plaited and bound with a fillet. On the neck, several necklaces are represented with pendants, one of which is apparently in the form of a man. A kind of fringed stole hangs below the upper garment in front of the knees.

The seated statuette of a lady, in the act of drawing the toga over her right shoulder, while her chiton is held there by a fibula. In her left hand, which lies

VENUS ANADYOMENE.

in her lap, is a round object like an apple or egg. On
her head is a coronet of leaves. Another female bears in
her left hand a swan, which thrusts up its bill as if to
caress her. Is this Leda? Another statuette, which
may well be referred to that mythical heroine, carries a
swan under her left arm, and seems to be drawing over
her naked figure a voluminous piece of drapery. Her
action is that of rising from the earth. A lovely statuette is that of a lady, who sits in a chair, having
her toga folded closely about her form, and nearly en-
shrouding it. She wears also an under-tunic. One of
her legs is crossed over the other, in the manner ascribed
to Juno Lucina. She rests the chin on one hand, while
the elbow of that side is sustained by her raised knee.
One foot is supported by a stool. This is the attitude of
a woman lost in thought : in this respect, the expression
of the face agrees. In the same technical style as the
last is the erect lady, whose hair is arranged in crisped
masses under a wreath. A third figure seems to be that
of a robust woman, having voluminously crisped hair, the
bulk of which is turned over her head to form a coronet
of plaits. This mode of wearing the hair is frequently
seen in Greek and Roman busts, as, for example, in
those of the Empress Crispina. There is also a statuette
of a woman seated in a chair, with a bird in her lap.

Contrasted with these is the grim, seated statuette of
an aged woman, whose much-mutilated form irresistibly
suggests that she was a leper. Her nose has been con-
sumed, both her arms have disappeared, her figure is
swollen and distorted, her gaunt face is seamed and
withered. She sits on a stool—a woeful figure of misery.
A still more hideous representation of an old woman grinning, without teeth, and with a tumid body, is in the
collection. Seated in a chair with a very high back is a
woman, who seems to be feeding a duck, or dove, in her
lap. On the hem of the tunic of a standing figure of

a lady, above her bust, is a clearly-marked double Greek key-fret interchanged, and coloured scarlet and deep red. Red occurs on the toga worn by this figure, as if that garment had been wholly of that colour; the tunic was quite white; a red ribbon, or carcanet, is to be traced on the neck.

A terra-cotta group comprises a naked Venus standing erect, in the attitude of arranging her ample tresses under a lunette coronet, and as if just risen from the sea. Behind the figure are sportive dolphins, on the shoulder of one of which is perched a Cupid playing on a shell lyre. On the other side is a second Cupid, holding an instrument like a double clapper (or shell box, as figured at page 79), the halves of which are attached to each other by a hinge. It is said that a rude instrument of this nature, which is used to produce a loud clapping noise, was in use in Cyprus not more than forty years ago, at the time of celebrating the death and resurrection of our Lord according to the rites of the Roman Church. It may be it is a mirror the boy holds before his mother. The tail of one of the dolphins has been placed so as to conceal the person of the goddess. Another statue of Venus appears riding on a goose, and wearing long thin drapery, so disposed that it falls from her head, and is held open before her to display her naked figure; it returns from her hands, and is folded over her lower limbs. About the feet of the bird, herbage or grass is represented. There is a third Venus, with wings, riding astride of a dolphin, which traverses the waves of the sea.

A very quaint and grotesque little figure of a Bacchante concludes my account of the female statuettes in terra-cotta in this collection. She is fat and old, much withered, and clothed in rags; her action is that of drinking from a small vase, while another such vase is suspended from her girdle, which likewise sustains a patera, or plate, on

TERRA-COTTA STATUETTE OF VENUS RIDING ON A GOOSE.

the back of which is a star-like figure, with traces of yellow pigment. She bears upright in her left hand a large vase, with two handles rising upright from its rim ; a large garland on her head, with large flowers on its outer margin. Her face has the expression of vociferous singing and tipsy jollity.

Fig. 207 represents a terra-cotta statuette of an actor, dressed in hairy skin, in the *rôle* of Silenus, or Hercules,

Fig. 207.   Statuette of an Actor.   *Terra-cotta.*

holding a banded club in the right hand, and a basket of fruit in the left ; it is referred to more fully at page 216.

The statuettes of children include several of Eros and some of nameless genii. Of the latter class, I may notice a boy genius, with wings, fluttering over the earth, and dragging behind him a reluctant goat, while he bears on his head a heap of fruit. A similar genius[1] is to be seen running, with a large bunch of grapes in one hand, and thus tempting a cock to follow him (fig. 208). He holds in the other hand a vase. There are traces of red, white, and pink on this group. On the back is the name of the

[1] The woodcut is kindly lent by the British Archæological Association.

maker. A similar winged genius, a little older than the above, carries on one shoulder a large amphora, and on

Fig. 208. Genius and Cock. *Terra-cotta.*

the other a lighted torch. His forehead is shaded by what seems to be a large wreath of flowers. Another

Fig. 209. A Genius riding on a Cock. *Terra-cotta.*

boy, clad only in a small mantle, carries under his left arm a swan. There is a second example of this design, in which the figure holds the swan in a somewhat different manner. It is obvious that both these figures were modeled by the same artist. There is a third similar statuette of a boy, a charming little figure, closely wrapped in a mantle, which he holds at his chest with one hand, while it is held at his shoulder by a fibula. He stands upright, and, with a smiling face, looks downwards. On his head is a wreath, like that which is often represented in such works as these.

A figure belonging to this class represents a kind of youthful genius, draped, riding upon a cock, resembling the fantastic figures of the Serapeus (fig. 209). From the inscription of the plinth in front of the figure, in Greek capital letters,

ΤΗΙ ΚΛΕΟΠΑΤΡΑΙ ΒΑΣΙΛΙΣΣΑΙ,

" To Cleopatra, the Queen", it is clear that the object is

Fig. 210.   Eros riding on a Horse.   *Terra-cotta.*

votive in character, and dedicated to one of the queens of that name. The coin of a Cleopatra was found with it.

I may here describe the subject of the accompanying illustration (fig. 210). A winged boy, perhaps Eros or

Cupid, wearing a kind of skirt fastened by a band round the waist, is riding upon a horse, designed after the Greek manner, which is walking or pacing in graceful action to the right. The face of the rider is turned to the front, so as to be full face to the spectator. There is no inscription on the plinth at the base of the group.

Another boy stands naked, except for a short cloak, wears a bulla, and carries a bag. A little naked boy, of the chubbiest form, stands with his hands against his hips, exactly in "first position" of modern military drill. It is excellently modelled, and proves to be the work of a skilled hand of a good Greek period. A crouching figure of a lad seems to be writhing on the ground in pain, if he is not in the act of playing with balls. In each of his hands is a ball as big as a large apple. Whatever the attitude of this figure may have been designed to represent, there is no doubt that the action is full of spirit and character. Like many antiquities of this material, it has been covered with a coat of thick white colour.

There are, besides the above, several figures of little boys, some seated, and others who are squatting on the earth, one of which plays with a bird; a second has placed a hand on a tortoise. There are other examples of this action. A third seems to be a snake-charmer, as he sits bound about the body and arms by a large snake, which is biting his breast. There is the figure of a man seated on the earth, about whose body a large serpent is wreathing itself, while, with his left hand, the man grasps the creature's head, and presses it to the earth. A fourth crouching boy holds in one hand a large bird; it may be a goose or a swan; in the other hand is a ball; on his head is an ample hood, or cap, turning over at the top, and furnished with large lappels, which fall on his shoulders; it is, in fact, the famous Phrygian cap, like that with which Paris is represented. Round

his neck is a thong-like necklace, with a pendant which strongly resembles a cross. There is a chubby figure, which, like the last, is naked, except for the cap he wears. This garment is, however, unlike the last-named example. It is formed into a high cone, like an old-fashioned English nightcap. This peculiar cap pertained to the inferior orders of the people. There is a draped figure of a boy, standing erect in a tunic, and wearing on his neck a collar, like that just now mentioned. He is crowned with a wreath. In one hand, he carries what seems to be a small bag or sack, while, with the other hand, he caresses a little dog with long hair and a bushy tail, exactly such a creature as that which is called a Siberian dog. Another boy has fallen back on the ground, and is assailed by a playful dog of the same kind. This figure is draped. The figures of babes are squatted on frusta of columns, or cylindrical pedestals, the fronts of which are channeled with undulating flutings.

There is a very pretty figure of a boy of about ten years of age, whose costume comprises boots, with pendant lappels at each side, and laced up the front. He is wrapped in a large and long mantle, fastened at the shoulder by a fibula, and enclosing both his arms and hands. Jauntily placed on one side of his head is a flat woven cap, exactly like that which the Spaniards call a *birréta*, and by the red, blue, or white colour of which the wearer indicates his political leanings. Doubtless, this figure represents an urchin going to school. The same cap occurs with other statuettes. What is nearly as much like a girl as a boy, stands and holds a dove on one arm. There is a fully-draped figure of a winged boy-genius seated on the ground, with its wings fluttering at its shoulders, and with a duck against its knee. On the head is a flat cap, rising to the back and front of the head, exactly like a cap which English ladies wore not many years ago. A winged boy-genius stands naked.

E E

holding a shield, which bears illegible blazonry, and wearing on his head a crested helmet, shaped in the fashion appropriated to Pallas, and leaning on a staff, the head of which seems to terminate in that which closely resembles a fir-cone. A half-clad boy-genius, whose body is bare, stands in a graceful and animated attitude, with his wings expanding from his shoulders. He is crowned with a large garland. He is leaning against a pedestal, with one foot in advance of the other. The execution of this charming statuette is so light and free, that it reminds me of works of the early *renaissance* sculptors even more than of that Greek art, of which, nevertheless, it is an unchallengeably delicate illustration.

We next approach a group of six statuettes, found by me in a single ruined building at Salamis, four of which are, doubtless, the work of one artist, a suggestion confirmed by the likeness of each figure to its fellows, in treatment, handling, and even in the faces. This is, therefore, a peculiarly interesting class of relics. The most attractive is a very energetic group of two little boys at play. The actions of the hands suggest very strongly indeed that we have here a representation of the extremely ancient game of Mora, which was played by throwing out the thumb, or one or more fingers of one hand, in order that the player's antagonist might guess the number of digits thus thrown forth. This game is still in vogue. The figure on our right is remarkable on account of its cap, which is of the flat, felted kind, like that worn by statues of Mercury, being detached from and independent of the head. The second figure is that of a winged boy-genius, Somnus, or Hypnos, lying on his left side, with one arm and one wing under his head, his knees bent up, and evidently fast asleep. The third example is that of a boy, who stands in a finely-animated attitude, with one foot before the other, and laughing gaily. One of the arms is lost. The modelling of this

pretty thing is very like, and quite equal to, that of
a work by Fiammingo. The fourth statuette, which is
clad in a short chemise, seems to have been intended for
that of a hermaphrodite, the freely displayed members,
the proportion of the shoulders and the hips, the plump-
ness of the contours, and the character of the head, all
agree in supporting this notion of the nature of the
figure. It is noteworthy that this very curious relic
has been treated in an unusually realistic manner. The
remaining two figures, or, rather, demi-figures, of this
company are fragments, of which the lower limbs have
been lost. The larger one is that of a lad in the action
of a warrior, holding in one arm a shield, and in the
other a sword, or spear. The expression of his features
could not be more energetic than it is, and it is extremely
well worth noticing, that the high-crested helmet worn by
this warrior has evidently been added after the head has
been modelled. A portion of its vizor having been broken
away, reveals the hair within. A belt is placed at the
hips of this statuette. The last work of this class is the
demi-figure of a boy in a casque.

A group of two boys, playing, or quarrelling, occurs
next. One of these urchins holds down his right arm
against his chest, while in the left hand he grasps a disk-
like object. It may be a cake, or even a garland, which
is in dispute between them. It is certain that the other
boy is in the act of grasping the extended right arm of
his neighbour, and biting the wrist of that member with
a good deal of passion. On the pedestal, rude representations of flowers and herbage indicate that this contest occurs in the open fields. Another group comprises
an almost naked boy and girl squatting close to each
other in loving attitudes, with one arm of each figure
over the shoulders of the other. There is a group of
rare elegance which comes next on my list. Two chubby
infants sit side by side; the girl, who is represented with

great detail, "cuddles" her companion with feminine energy. A flower-holder, in the form of a foot, like those which occur occasionally in glass, has lost its upper portions, but preserves the representation of the shoe and sole attached to it. The bottom of the sole is curiously marked, indentations answering to the stitches, by means of which it was sewn to the body of the boot.[1] On the front of the foot, a chubby child is reclining, as if asleep, with his hands placed under his head and among his abundant tresses.

The erect naked youth, in the act of walking, wears a mantle, in the folds of which he has wreathed one arm. In one hand, he holds a short sword of the Greek form. There is a Cupid, sleeping at ease in the hollow of a large shell, which, as if it floated on the sea, is supported, or driven, by two dolphins. There is a standing boy, or Autolycus, in a scanty shirt, which does not completely cover his body, holding to his breast a large bunch of grapes. He seems to be laughing. On his head is a broad fillet with three pendants, one of which is shaped like a shield. The next pendant is more like an alabastrum on a very small scale; the third pendant is placed in the centre of the forehead, like the phylactery of a Jew, and, like that object, the lower part of this one is oblong, and seems to comprise a frame enclosing another article, probably an amulet. A small circular object rises, and is attached to this oblong one. These articles or amulets occur on one side only of the boy's head, his hair braided from back to front. At his side stands a large cock. The bird leaps up with one foot raised. On the pedestal of this work is a bas-relief of Cupid in a chariot drawn by two lions, and preceded by a winged genius.

A curious class of terra-cotta figures comprises those which appear in the act of riding. In one instance, a chubby girl is astride of a huge cock, and, being clad only

_____
[1] It is figured in the Chapter on Lamps.

in a mantle, seems quite at ease, while the bird carries
his burden well. At foot is in Greek characters the
name of Cleopatra.[1] A boy guides the cock, which carries him, by means of a bridle. A third figure of the
same class shews another boy mounted on a cock and
wearing a crown like a *nimbus*, with rays exactly like
those appropriated to Phœbus Apollo. The same *nimbus*
occurs in other cases in my collection of antiquities.
This cock is almost a grotesque, the head and beak being
unusually large. Another boy, wearing a close-fitting
military dress and round cap, is seen galloping on a pony,
with a high action of its forefeet. A boy, wearing a
mantle and Phrygian cap, sits his horse easily, and looks
aside, while the animal walks towards our right. A
winged genius is mounted on a horse, which is rapidly
trotting in the same direction. The horse's mane has
been "hogged" in the Greek manner. The expression of
his head in chafing of the curb is full of spirit; indeed,
could not be better than it is.[2] There is a statuette of a
little boy, who, lying on his back, between the shoulders
of a large goose, or swan, seems to be fast asleep.

Like the before-mentioned group of a boy, who plays
with a dog, and has fallen on the floor, is the other naked
boy, who is assailed by a cock half as big as himself. A
boy-genius, riding on a dolphin over the sea, has been
already mentioned.

A few groups, comprising boys in pairs and with girls,
may now be mentioned. These are a boy, clasping in his
arms, as if to draw it towards him, an hermaphrodite.
The double sex of the latter is unmistakeably expressed
by the bust, hair, and other details ; both these figures are
winged. Likewise winged are the statuettes in a group
which may represent Eros and Psyche embracing. They
stand side by side, she has the wings of a butterfly, both

[1] Compare fig. 209, page 206.
[2] Compare fig. 210, page 207.

wear large garlands, she only is draped, and her form is
thus partly covered.   There is a similar group of larger
figures, which are in the act of kissing; this female is
more covered than the former one.

There is a bust of an infant, formed of peculiarly white
terra-cotta, the face of which is laughing with a very
lively expression; on the forehead, on one side only, as
in the previously-mentioned instance of the statuette of
the boy with grapes and a cock, is a fillet sustaining
pendants of circular shapes, like the coins still worn in
the same manner by innumerable women in the East.
Round the neck a ribbon carries a round object like a
bulla.

Among the adult male figures, besides the animated
statuette of Hercules, is an Apollo seated on a rock, on
which he leans one hand, while the other hand, in a very
graceful way, is cast over the side of a lyre, which rests
on the rock at his side.   The closely-clad effigy of a
youth, with wings displayed from his shoulders, suggests
an older Eros.   The head is wrapped in drapery, and
bound with fillet in that which may be called the Phrygian mode; two long tresses escape from this hood, and
trail before the shoulders of this statuette, which wears
likewise a tunic fitted loosely to the torso, bound by a
girdle at the waist, and falling thence to the knee.
Loose trousers, like those the Romans considered the
dress of the barbarians, and which are many times represented on the Column of Trajan, as well as in more
ancient Greek examples, occur on the legs of this work,
which is in the attitude of standing, with one of the
feet crossed before its fellow, while each hand rests on
its proper hip, and the slightly advanced head bears a
cheerful smile of enquiry on its youthful features.   There
is a very elegant and well proportioned male figure
standing erect, as if about to walk forward, wrapped in
an ample, beautifully disposed toga, which, while it en-

closes the hands and arms (one of which is placed against
the breast, the other hanging at the side), is fastened on
the left shoulder by a fibula. There is another in an
attitude nearly identical with the above, the execution
of which is not nearly equal to that which gave a nameless grace to the fine Greek relic. Slung by a strap on
the shoulder, and lying against the back of this figure,
is what looks like a flat cap.

The remaining adult male figures are all more or less
ludicrous and homely; some of them are grotesque. A
very remarkable one shows an elderly man seated on a
rock, with, by way of clothing, only a girdle, the ends of
which descend before his figure, and a conical cap, which
is on his head. He holds, in his left hand, a large re-
ticulated bag, or net-pouch, completely filled, although
what it contains I cannot guess. In his right hand is, at
present, a rod of ivory, about the size of a bodkin, one
end of which appears in front, and is covered with gold,
as if it were intended for a sceptre, or staff of another
kind; the other end of this implement—whatever it may
be I have not been able to discover—protrudes behind
the statue, and proves to have been broken: no gold is
on this part. The face has a squalid, ugly, and degraded
character; the features are mean and wasted. These
circumstances, and the general aspect of the work, as
well as the bag at its side, induce me to think that this
is the statuette of a begging priest of antiquity, one of a
class analogous to the dervish of the Mohammedan world;
unless, indeed, it is a fisherman.

The next instance is that of a water-seller who is naked,
except in respect to a very short tunic, which extends
from the hips to the knees. He carries on one shoulder
a large amphora with two handles, the foot of which
he grasps with one hand, while its weight makes his
shoulders and his knees, brawny as they are, bend. The
back is further burdened by a cask intended to hold

a store of liquid, the spout, or leathern tap, of which comes to the front, and is grasped by the right hand of the bearer. A wine-presser, squatting on the ground in the manner of an Indian *fakir*, comes next; his knees are raised, and the downward extended hands are crossed before his person, and hold a rammer, or pestle, with which he crushes grapes; all the body to his legs is covered by a rough skin, probably that of a bear, from which the hands, the head, and the legs issue; the feet are in loose boots, or buskins. He sits in a large bowl, or pan, and seems, with the rammer, to be pressing grapes in it; the spout of the bowl is seen in front, between the feet of the figure. The bearded head is crowned with a wreath, and the face bears an absurd expression of sottish gravity, suggesting that the owner meditated on the deplorableness of drunkenness. This is a complete refutation of the assumption which obtained with many writers that nothing exists among antique sculpture of a satirical, or even ludicrous character. So far is this from being the case, that the obscene statues, statuettes, bas-reliefs, and other works on lamps and plaques, might well have suggested that the assumption was fallacious. During the past half-century the discovery of relics of the category, which is so well represented by the *Figu-rines de Tanagra*, has effectually dispelled the idea that the nations of antiquity had no ideas capable of ludicrous reproduction in plastic modes.

Another grotesque figure is that of a bearded Hercules of a very archaic type, and clad completely in a lion's skin, the head and ears of which are placed on his head, so that the ears project on the right and left.[1] His beard falls on the breast of the statuette, the bare face of which has a stony and energetic expression. In his right hand is a monstrous club, strengthened with bands of metal; it rises to the owner's shoulder. In his left

[1] See fig. 207, p. 205.

hand is a large basket or dish, filled with fruit of different kinds, as well as a piece of flat bread or cake ; his hands and feet are bare.

The seated figure of an elderly man comes next ; his face is portrait-like in its quaintness and gaunt character ; he seems to be in the act of calling aloud, as if he noisily solicited alms. He is naked, except a short cloak, falling from his shoulder, and fastened under his chin. At his left crouches a dog of long and lean form, with a slender muzzle, and, in its general aspect, like a greyhound. The man fondles the dog with his left hand, and holds in his right a round object, probably a ball. The groupings represent Ulysses and his dog. Simonides and Anacreon were similarly represented. A similar object occurs with other statuettes. With this group may be classed a figure of a bearded man clad in a lion's skin, standing erect, and, like the before-described woman, carrying a draped child on his left shoulder, and clasping the feet of his burden with one hand, while, in the other hand, he carries a long *thyrsus*, the fir-cone head of which rises above his right shoulder. As in the above-named skin-clad examples, the hands and feet are naked.

There is shewn, also, a great deal of spirit in the standing youth, who wears a tunic of the proportions of a loose shirt, reaching from his shoulders to his knees. He seems to have cast over his head a short cloak, and is in the attitude of a playful lad, who shelters himself during a shower. Holding, one in each hand, before him, the fore-hems of the cloak, he looks from between its folds. On his head is a large garland, with a horn-like protuberance over each temple ; the feet and legs are uncovered. This figure may be in the act of playing at "bopeep". Perhaps it is a figure of Telesphorus, the companion of Æsculapius.

A group of extravagant grotesques must now be de-

F F

scribed. The first of these is (fig. 211) the laughable representation of a player, or actor, in the character of a pack-man, trudging with a huge pack on his shoulders, and exactly in the manner of a Scotch pedlar, or pack-man, of our own time. He carries the pack by means of a flat stick, the hook at one end of which passes through a strap bound about the burthen, and thus keeps it in its place on his back. The stick passes before his chest, and is furnished with a stud-like second hook. Over this

Fig. 211.   An Actor.   *Terra-cotta.*

hook, the handle of a small bag or gourd is placed. He grasps the stick with one hand, and in the other, which appears pendent at his side, is a second bag or pouch. That this is the figure of an actor in character is obvious, by means of the comic mask he wears, the mouth of which is shewn, as well as the hair which surmounts it. A broad belt, or scarf, binds his belly below a twisted scarf, or girdle, which he wears. There are other figures very like the above. One, smaller than the last, represents a man in a short tunic, holding up a portion of the mantle which covers this garment by twisting it about his left hand and arm. By this means, a very remarkable phallus is displayed. Before the face is a large satyric mask. Another of an old man standing, whose tumid body is distinctly seen under his toga and tunic. He holds with his left hand a nearly flaccid pouch ; his head is disproportionately large, and its ludicrous features are distorted to resemble a mask of extremely *bizarre* character, and almost Chinese in its grotesqueness, with round, staring eyes, and large, pendulous lips.

Appearing below a long beard, the demi-figure of a man, perhaps Silenus, may be noticed, whose head is shrouded in part of his toga, which expands on each side, as if distended by the wind. That such is the case is supported by the manner in which the drapery is pressed against the bust. He has a thin, peaked beard. Another represents a fat fellow rolling on the ground, with a two-handled amphora of Rhodes at his side. The mouth of this vessel is closed, and secured by a band, which crosses it, and seems to be attached to the handles. He wears a satyric mask encircled by a wreath. He is an actor in a drunken character, and this subject is represented with great spirit. I may draw attention also to a similar figure of the same subject which may be studied, comprising a much larger amphora, on which the man reclines. The example has been adapted as a lamp. A demi-figure of a man in a satyric mask, the features of which are coloured of a deep, still perfectly fresh and sound red, while the hair of the head and beard is coloured a deep yellow. The execution is fine and carefully finished, and the fragment pertained to an incense-burner.

Four grotesques of pig-like figures, which come next, were likewise designed as incense-burners. Of these, one (fig. 212) is the caricature of a pedagogue squatting and holding a scroll extended between his paws. On the scroll is "A B Γ Δ", in archaic Greek characters. The others are the caricature of a priest in the act of speaking, with both arms raised ; a similar figure holding a wreath ; and that which holds an object of a serpentine form not easily understood.   When some of these relics are placed

Fig. 212.   Statuette- A Pedagogue.   *Terra-cotta.*

horizontally and face downwards they represent swine. We may examine a group of three erect, fully-draped figures, each with a staff in its hand ; two have satyric masks, the central one is bare-faced, and its features have a grotesque character.   There are traces of yellow on the satyric masks.   They are actors in characters. Among the grotesques, one represents a large ape. Another is a Bacchic figure of a bloated old man, crowned with a huge wreath, hugging himself with both arms, and having a perfect expression of drunkenness. On the head is a large wreath.   It is a Silenus.

A statuette which resembles a gladiator holds a large weapon like a *bipennis* in the left hand, and raised as if on guard.   It may be that this is a trident, or relates to the net of a *retiarius.*   The right hand is extended, with the fist clenched, as if a second weapon had been grasped by the man.   The lower part of his body is protected by armour suspended by a wide strap.   Another work has a greave on one leg.   In its right hand has been a weapon ;

the left hand is lost; the body is naked. Near these specimens were found tiny models of weapons in bronze, the one a lance, or axe, with a very long and heavy blade, like a celt; the other, a mace, with a ponderous ball at one of its extremities. With these articles, and probably belonging to one of the figures, was found a gladiator's helmet, modelled, of course, in clay, and intended to cover the head of the wearer down to his shoulders; it is crested, and pierced with eye holes. With the same was discovered a wheel of a chariot with four spikes and a tire. Although of terra-cotta, this wheel evidently represents a bronze original. With the above were found the body and head of a very beautiful horse in the attitude of galloping. It probably belonged to the chariot to which the wheel pertained. All these things were discovered with a sarcophagus of terra-cotta in a tomb at Salamis, which comprised many fragments of other objects. These, being more or less crushed, could not be adjusted. The whole were disposed in an amphitheatrical form, as if the figures and their accessories represented a dramatic performance. The falling in of the cover of the sarcophagus had been followed by the disarrangement of the original order of the relics, and the breaking of most of the figures.

CHAPTER XVIII

TERRA-COTTA.

(Continued.)

SACERDOTAL AND SACRED EFFIGIES.

E have come to a very remarkable class of antiquities, which, unlike those above named as having been found in the ruins of domestic and civic structures, were invariably discovered in the built vaults of ancient erections, probably temples, together with larger figures of stone, which were usually broken into fragments either by direct violence of iconoclasts, or by earthquakes. The places in question were not parts of tombs, or other mortuary edifices ; no sarcophagi were found with these figures. The most important of the relics of this class is a statuette, three feet and a half high (fig. 213), of Ariadne, or a lady of great dignity, magnificently adorned with jewellery. She is in the act of carrying offerings to the temple, and the character of the figure is precisely the same as that of the canephoroi of Greek and Roman architecture. Her tunic and body-robe are disposed with rare skill, proving that this work is due to a fine Greek period, though, doubtless, it was executed by a provincial artist. The right hand, hanging at the side of the statue, holds easily the folds of the upper garment. The left hand and arm support a kid—

the offering the lady is about to make. Extraordinary wealth of ornaments distinguishes this figure. On the wrists are large twisted bracelets; round the neck are two carcanets, the smaller and upper one of which is formed of circular beads; the lower and larger carcanet comprises pendants of fir-cones suspended to the cord at the intervals of large oval beads, and in the centre is an ornament of square form, and resembling a quatrefoil. The hair is carefully dressed, brushed off the forehead, and falls in four large tresses on the shoulders. Large earrings are composed of a rosette with a fir-cone pendant. On the head is a magnificent tiara or coronet of extraordinary elevation and sumptuousness. This superb mass of jewellery rises from a broad lunette, or fillet, above which is a line of rosebuds. Over this is a row of disks, pateræ, or rosettes (fig. 214). Above these is a line of eagles, or doves, with their wings displayed, and alternating with balls. Between the wings of the eagles, a still higher tier of ornaments has reared itself, but it is now too much injured to be described. Its elements resemble honeysuckles. Much red colour may be seen on this figure.

Fig. 213.
Statuette.
Terra-cotta.

There is another standing statuette of a lady, very similar in many respects to that which is above described. The figure holds on the left arm a kid. This is her offering. The right arm is lost, but enough remains of the indications of that member to enable us to decide that the position of the limb was not unlike that of the arm in the previous example. Considerable traces of strong red pigment remain on the tunic of this figure. The jewellery which it bears is less magnificent than that of the other work. These ornaments comprise a lofty coronet, consisting of a lunette, surmounted by a row of large balls, or roses. Over this is a fillet, which, in its turn, is topped by a row of flowers and leaves,

Fig. 214.   Details of the Head-dress.   Terra-cotta.

alternating with disk-like enrichments. The last-named elements are supported behind by a flat lunette, which seems to belong to the body of the coronet. The earrings comprise annulets with fir-cone pendants. There is no carcanet.

The collection comprises also the half of a statuette which represents another lady, apparently the personification of a city, with an offering, which in this case is a dove. Two carcanets are on the neck, one of which is comprised of oblate beads, while the other exhibits a row of pendants like fir-cones, such as occur with others in the same class. The head-dress of this figure

is not inferior in richness to that of either of the above
examples. Lowest of all its elements is a narrow fillet.
Over this is a row of balls, next a row of rosettes,
which are identical with those which are so frequent in
Assyrian modes of decoration, that they are habitually
associated in our minds with the art-works of that
nation. Next is a line of eagles with their wings displayed, the decorative effect of which is analogous to
that of the well-known *anthemion* ornament. The sum-
mit of this extraordinary structure represents distinctly
a mural crown, or line of lofty and battlemented towers,
connected by curtain walls ; in fact, here is the figure of
a fortress of the same kind as that so frequently represented by Assyrian sculptures, and including the well-
known crenellations of the battlements.

The loftiness of such crowns as these is shewn by the
proportion of this example to the face of the statuette it
enriches. This proportion indicates the altitude of the
ornament to have been about fourteen inches. Such
crowns must have been extremely light ; and that they
were formed of gold leaf, laid on a stiffening body, may
be surmised. The right hand of this figure seems to
have held a small animal, such as a hare, of which the
legs alone remain, attached to the drapery of the statuette. Unlike other examples, the lady's girdle is shewn
in this instance. The unbroken car-ring—its fellow has
been defaced—has a very long pendant to a large disk.
It is an ornament such as is frequently represented on
Egyptian paintings.

A further example likewise exhibits the Greek costume and a coronet of roses, and other ornaments too
much defaced for recognition, and is, like the above, a cane-
phoric figure of a lady. She carries in one hand a dove,
by way of offering to the goddess. A kid is in the
other hand of the figure. The edges of a veil which
descends over the shoulders are cut in vandykes, as if a

G G

fringe of some sort was worn there. This statuette is
distinguished by three carcanets, all comprising pendants.
The lowest of these ornaments is made of fir-cone-shaped
jewels, or bottles, of unusual dimensions, and in their
form not unlike amphoræ. Very distinct traces of a
jewel representing two human figures, which seem to be
struggling, or embracing, occur at the centre of and
below this carcanet. They seem to belong to it, and
may be parts of its largest pendant. The second carcanet exhibits a row of amphora-like pendants. The
third consists of pendent beads, or roses, attached to a
fillet, or chain, in the centre of which is an unusually
long pendant, the much-injured contours of which suggest
that it was a bottle in the form of a date fruit, which is
represented here, similar to those which have been described above as formed of moulded glass. What looks
like a chain, or garland of roses, crosses the front of the
body of this statuette. Another figure wears the Greek
costume, including the knotted girdle, two carcanets, a
towering coronet, ear-rings with long pendants, and
shoes. In her right hand is a dove, held against her
breast. With her left hand, she seems to grasp a kid by
its fore paws, the creature's body hanging down before
the bearer's figure. Two others, although differing in size
from the last, are almost identical with it in other respects.

It is noteworthy that all the above-named effigies exhibit not only the Greek costume pure and simple, and
carry offerings like the canephoræ on their way to the
temple of the goddess, while their lofty coronets are to
be closely associated with those still worn by brides in
more than one province of the Turkish dominions in
Europe and Asia Minor, but their faces, as regards the
expressions, characters, and forms, even to those which
are due to the skulls themselves, are Greek, and of the
noblest type.

The next company of statuettes display facial and

cranial characteristics of an entirely different order, and intellectually, if not morally, speaking, are of an inferior type to that of the above. This type represents that which appears in numerous statues and statuettes in stone, and other materials, found in Cyprus by Mr. R. H. Lang and others, and is so peculiar as to be distinguished as the Cypriote type.

It must be remembered that in the so-called Cypriote type of sculptures certain conventions of execution appear to have been in force, and that these conventions were evidently analogous to those which ruled the artists of the Nile. Some part of the peculiar appearance of the sculptures in question may be due to these conventionalities of treatment, but I think this does not account for the whole of that degrading contrast which occurs between the above-named Greek types, which I have already described, and those to which I have now to call attention as more peculiarly Cypriote. It may be that the latter class are exclusively sacerdotal representations, or that they are of greater antiquity than the former. The aspect of these "Cypriote" sculptures is very like that of the Aztecs. Its broad elements consist of unusually large and prominent eyes, which must have been very quick in moving and lustrous; the noses are uncommonly large, of an exaggerated aquiline contour, and thin in section; the low, conical foreheads slope backwards greatly, suggesting defect of mental, if not moral powers; the lips are lean, the muzzle is short, the lower jaw is narrow and pointed. In effect, it is to be noticed that of the three regions of the face, the central, or sensuous one, is out of proportion to the upper, or intellectual one, and to the energetic or physically potent one, which is the lowest of the three. Considering the size of the head as a whole in proportion to that of the body of a person of this type, it is obvious that this divergence from a fine model is due, not so much to the

excess of size in the central elements of such physio-
gnomies, as to the uncommon smallness of the upper
and lower elements of the same. If such is the case, it
is not difficult to recognise physical characteristics which
assort well enough with what we are led to expect by
the history of the Cypriote people,—a facile, voluptuous,
sensuous race, submissive and light-hearted, capable of
receiving impressions from all around them, but not qua-
lified to retain, and still less likely to improve on, these
foreign impressions.

I presume that the statuettes I have now to describe
represent members of a peculiar and, doubtless, sacerdotal class of persons, natives of Cyprus. Their external
physical characteristics I have already mentioned. Their
costumes are extremely like those still in vogue with the
Roman Catholic hierarchy, which are admitted to be of
great antiquity, and adopted of yore for sacerdotal
offices. Many of these figures bear, hanging before them,
the well-known stole, which is used by priests to this
day, and comprising those fringed ends which are still in
vogue. The surplice, which is familiar to us all, occurs
in several examples. Something which strongly resembles a cope is on the shoulders of two figures. The
tunic, or petticoat, is the same as in the above-described
Greek figures, and in those which I call Cypriote, as well
as in Christian ecclesiastical costumes.

All these Cypriote terra-cotta figures are females.
Many of them exhibit a characteristic attitude of standing with both elbows bent before the breast, while the
hands respectively hold the mammae. Of this type
there are at least a dozen more examples. This attitude
may be ceremonial, and due to the peculiar *cultus* of the
island. All the figures which exhibit it wear stoles as
distinctive parts of their costume. Other figures, although holding their mammae, wear no stoles; while such
examples as that figure which is in the act of playing

on a lyre, display the stole, but are not in this peculiar attitude. This effigy belongs to another class.

Several figures wear stoles, and carry offerings, one of which grasps a dove by its wings with the left hand. Nearly all the statuettes in question have fully-developed busts.

One of the most remarkable of the " sacerdotal" class, which I am now describing, is an unusually large one. It is the portly figure of a lady, or priestess, standing erect, with the above-mentioned action of the hands, and wearing surplice, tunic, and stole. On her head is a crown of disks ; below, a wreath of laurel. Her hair, which appears to be braided, is spread on her shoulders, as in another remarkable example of the same character. Three carcanets are about her neck. Two of them consist of amphora-like pendants, with other pendants in the centre, one of which is a disk ; the other (as before) like the fruit of a date tree. The third necklace consists of beads, with a central disk ornament and its trefoil pendant, as in other examples mentioned below. In front of the waist of this figure, and attached to a large ring, which is suspended round the neck by a chain, or yoke, are depending three of the objects we are accustomed to call "keys", to the size of modern examples of which, as in other respects, they bear but a very remote likeness indeed. They are not quite unlike " iron hands", or tongs intended for use in gathering the articles together from a distance towards the person who uses the apparatus. This resemblance is rather fanciful than exact, and it is due, not to the forms of the object singly, but to them when grouped and as a whole. They consist of flattened oval rings of metal attached to a seal ring. They thus afford illustrations of the use and mode of carrying large personal seals, such as those which are comprised in other sections of this assembly of antiquities. Similar articles, or " keys", occur in other

statuettes, some of which are of inferior mark, all of
which wear the stole and chasuble, as noticed above.
Two seem to be the work of the same artist. The
"keys" are very large in one of them, while to one of
these keys is suspended an ornament, utensil, instrument, or what not, which in modern parlance would be
called a "charm", and is in the human form. It is, in
fact, a tiny statuette. Such an object is to be seen
with another figure, in company with precisely similar
"keys". For tiny statuettes, the reader may refer to the
notes on gold ornaments in another part of the work.
Both of the above-named figures wear large armlets just
below their shoulders, and making two "turns" round
the limbs in question. Such armlets occur with a statuette which grasps a dove, by the wings, in its left hand.
Unlike the others, this one wears a lofty coronet of a
design differing from that of any one of those described
above. Otherwise, the jewellery and hair of this figure
resemble those of the majority of the statuettes with
carcanets.

It has been suggested that some of these figures with
the lofty coronets, especially the "key" bearers, and
that with the mural crown, are really representations of
goddesses, Asiatic in their characteristics, and in respect
to the *cultus* of which they may have been the objects.
Professor Sayce has recognised a likeness between some
of these relics and those of similar aspect disinterred by
Dr. Schliemann in his *Troy*. The same distinguished
antiquary has acutely remarked that works which we
know to have belonged to that great people the Hittites,
whose memorials are but now emerging from the earth
and the gloom of ages, bear a considerable resemblance to
both these classes, *i.e.*, the Cypriote remains, and those
from Hissarlik. It is presumable that the whole of
these antiquities may belong to a widespread and even
long-continued *cultus*. The subject is still so obscure

that I dare not venture to write of the crowned and
jewelled effigies, whether they are "key" bearers or what
not, in other terms than the above. To them I have
applied the old English term "ladies", and I leave it to
future students, after wider researches, and with larger
opportunities than now offer themselves, to determine
whether these be goddesses or mortals, priestesses, worshippers with offerings, or ministrants. In respect to the
suggested divinity of some of the examples, I may point
out that several of the figures with lofty coronets bear
animals, which can hardly be other than votive offerings.
Whether the mammæ-holding females are devotees,
priestesses, or goddesses, I cannot take on myself to
determine; but I think it more than probable that the
examples owe their origin to different periods of time,
the aggregate of which may be centuries. Difference of
style in the sculptures seems to suggest this notion.

To continue my remarks on the similarities of costume
in these figures, and the dresses of the Roman clergy, I
may observe that fringes are to be distinctly seen on the
wrists of one, which is clad in a fringed cope. In
this example, the features, as is the case with most of
the bearers of offerings, are decidedly Greek, not "Cypriote" or sacerdotal. Returning to two already described, of which the faces are markedly "Cypriotic", the
dressing of the heads is to be noticed as altogether different from that of the crowned figures. The former
work shows the hair bound by a fillet just above the
forehead and ears, and enclosed by a net, while a long
veil, similar in form to a veil which occurs in another
statuette, is suspended from the back of the head. The
crisped hair of another is bound by a broad, flat fillet,
and half covered by a drooping veil. One of the mammæ-
holding effigies has keys at her girdle, large pendent earrings, "Cypriote" features, a chasuble, tunic, and head-
fillet, likewise a very voluminous veil falling over the

wrists, and ample braided tresses falling, like those of
the large statuette already described, upon the shoulders.

There is the half of a figure, of which the head-dress
differs from that of any one of the above-named examples.
It includes a conical cap, substantial enough to hide the
hair entirely. The peak points backwards, and the front
of this garment bears a row of large disks, with smaller
disks placed upon them. This fragment exhibits uncommonly large ear-rings, one of which comprises three
finger-like appendages to large roses, or disk-like elements. No statuette exhibits more elaborate jewellery
than a work which has the "Cypriote" features, a very
large and prominent example of head-gear, consisting of
two lines of roses and a third intermediate line of
ornaments, shaped like little calabashes. The pendants of the ear-rings, which are oval amulets, are comparatively immense: three carcanets and the yoke-like
ornament which occurs on the figures of the priestesses (?)
with the keys. The pendants to these carcanets are—*a*,
at top, a rosette with three leaf-like appendages, exactly
like those described in the notes on gold ornaments. The
second pendant, *b*, seems to have the form of an alabastron, or fir-cone. The third pendant is a large disk, with
a mammillary stud in the centre. The last-named ornament hangs between the mammæ of the wearer, whose
dress is cut "square", or straight across the bust, and
low enough to expose the throat and half the bosom.
This is the mode of leaving uncovered the bust, which is
still in vogue among the women of Greece and the islands.
Similar coronets to those above described are still worn
by bishops of the Greek rite.

Some of the heads of these terra-cotta statuettes have
the brows encircled with fillets, which exactly represent
the gold chaplets, or coronals, which I have mentioned in
the chapter devoted to the gold relics. I may here introduce figures 215, 216, of two gold leaf relics of this

FIGURE OF A FEMALE MUSICIAN.

nature which will supplement those given in the earlier part of the work. They are the exact types of those carved on some of the heads.

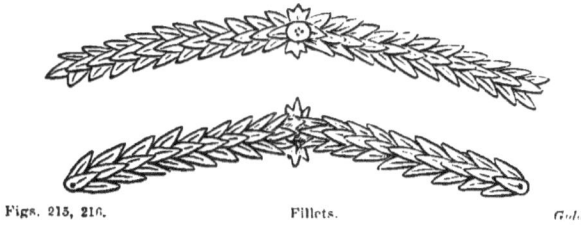

Figs. 215, 216.   Fillets.   Gold.

THE CHOIR, OR MUSICIANS.

In this rather numerous company of statuettes we have a curious and valuable category of worshippers. They are to be conveniently divided into three classes, although every individual carries a lyre; but these instruments differ from each other in greater or less degrees. The first class consists of women whose physiognomy, stature, carriage, costume, and coronets are unquestionably Greek, in which respect they resemble a body of similar personages whom I have already described as bearing offerings of animals for the goddess. The second class consists of figures clad in tunics and togas, carrying lyres, but wearing no lofty coronets, their hair being bound by fillets, while the heads of some of them are partially covered with veils. The third class appears to be more distinctly sacerdotal than the second, although both of these classes differ from the first in exhibiting the "Cypriote" types of features and forms, as described before. I distinguish the third class as stole-wearers, on account of the stoles which accompany their togas.

In the first class, one holds a nearly perfect lyre, of the Greek form, which distinctly shews the use of the

H H

little ivory rods with bronze brackets, to which I have
already alluded while dealing with examples of the former material.[1] The jewellery of the wearer is very
clearly shown in this work. The second class wear garlands, usually of large flowers or disks. Nearly every
example of the whole company of three classes shows a
large bracelet on its right wrist. Red colour occurs on
most of these relics. These members of the choir remind us of the well-known line descriptive of Cyprus:—

"Insula læta choris; blandorum et mater amorum."

---

[1] See pages 74, 75.

CHAPTER XIX

TERRA-COTTA.

(Continued.)

MASKS—CARICATURES—ANIMALS—CHARIOTS—WARRIORS—TOYS—
AND OTHER OBJECTS.

 CLASS of small terra-cotta masks, or rather half-heads, of which there is a considerable number, being works of great spirit and variety of character, ought to have place here. One represents an aged faun (fig. 217) wearing a garland and a very long beard which

217.

218.

Figs. 217, 218.   Masks.   *Terra-cotta.*

streams downwards in hanks of hair; another is the half-head of a very young man (fig. 218), the expression of the features of which admirably represents drunken hilarity; another is crowned with ivy leaves and is a

true mask of the satyric order, as the form of the open
mouth attests (figs. 219, 220). A large garland, inter-
twined with ivy, projects far over the forehead. The

219.   220.

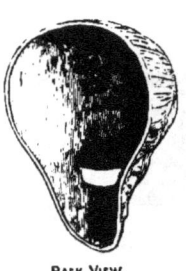

BACK VIEW

Figs. 219, 220.   Satyric Mask.   *Terra-cotta.*

last is one of the most animated and beautifully executed
works of its class, and it deserves a high place in that
category; traces of deep purple pigment appear on the
features.

These examples may have been intended for puppets, to
be suspended by strings from above and used in a show;
to this end the two small holes at the top of each head
might be applied. But it is much more likely that they
served as handles to vessels, probably table vases of a
very fine order. A class of larger masks, evidently derived from bronze or carved-wood originals, may follow
here. Another of these, about three inches high, represents the tragic expression, and seems to be of much
older date than the above-named three; the surface is
greatly corroded. There is also a quaint satyric mask
(fig. 221) nearly life-size, comprising a large aquiline nose
dropped over the mouth, a pair of round staring eyes;
the mouth is made more than usually ludicrous by the
absurd upward curving of its ends, and by the placing
of a pellet in each side; the hair and beard are braided.

It is a mask of the same character as to this day appears in use, during festivals, in Milan and other parts of Italy.

Fig. 221.　　　　　　　Satyric Mask.　　　　　　　*Terra-cotta.*

A very impressive female tragic mask, with the lips closed, 'is of archaic character, and very fine execution,

Fig. 222.　　　　　　　Female Mask.　　　　　　　*Terra-cotta.*

(fig. 222). Then may be placed a bacchic mask (fig. 223)
crowned with ivy leaves and berries, and with bunches
of grapes indicated at the side of the head, which represents a very young woman; the holes by which this
mask was affixed to the face are distinctly seen at its
sides and above the forehead. Traces of deep red colour
are on the hair. It may, perhaps, represent Ariadne.

Fig. 223.   Female Bacchic Mask.   Terra-cotta.

There are fragments of other masks, including one
which is that of a child—a fine, tragic face of a little
more than half life-size, and with a lofty coronet of hair,

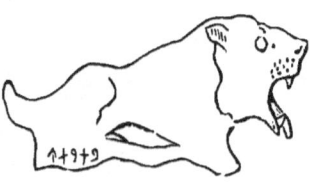

Fig. 224.   Inscribed Lion.   Terra-cotta.

crowned by an ornament of the usual kind. Another
represents by its much-injured features the signs of a
fine style and period of art.

A considerable number of lions, one (fig. 224) inscribed

with ↑ ↑ 9 ↑ 9, partly Cypriote, partly Phœnician characters; dogs of various breeds, one inscribed with the word ΔΩΡ, part of a word, or "a gift" (fig. 225), pigs, cocks, swans, eagles, foxes, horses, a dove with a ribbon round its neck, and other doves in different attitudes occur. One of the fragments of horses bears trappings about its head, with very distinct pink colour and wreaths. Another is likewise enriched with wreaths. It is entirely painted. A sow is beautifully modelled. There is a shaggy dog with a necklace and pendants over his shoulders, and

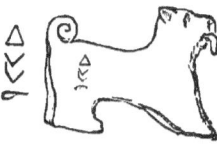

Fig. 225.   Inscribed Dog.   *Terra-cotta.*

what looks like a garland encircling its body. These objects are probably votive in their nature. A great number of similar works were discovered at Alambra, in Cyprus, near Dali.

The collection of terra-cotta toys, if such they are, and not insignia of the dead, is very curious. They amount to almost four hundred in all. Among the creatures represented by these remains are rattles in the forms of pigs, which retain the pellets inside, a donkey with panniers, a bull, and various domestic animals. Probably the most curious of all is a *tethrippos*, or war-chariot, drawn by four horses (fig. 226) yoked in pairs (fig. 227) by heavy bars of wood, cylindrical in form, painted yellow, perhaps to represent wood, and passing through straps or head stalls behind the ears. This mode of harnessing is still in vogue whenever bulls are used in agricultural operations. The horses are in a line, like other horses in this collection. Each animal is painted in stripes of deep red and black; the head-gear is painted black. The chariot is of the true Greek form, but it has no pole. The wheels, which appear to have been made to represent wood, are painted with a deep, bright red ground, on which black radii, felloes, and tires are painted. Red and black ornaments are depicted on the chariot. The back of the chariot-body shews the door, by means

Fig. 226.   Tethrippos or Four-horse Chariot.   *Terra-cotta.*

of which the riders ascended to their places. The riders are shewn to be the warrior in a high conical helmet, the cover of which, painted black, falls about the shoulders like the camail of a mediæval or oriental warrior. The

Fig. 227.   The Yokes.   *Terra-cotta.*

lappels, like the laces of a modern helmet, fall by the sides of the face, and are united in front of the breast by a brooch, or stud. A band, or coronet, which extends across the forehead, comprises rosettes at its extremities, and a single rosette in the centre. The hinder part of the head-covering falls, like that of a hood, on the neck. The loose body-coat of this champion is now of a pinkish orange, or brown; it was, probably, originally black. A baldric of crimson crosses two belts on the body. The face is painted to imitate nature with a brownish carnation. The arms of this figure comprised a shield, on the surface of which are a large central boss and seven spirals, ending in as many studs, arranged about it. The ground is of the same vivid red as that of the chariot wheel. Radial curved lines of black have been drawn with a brush, so as to form a pattern with the boss and studs, which are likewise painted black. In his right hand is a weapon—a sword, or lance—which has disappeared.

Squatting low between the knees of the fighting men is the other figure, the driver of the chariot, with his arms extended as if holding the reins and guiding the horses. His black face and the forms of his features indicate that he is a negro. He wears a high, peaked cap of very brilliant red. This very extraordinary specimen of archaic type was found at Salamis in a vase of terra-cotta, and bedded in lime, to which circumstance the brilliancy of the red colour may be due, as well as the perfect preservation of the relic. Traces of the lime are still distinct on the surface of the group.

There is another chariot, likewise found at Salamis, in the form of a flat tray mounted on wheels, which still turn on the axletree, so that this is a "practicable" toy. In the front of the tray a cylindrical socket occurs, with a hole, into which, probably, a stick was driven, in order that the child-owner might drag the vehicle after his own footsteps. In the tray reclines a lady, with one elbow sustained by a cushion; the cushion is still red. This colour was burnt in, and is, therefore, permanent. This lady's head is decorated with a large garland; a large disk-like earring is attached at each side of the head; the open mouth is of a deep red. Traces of a similar colour are on the robe of the lady and the

chariot.   On the robe are more traces of bright
yellow.

Another biga or two-horse chariot (fig. 228), of which
the wheels are still in perfect order, is adorned with a

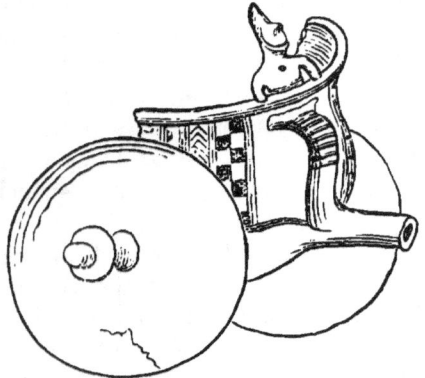

Fig. 228.   Chariot for two Horses, with Warrior.   *Terra-cotta.*

band of chequered, and a band of chevroned pattern, on
each side.   The front is semicircular, and has a socket,

Fig. 229.   Chariot for two Horses.   *Terra-cotta.*

into which the pole was fastened before the two horses
were attached.   A warrior stands within the chariot,

wearing a tall conical helmet. This object is of a very
archaic character.

Almost similar to the above is a chariot (fig. 229), also
for two horses. The wheels in this case are still perfect,
but there is no ornamentation upon the body of the
relic as in the former instance.

Another extremely quaint toy of terra-cotta represents
a centaur (fig. 230) which appears to be a hermaphrodite,

Fig. 230.   Armed Centaur.   Terra-cotta.

if we compare the female bust of the figure, with the
emblems of virility below. On the head is a high helmet, the crest of which is like a cock's comb; a small
buckler, with a cross device, is on the left arm; the right
arm is in the act of brandishing a now lost weapon.
This figure is painted with red and black, including
bands, and a harlequin pattern of these colours. These
colours have been burnt in.

We have next a soldier-toy standing, wearing a conical helmet painted red, and a buckler with a rosette pattern painted black; the right arm is raised near the ear, like a modern soldier in the act of saluting his officer. This odd figure stands on a bell-like base, and its feet hang loosely within, so that the child to whom it belonged could, by shaking the toy, produce a sort of tintinnabulation. A similar and taller toy represents a soldier with a conical helmet and a long spade-like beard; the cheek-pieces of the helmet are peculiar. Traces of green pigment occur on this relic. Another article of this class represents a woman carrying a *hydria*, or water vase, on her head. A trumpet of terra-cotta, about three feet long, and shorter examples of the same kind, and a model of a boat, seemingly hollowed out of a tree, must not be omitted even in an enumeration of this extraordinary treasury of toys,—if toys they were, which has not yet, I believe, been entirely decided. It is certain that considerable numbers of such things have been exhumed.

This class embraces rudely-designed figures of goddesses, chiefly Venus, with broad hips, narrow ankles, a triangular hatched ornament on the pubes, large ears with terra-cotta rings in them, the arms brought round and laid upon the breast; men wearing conical helmets, and many without legs, seated upon horses, or animals at any rate intended, by a stretch of imagination, for horses, which they hold by the neck or ears; striped animals of uncertain nomenclature; and swine with the mouth so disposed with a funnel-shaped termination, that the object takes the form of an unguentarium or aryballos when set up on its end.

CHAPTER XX.

TERRA-COTTA.

(Continued.)

HE number of these objects in this collection is very considerable indeed, not fewer than four thousand pieces in all. These comprise amphoræ of various sizes, from about four feet high to the smallest examples, and of various origins, being Phœnician, Cypriote, and Greek ; some of them bear inscriptions in one or other of these languages respectively. Among the vases of this class, more than two hundred exhibit beautiful patterns painted on their surfaces, including birds, bulls, and other creatures; many of those are extremely precious works, some of them are believed to be unique as to the decorations they bear and as to their origin; it is supposed that these remarkable instances are pure Phœnician; their decorations agree in general respects with those of other vessels to which the name of the Phœnician nation has been given.

The accompanying illustration represents a Phœnician vase of considerable dimensions (fig. 231). It contains an inscription of five letters in the Phœnician language, of which, according to M. Pierides who has examined it, the Hebrew transliteration is the following—בלחמן, *Baal-Hammon; i.e.,* " Baal Solaris, or Baal the Sun".[1]

Fig. 231.   Inscribed Phœnician Vase.   *Terra-cotta.*

One of the workmen whom I had employed in my excavations found a conical urn or vase, similar in shape to the foregoing specimen, in a tomb to the south-west of Larnaca, and outside the walls of the ancient city of Kitim. The vase is of the ordinary terra-cotta of the island (fig. 232) and bears the Cypriote inscription now engraved in the accompanying illustration.

On being informed of this discovery I proceeded to the spot, and found that the tomb was about nineteen feet and a half below the surface of the ground. It had been

[1] See Gesenius, *Script. Phœnic.*

constructed of large stones, cemented together, as they
were laid on the earth, with lime. It had an oval shape,
except at the bottom, and was six feet nine inches deep,
and little more than six feet wide. The entrance had
been closed with a square slab of stone, roughly hewn.
The earth, sodden with the rain, which had percolated for
ages through the defective cementing of the roofing
stones, covered the floor to the extent of more than eight

Fig. 232.   Inscribed Cypriote Urn.   *Terra-cotta.*

inches; but as there was no sarcophagus in the tomb,
and the body which the tomb had received was laid on
the earth, I could find no other vestige of humanity
than a small piece of bone which perhaps belonged to
the head of a child. No sooner did this relic come into
contact with the air than it crumbled away to dust.

The inscription upon this vase is, I am told by Dr.

Birch, to whom I have submitted it, of a doubtful signification. It appears to read:—

mi . e . o . sa . ti . ja . ta .

But the first two characters on the right are uncertain.
It is evidently the genitive case of a proper name pre-
fixed to the verb *emi*, *I am*, or *I belong to;* and may
perhaps be read "I belong to Tajatisas, or Tathasus".

A vase very similar to this in general shape has two
handles on the shoulder.

There are about eighteen hundred lamps, partly Greek,
partly Roman, of which nearly three hundred bear inscriptions of the names of the potters. The designs
moulded, or impressed on these lamps, are of the usual
character, mythological, historical, domestic, satirical,
and obscene. They will be treated of in a subsequent
chapter.

A large bowl of Samian ware is enriched on the body

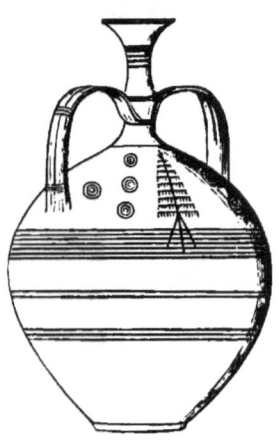

Fig. 233.   Archaic Red-ware Vase or Diota.   *Terra-cotta.*

with several dancing figures, some of which are
winged, while others bear musical instruments. It is
precious, on account of the spirit and elegance of the

design. A description of this will be given further on.
Two red ware vases deserve especial mention, because
they are unique in exhibiting figures painted in black
on their bodies. On one of these (figs. 233, 234) is a

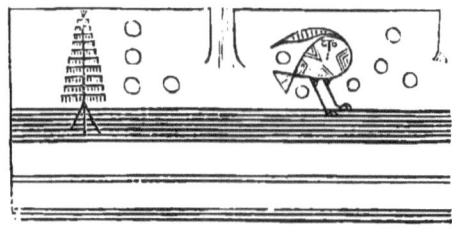

Fig. 234.   Details of Fig. 233.   *Terra-cotta.*

standing owl, or swan, and opposite to it a tree of the
sacred or "*Hom*" kind, the emblematic palm, or date

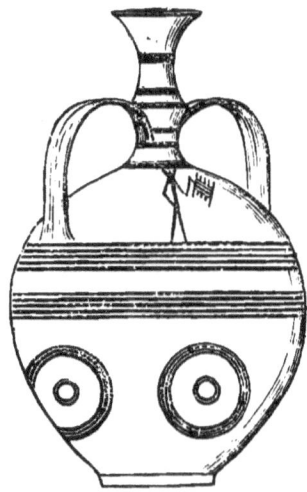

Fig. 235.   Archaic Red-ware Vase or Diota.   *Terra-cotta.*

tree, which was found significant over many regions in
Asia, and has been frequently recognised in Assyrian
remains, even on the breastplates of the kings in Chal-

K K

dea, Egypt, India, and China. What may be a remi-
niscence of the "*Hom*" is often seen to this day in Turkey
carpets. The Greek anthemion, or honeysuckle ornament, has been referred to as the Greek variety of this
symbol degraded into an ornament, and with no other
significance than that which is due to a lovely combination
of harmonic lines.

On the other vase (fig. 235) are the figures of two
men, both in the act of walking, and carrying bundles of
wood, or fascines, such as we call "faggots". Doubtless
they may be about to attend a funeral pyre. These
figures give extraordinary importance and value to the
vase on which they appear.

Among the thousands of vessels of this kind, no other

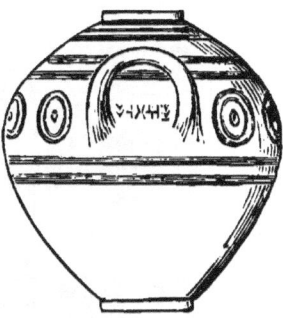

Fig. 236.   Inscribed Archaic Vase.   *Terra-cotta.*

that is known to me bears a representation of the human
figure, or bird, or tree. All other enrichments of this
category are geometrical, as, for example, in the accompanying woodcut (fig. 236), which represents a double-
handled vase, perhaps a *stamnos*,[1] enriched with three
double rings and a series of disks or double annulets
round the widest part of the body, with a dot in the

[1] See Dennis, *Cities and Cemeteries of Etruria*, New Edition,
vol. I, p. cix.

centre. On the space between the insertions of the handle is the following Cypriote inscription :—

$$\vee \dashv \,)(\; +\!\!\mathbf{I} \; \vee$$

thus read by Professor Sayce :—

ma . ta . ru . e . o .

or in Greek equivalents :—

ὦ ἔρυ[ε] θαμά.

"Oh, carry often".

The great variety of shapes exhibited by terra-cotta vessels, ornamented with spirals, bands, geometrical devices, animals, and flowers, can be scarcely conceived without a personal view of them. There is hardly a shape known to archæologists that is not represented by them. Among them may be mentioned large jars with wide mouths, heart-shaped bodies, and two loop handles (see fig. 237), globular bodies with narrower necks, and only one handle (see fig. 238); hemispherical bodies, with a mouth having a diameter but little reduced from that of the body itself, and with one handle, the wine jar; true amphoræ of the Rhodian style, as well as the allied forms, the *cadus*, *orca*, *lagena*, and *sena*; the *kylix*, the *kantharus*, the *diota*.[1] The *oinochoe*, or wine-jug, which evidently ministered the dark sparkling wine at festive entertainments, of proportions sometimes truly heroic; the *hydria*, or water-pot; the *kalpis*, *skyphos*, *depas*, *pelike*, *crater*, and *prochoos*; *tetinæ*,[2] with

[1] See Birch, *History of Ancient Pottery*, new edition, p. 180.

[2] Mr. H. Syer Cuming's Paper "On Early Tetinæ", in the *Journal* of the British Archæological Association, gives illustrations of a large number of these objects. The writer quotes Fosbrooke's *Encyclopædia of Antiquities*, s.v. Nursing, to show that "among the Greeks the nurses, during the time of sucking, used to carry the children out to air, having with them a sponge full of honey in a small pot, to stop crying". None can doubt, he continues, that in ancient, as in modern days, there were

tiny spouts inserted at the widest part of the body,
either to enable the holder to pour out a libation in a
thin, trickling stream, or to allow a nurse to feed an
infant by pouring a few drops of milk at a time into its
mouth ; wine-cups, with or without handles, long, narrow, and truncated *lecythi* ; and the *nasiterna*, or nozzle-
mouthed jug, so called from the length of its spout,
many of which are ornamented or enriched with a series
of small loops or eyes, either singly at intervals, or in

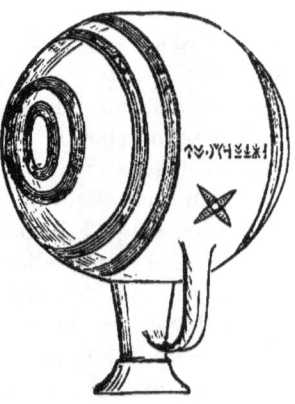

Fig. 237.   Inscribed Archaic Vase.   *Terra-cotta.*

pairs, regularly placed along each side of the body.
These are generally glandular or ovoid in shape, with
narrow spouts elongated on one side, and pinched together at the extreme end, in order that the liquid
contents may be delivered in a very thin stream.   Some

---

many instances in which hand-feeding was forced to take the place of
the breast ; and the question is, how was that feeding effected ?   In
this country and abroad, many antique vessels of terra-cotta have been
discovered, which were formerly regarded as oil-cruses for the service of
lamps ; but they are now accepted as infants' feeding-bottles, upon
which the title of *tetina* has been bestowed.

of this last kind of vessel have three or four short feet, to enable them to stand upright more securely.[1]

An archaic globular vase, perhaps an *askos*, decorated in a somewhat similar manner (fig. 237), has a star under the inscription of the handle, and is in like way enriched with an inscription in the Cypriote character :—

↑ ⌄ ·)˘(⊣ ≳ ↓ ✳ ⊣

which Professor Sayce reads :—

ti . pi . ma . ta . o . te . e . ta .

that is—

τὰ ἤδεο δαμά πῖθι,

"What you liked, often drink."

or—

τὰ ἔθεο θαμά πῖθις.

"What thou hast put (here) drink often."

Another vessel, or amphora, of the Græco-Egyptian or

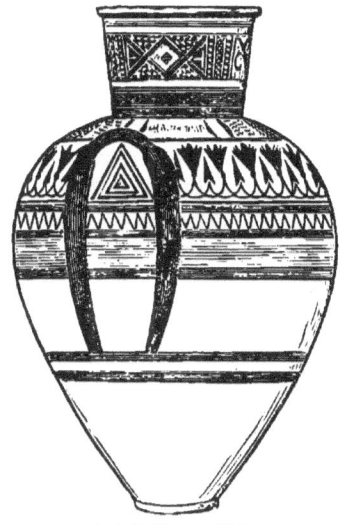

Fig. 238.   Archaic Vase or Diota.   *Terra-cotta.*

[1] For the names of the various forms of archaic Greek fictilia, the reader may consult the concise and lucid " Appendix on the Forms and

Alexandrian style (fig. 238), is of very large dimensions, and beautifully adorned with geometrical patterns, filled in with chequered ornamentations, annulets, and spirals, as shewn in the illustration of enlarged details (fig. 239). The height of this vase is 4½ feet. On the shoulder is the inscription, in Greek capitals, ΑΡΣΙΝΟΗΣ

Fig. 239.   Details of Fig. 238.   *Terra-cotta.*

ΦΙΛΛΔΕΛΦΟΤ, evidently purporting to belong to Arsinoe Philadelphus, wife of the second Ptolemy.

The accompanying figure (240) illustrates a vase, which,

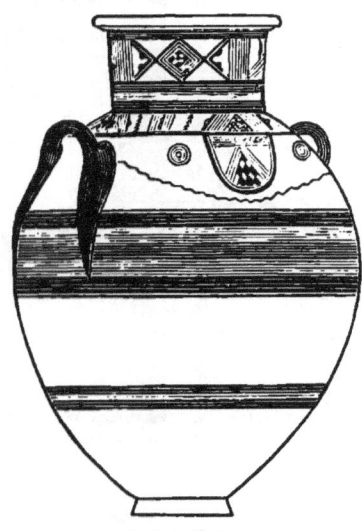

Fig. 240.   Archaic Vase.   *Terra-cotta.*

Uses of Greek and Etruscan Vases", in Mr. Dennis's new edition of the *Cities and Cemeteries of Etruria*, vol. i, pp. cv-cxxvi, where a large number are figured and described.

while in other respects resembling many others of the
same class, both in the Lawrence-Cesnola and in other
collections, has a shield-shaped addition upon the
shoulder between the handles, adorned with chevrons

Fig. 241.   Details of Ornament on Fig. 234.   *Terra-cotta.*

and small chequered squares. It is 4 ft. 2 in. high. The
details of the neck of the vase are given in fig. 241.

I give here some examples of the geometrical details
found upon corresponding parts of other large vases in

Fig. 242.   Details of Ornaments.   *Terra-cotta.*

the Lawrence-Cesnola collection. These comprise che-
quer patterns, lotus or other flowers, wheel-shaped circles
(fig. 242), with spokes or radii, zigzags, wavy lines or

Fig. 243.   Details of Ornaments.   *Terra-cotta.*

chevrons, and a peculiar tear-like thickening on the
middle of a black line, as seen on the left hand side of
the last example (fig. 243). The collection contains a
good number of these large vessels. The kind of vases

Fig. 244.   Details of Ornaments.   *Terra-cotta.*

shown in figs. 238, 240, are always found inside tombs, full of bones. I think that in ancient times the owners of the tombs prepared for new arrivals by preserving the bones of previous occupants of the tombs in these vases. Two or more of these vases have been found in one tomb.

Fig. 245.   Archaic Jar, with Four Handles.   *Terra-cotta.*

Fig. 238, with the Greek inscription, I think probably more ancient than the inscription, through the inscription not being burnt in when the vase was made; or possibly the vase was made in the ancient shape in the time of Arsinoe, and this is rather confirmed by its bright

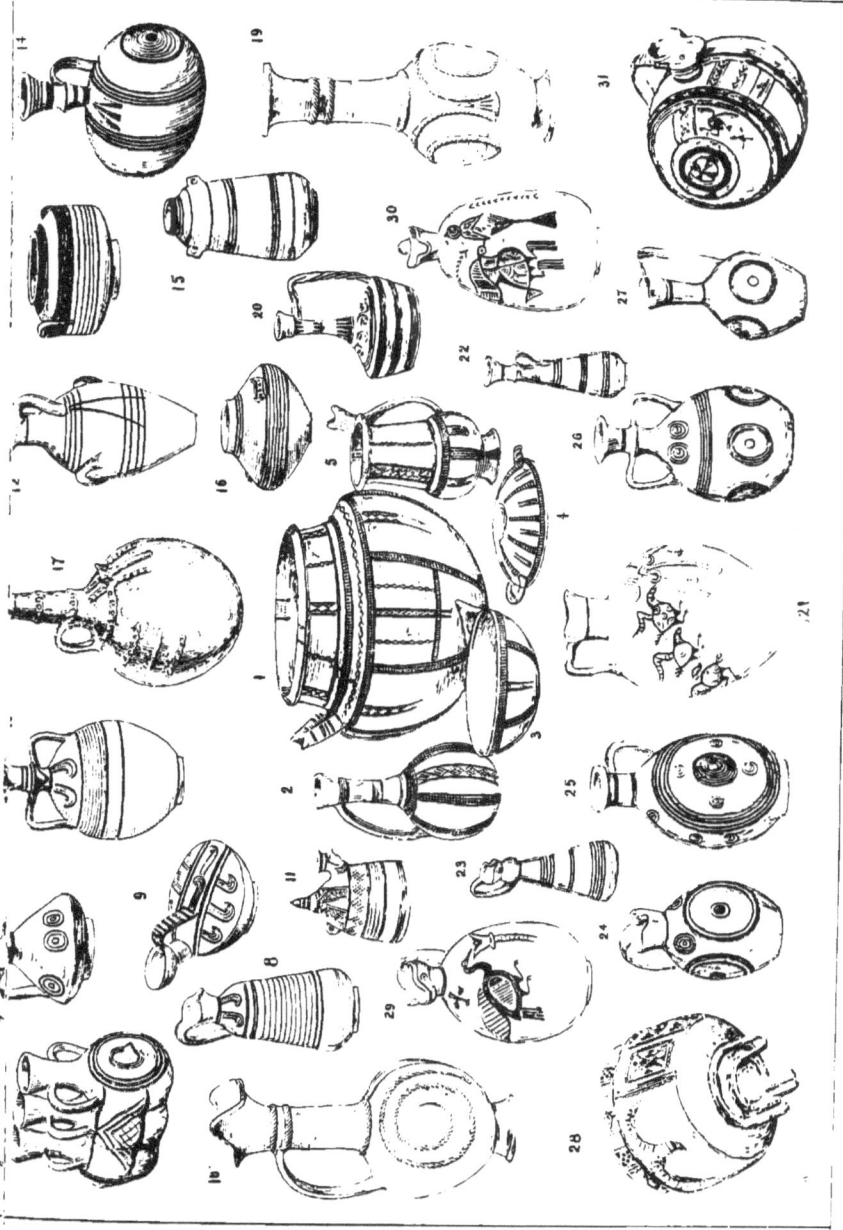

ARCHAIL. TERRA COTTA

—

colours and perfect state of preservation, which is different to fig. 240 ; that appears much older.   In Cyprus,
at the present day, there are vases of ancient shape in
common use, particularly water jugs, which have two
little reliefs in form like the female bosom, and tradition
says that it represents the bosom of Venus.   My learned
friend Mr. D. Pierides is of the same idea.   It is only
another instance of the survival of ancient types.   A four-
handled *stamnos*, jar, or urn (fig. 245) of this style, with
two narrow bands or rings, and one of wider dimensions, is
elegantly painted with four palm trees in a natural
manner that is very remarkable.   This vase has an ivy
leaf on the shoulder within the area of each handle, and
a circular lid with a hole in it, and a knob-shaped handle
to it.   On the knob are six Cypriote characters.   It is
2 ft. 6 in. high.

An elegant aryballos of the oldest Greek style is

Fig. 246.   Archaic Aryballos.   Terra-cotta.

shewn in the accompanying illustration (fig. 246).   It
was found with other archaic remains at Paphos, not
far from the celebrated Temple of Venus, which has been
described in other works upon the antiquities of the
island.   The ornamentation upon neck and mouth, the
style in which the swan, or eagle, is drawn and coloured,
the radiating tears, or leaves, at the upper and under
surface of the body, and the rosettes, or flowerets, which
are placed in the field, may all be compared by the

L L

reader with similar details shewn upon the archaic
oinochoe, and the archaic aryballi and other vases in
Dr. Birch's *History of Ancient Pottery* (pp. 184-188, new
edition).

In the accompanying illustration of a group of early
fictilia, the first is a kind of *stamnos*, or honey-jar, but
differs from the true form, of that name, in having a single
loop-handle over the mouth terminating in lions' heads,
instead of two more erect handles at the sides (fig. 247).
The second figure (248) is an early *hydria*, shewing the
transition from purely exclusive geometric forms of orna-

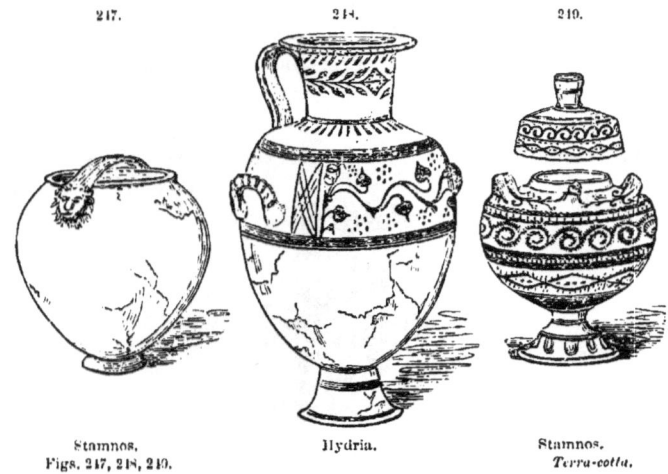

247.   248.   249.

Stamnos.   Hydria.   Stamnos.
Figs. 247, 248, 249.   *Terra-cotta.*

mentation to a style where the geometric patterns are
interspersed with chaplets of leaf work and wavy scrolls of
ivy leaves and berries. The last figure in the group (fig.
249) is probably a *stamnos*, from Salamis, called the "Apu-
lian stamnos" by Dennis,[1] a small and late variety of the
stamnos. It may have served to hold honey or sweet-
meats. It is a variety of the amphora. The ornamentation of this example is elegant, and of early date.

[1] *L.c.*, cix, cx.

The two following vessels, found by me in the ground at Curium, are of considerable interest, being of archaic insular style. The first (fig. 250) is evidently a water-bottle, not

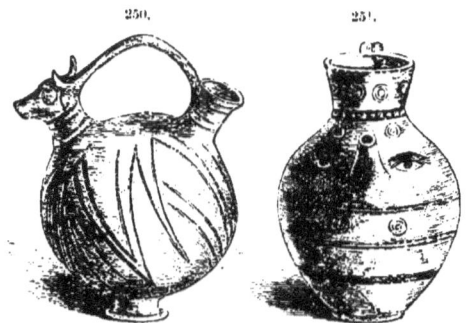

250.   251.

Figs. 250, 251.   Water Vessel and Jug.   *Terra-cotta.*

unlike the Moorish water-coolers, made of red clay in Spain, Portugal, and some parts of the northern littoral of Africa to this day. The head of the ox, which adorns the spout, and the acute-angled lines which embellish the surface, are, however, peculiar to this example. The other (fig. 251) is a pitcher, or jug, of an archaic style, having two eyes, with a spout between them for sprinkling libations, or feeding purposes. It is also enriched with a number of sets of concentric circles.

At Curium, I found an interesting specimen of the *oinochoe* of transitional archaic Greek style, painted with lions face to face (fig. 252). It may be compared for its shape and style with an *oinochoe* adorned with animals and flowers, figured in Dr. Birch's *History of Ancient Pottery*.[1] The custom of adding small ornaments like those above, as well as fylfots, chequers, spirals, and so forth, is commented upon by this authority in the same part of the work mentioned.

Among the homely curiosities of this collection of

[1] New Edition, p. 185.

terra-cotta utensils are several which deserve particular
mention.   I do not now allude to the numerous stately
and beautiful vases, of many sizes and divers fashions in
decoration, with which this collection is unusually enriched, nor even to those examples of the same use which
are doubtless of greater antiquity, as well as less charmingly decorated than the latter.   I allude to the group

Fig. 252.   Œnochoe.   Terra-cotta.

of fumigators, incense-burners, or foot-warmers of terra-
cotta now before us.[1]   I have called them fumigators,
because they were evidently intended to contain char-
coal, or peat, and emit the fumes by means of the holes
with which the sides of the vessels are furnished.   They
were, I think, really designed as foot-warmers, and intended for winter use in Cyprus by a luxurious people.
The Dutch, and other northern nations, still employ

[1] See Plate xx, figs. 18, 20.

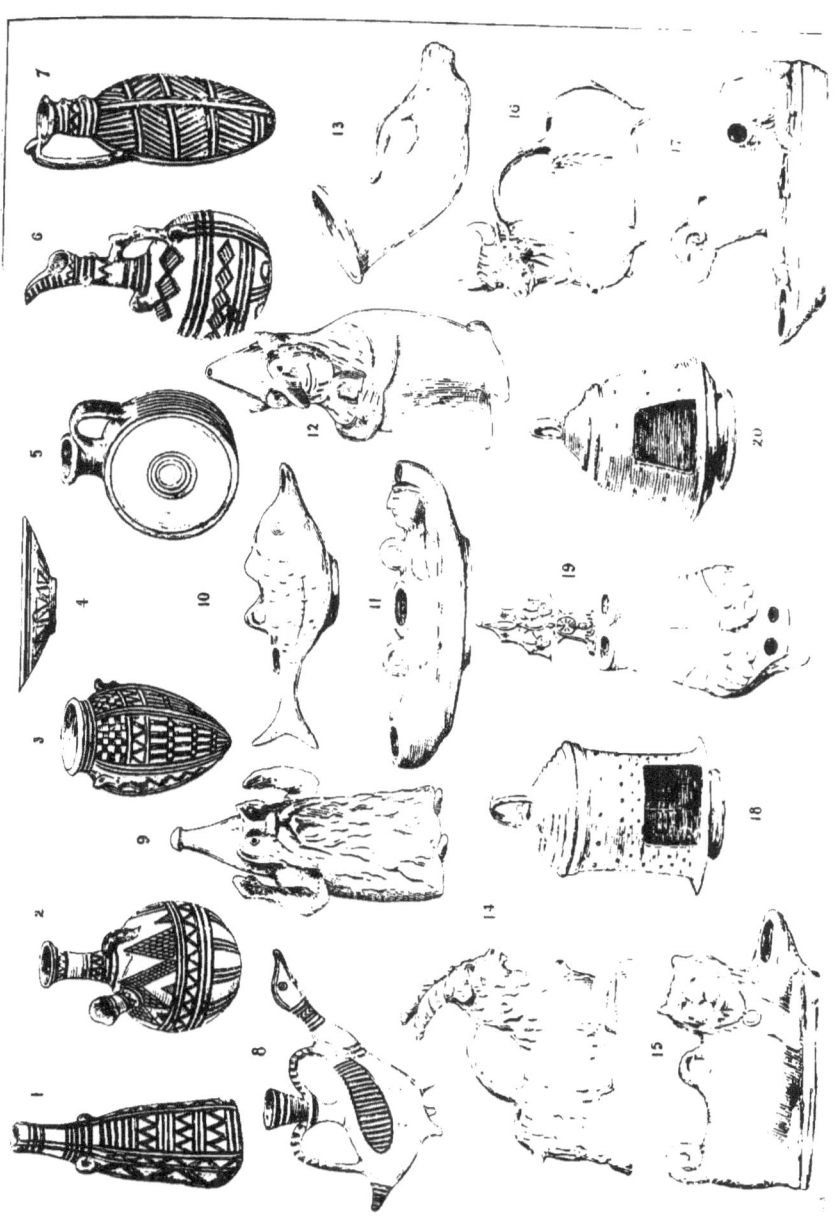

analogous utensils. The ladies of Holland are accustomed to sit with such articles, when made of brass or copper, under their petticoats. The like are not unknown in Venice likewise. Most of them are furnished with handles arching over the tops, so that they may readily be taken from place to place even when ignited. Being about fifteen inches high in the body, exclusive of the foot and overarching handle, one of these utensils would contain sufficient fuel to supply heat for a considerable number of hours, if it was allowed to stand still. They could not have been designed for incense-burners, being on too large a scale for that purpose, although they might have served as fumigators. It is much more likely that they were foot-warmers.

Two shallow bowls, perforated with triangular holes, and marked with chevron patterns, were obviously intended for use as strainers. Not more than half a dozen rhytons have been found in this collection. They are not large, nor rich in ornamentation. They appear to be of Roman origin.

As to the amphorae, jars, jugs, ewers, and bottles proper, apart from bowls, paterae, and such like flat vessels, the number before us is very considerable indeed. They are of all sizes, and, I doubt not, within the chronology of the ancient world of nearly all dates. It seems probable that the greater portion are of native manufacture. Cyprus still supplies clay for the potter in the neighbourhood of Famagosta. I consider these works to be mostly of native manufacture, notwithstanding the well-known practice of the ancients to export pots to all parts of the world then known to them. I recollect that even in the remote Britain, countless specimens of Samian ware have been found, as well as examples of the craft of the indigenous potters. The repeated discovery of numerous pieces of foreign earthenware near the foot of the cliff at the mouth of the Thames, where now stand the

Reculvers, is believed to indicate that a vessel must have been wrecked at sea near that point, and that parts of her cargo were recovered from time to time; unless, indeed, the sea now covers the site of a manufactory of Samian ware. Fragments of Roman pottery have been dredged up from below the waves, off Winchelsea, and other parts of the southern coast.

It is only the pattern depicted in black or red, or incised on the dark grounds of some of these vessels, which give us anything like a clue to the age, nation, or mode of design to which such works are due. It must be remembered that a large number of such antiquities are without patterns, and exhibit shapes so simple and characterless that they may belong to any period except the rudest. Observers of such relics never allow themselves to mistake simplicity or, to be more exact, defect of character, for the proofs of ancientness, or the expression of extreme antiquity. No shrewder trap for tyros than this one is known to exist. On the other hand, it is often true that productions of the finest period of ceramic art are absolutely simple even to severity. Indeed, severity, if not plainness, is an essential in the finest mode of art as applied to "pots", and to everything else. Amphorae and jars are comprised in this collection, than which nothing could be less ornate; and, yet, they belong to the best style of Greek design, and are unrelieved by patterns in colour or otherwise.

Doubtless, the greater number of the vases before us are Greek. There can be no question that the largest amphorae, some of which are between four and five feet high, and capacious enough to contain a well-grown man, are of the Greek period, although they exhibit the Egyptian lotus (see fig. 238) in exquisite compositions as to lines and proportions. There is nothing archaic or stiff in the enrichments of these vessels, and we could not fail to expect such characteristics as these in works

which were due to the Egyptian domination in Cyprus.
The contours of these great vessels are perfectly and
purely Greek; the lotus occurs often enough in Greek
decorations when combined in the mode before us. The
accessory ornaments on these amphoræ are exclusively
Greek. There are two amphoræ of the second order as
to size, which bear traces of Assyrian influence in some
of their decorations; but even these are not without
testimonies to the effect of Greek taste on the minds of
the makers. The taller of these has dark handles, and
round its neck a very broad band, within which, besides
other elements, is a floral conventionalised pattern of
a volute enclosing within the "horns" respectively a
rosette. The other work of the two in question is
smaller, has a broader base, less elegant proportions of
handles, neck, and body, and is of inferior workmanship.
About the shoulders, on the line of the handles, are
groups, four in each, of the concentric ring ornament,
which is more Assyrian than Greek, and less Egyptian
than either. This example seems to me older than any
of the above-named instances of the first and second
class in the order of size. It may be, however, that its
insufficiency is merely a proof of the comparative incom-
petence of the maker than a sign of the ancientness of
his handiwork. There is a fine specimen, in the second
order as to size, of Greek art, comprising the lotus (see
fig. 238) in the band at the line of the handles. This is
very typical. The throat of this example comprises the
guilloche in upright lines, and compartments of crossed
and reversed chevrons, forming a diaper. The handles
are unpainted, and not very well proportioned.

Of the third order, in respect to size, is a numerous
group of vases, bottles, jars, jugs, or pitchers. Great
variety of decoration has been employed on these examples, and, so far as it is possible to judge, I am willing
to accept the idea that two classes of this order are

Phœnician, or, at least, less Greek than either of the
others. The Egyptian and the Greek artists never, I
believe, departed from the true logic of design in en-
riching anything which came to their hands for the purpose of being decorated. They could, I sincerely believe,
never have brought themselves so far to outrage the
sense which was within them as to depart from its
instinct, and place on a vessel an ornament which did not
more or less completely harmonise with the contours of
the article itself. Concentric circles, enclosing diapers or
collars, of running patterns, as in the lotus bands before
named, all of which are continuous and complete in themselves, whether they include rosettes or chevrons, or
what not else, pertain to the Greeks, or their teachers,
the Egyptians.

Violations of this devotion, this instructive logic of
propriety, seem to me to indicate the art of a people
whose æsthetic conceptions were not high; and as to who
that people were, I think, admits no doubt. The Phœnicians alone, it seems to me, deserve the credit of
making "pots" on which circles are drawn which absolutely contradict the harmonic principle by existing in
upright, instead of horizontal, positions. There are very
many specimens of this nature, and they are all defective
in respect to grace of contour, the proportions of the
handles, and the positions of the handles where such
members occur, as well as in the proportions of the decorative elements to each other, and, above all, to the
vessels to which they character. Many of these relics
exhibit the concentric ring ornament which I have already associated with an Assyrian mode; nevertheless,
this does not militate against the reasonableness of the
notion which refers these ill-proportioned vessels to the
Phœnicians, or, at least, to a predominance of their
influence in Cyprus.

As a rule, Greek pots were so far "reasonable", that is,

logical, in the relationship of their construction and ser-
vices, that they do not fail to stand on their own bottoms.
Unless they were amphoræ, and devised to lean against
one another, be buried in sand as cisterns, or otherwise
serve as fixtures, or be propped on stands made for the
purpose—removableness not being essential in their cases
—all the Greek vessels subserve this rule of being capable
of standing upright. Now, on the other hand, but a very
small proportion of the so-called Phœnician vessels have
the slightest power of standing on their bottoms, for the
fact is, they will stand in any other position than the
upright one. Those which are furnished with base-rings,
and are, therefore, enabled to stand upright, have less of
the apparently indispensable elementary power of standing on their bottoms. Of course, there are Greek rhytons
which will only rest when inverted; but there was a
reason for that odd arrangement, which does not at all
affect what I have ventured to suggest.

Of late style, reminding one in some respects of the

Figs. 253, 254.   Jug.   Details of Fig. 253. *Terra-cotta.*

mediæval bellarmine, I discovered a jug (fig. 253) with
pyriform body, broad ribbon-shaped handle, and narrow
neck. The front of the neck and lip is ornamented in
a somewhat unusual manner with the bold relief of a

*   M M

female figure (fig. 254), closely draped, carrying a fictile vessel of a shape almost identical with the modern pitcher. This may, perhaps, be attributed to the fancy of a potter, rather than to the conventionalism of a type. The vase itself is 1 ft. 6 in. high.

The forms which are affected by *aryballi* are very various. Among others, one in the collection, nicely

Fig. 255.　　　　　Aryballos—Hercules.　　　　　*Terra-cotta.*

moulded, takes the form of the head of Hercules (fig. 255), covered with the skin of the lion's head, the ears, nostrils, and teeth of the vanquished animal being clearly shewn (fig. 256). The orifice by which a small portion

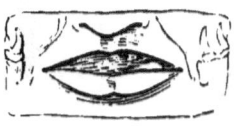

Fig. 256.　　　　　Details of Fig. 255.　　　　　*Terra-cotta.*

of the liquid to be preserved was introduced into the hollow interior of the vessel is placed at the top of the head. It is not improbable that this vessel, and others of a similar character, were purely ornamental in character, and, like the chimney ornaments of the present day, never employed to contain anything.

The excavations which I conducted at Kitium dis-

Fig. 257.   Aryballos—Silenus.   *Terra-cotta.*

closed an aryballos (fig. 257) in form of a Silenus, with heart-shaped beard, kneeling, with the hands placed upon

Fig. 258.   Aryballos.   *Terra-cotta.*

the thighs. The body is hollow, and the mouth is formed upon the top of the head of the figure.

Another aryballos is in form of one of the mis-shapen

Kerkopes, or thieves of Ephesus (fig. 258). The upper
part of a human figure, clasping the hands over the
stomach. is united to the hind legs of an animal. These
droll and thievish gnomes are reputed, according to the
legend, to have robbed Hercules while he was sleeping.
Some place the scene of their tricks at Thermopylæ,
others at Œchalia in Eubœa, or in Lydia.

Other moulded vases, chiefly of the class designated as
aryballi, take the shape of a goat reposing, with the head

Fig. 259.   Aryballos in form of a Goat.   *Terra-cotta.*

turned to the front (fig. 259); of a dog in a similar attitude (fig. 260); of a sheep, or she-goat (fig. 261). All

Fig. 260.   Aryballos in form of Dog.   *Terra-cotta.*

these figures have the orifice, or neck of the vessel, placed
in a small mouth fitted with a lip in the middle of the
back of the animal figure. They were found at Kitium,

one of the most prolific sites in the island of Cyprus with respect to archæological discoveries.

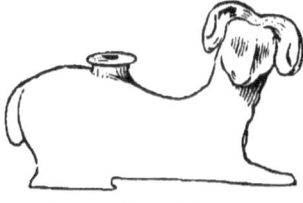

Fig. 261.   Aryballos in form of a Sheep.   *Terra-cotta.*

Of the same class is a cock (fig. 262), having the mouth of the vessel placed in the same position as in the

Fig. 262.   Aryballos in form of a Cock.   *Terra-cotta.*

preceding objects. This also comes from Kittium, and the general resemblance of these four little aryballi makes it reasonable to believe that they owe their origin to one and the same designer.

Among the curiosities of pottery to be found in this numerous aggregate is a basket, like a carpenter's basket, containing a bottle, the neck of which emerges at the side, while the edges of the basket have been sewn over the bottle. This relic (fig. 263) has evidently been made in a mould taken from "nature", *i.e.*, from a real basket and bottle, the meshes of the woven rushes are unmistakably due to "the life". The inscription in relief on one side is ΔΙΟΔΩ; on the other, ΔΙΟΩ—perhaps abbreviations of ΔΙΟΔΩΡΟΣ ΔΙΟΩΚΛΕΟΤΣ—"Diodorus, the son of Diocles".

Some of the oddly-shaped articles in terra-cotta are undoubtedly bottles; there is, of this class, the figure of a

Fig. 263.   Aryballos in form of a Basket and Bottle.   *Terra-cotta.*

goose, thrusting forth its head; another is a squatting
hen or duck about to take to the water; a third is a

Fig. 264.   Vase.   *Terra-cotta.*

Terra-cotta.

Subject of Fig. 264.

Fig. 265.

dove crouching, as if on the ground. A strange bottle is that which resembles an inverted amphora, with a neck stuck in itself; this is a monstrosity which would have shocked a decent Greek. Among the oddest of these things is that rather large one shaped like a child's whipping-top, and furnished with three bottle-necks. Several examples illustrate the same types of design, in form and direction, which Dr. Schliemann found at Hissarlik; a great many of them are so *bizarre*, that not all the courage and learning of that explorer could account for them.

Of later styles, I place here a vase, perhaps a variety of the *olpe*, resembling a lecythus, with a bowl-shaped body (fig. 264) and ample handle, the lower part adorned with petals or leaves, and the upper part of the bowl ornamented with a narrow band or frieze of ivy leaves. Round the bowl is painted in black colour a scene, which commences with a tripod or altar and a faun dancing before it, as in the accompanying wood-cut (fig. 265). Two winged boys, play-ing on a pipe or trumpet; a female harpist, resembling a terra-cotta statu-ette of a harpist in the collection, to which I have already drawn the atten-tion of the reader; two seated figures with the knees crossed, and the hands resting on them in a pensive and atten-tive attitude; and three groups of a male figure apparently lifting or sustain-

ing the frenzied or fainting form of a bacchante or
mænad who has become exhausted by the music and

Fig. 266.   Roman Vase.   *Terra cotta.*

revelry in which she has probably borne a conspicuous
part. Professional players on the harp and pipe are not
uncommon subjects upon painted vases (Birch, *Hist.*, 284).

A capacious goblet-shaped Roman vase (fig. 266) has
a frieze or upper border of masks or faces, evidently
satirical, and the subject painted upon the body appears
to be a parody or burlesque of some scene, perhaps of
the myth of Circe, the enchantress, in the ancient
theatre. It is well known that parody and caricature of
myths and historical legends were largely introduced
among the subjects of later painted vases. The subject
on the reverse side of this remarkable relic is reproduced
in fig. 267. It may possibly represent a scene in connection with some of the ancient Mysteries; subjects relating
to these being of sufficient frequency and importance to
be placed by Millingen in a separate class in his classifi-
cation of vases. It is 21 in. high, and 15 in. broad.

I am now compelled, by want of space, to conclude these chapters upon the terra-cottas, which might have been

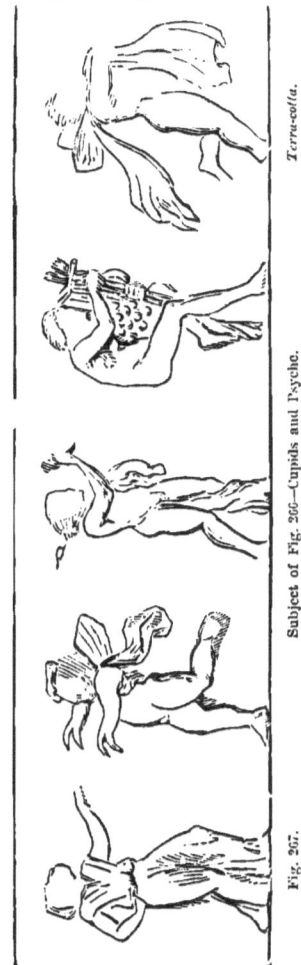

Terra-cotta.

Subject of Fig. 266—Cupids and Psyche.

Fig. 266.

easily augmented in size had I described all the interesting points in the vast collection of *fictilia* that the fertile soil of Salamis has, not without trouble and fatigue, yielded to the Lawrence-Cesnola collection. It has been my aim on this occasion, not so much to dilate upon every specimen which I was fortunately enabled to rescue from the silent site where it has slept for hundreds or thousands of years, as to put before the indulgent reader my own account of the points and details which seem to me to be most marked, and to call more especially for pictorial or descriptive illustration.

By these means I have endeavoured to convey to the archæologist a faithful idea of the ways and means of domestic life in the ancient days of Cyprus, mirrored alone, as is the case with other ancient sites, in the sepulchral surroundings of the shadowy homes of the dead. The field of Greek and Roman archæology had been, we are told by one who stands in the first rank as the historian of ancient pottery, almost exhausted by the labours of the learned for two centuries, but the discoveries which recent excavations in Cyprus have revealed, have thrown a new glamour over the ardour with which researches into early and archaic features of any art have always been prosecuted, and in some cases a modification of hitherto accepted opinions has resulted. The rearrangement of the archaic pottery of Hellenic origin in the new "First Vase Room" of the British Museum is an important outcome of the hypogeal harvest which those who have eyes to see may gather plenteously in the

Fumigator. *Terra-cotta.*

island of Cyprus ; and a very cursory inspection of that richly-freighted room is sufficient to show how greatly the island contributes to the unrivalled exhibition there made of early strivings of human art in this particular direction,—trammelled by technical difficulties in its inception, influenced by a nascent feeling of beauty in simple natural objects in its earlier stages of progress, and ultimately adopting, during its finest period, the forms of these very objects, and rendering them subservient to rules of conventionalism and practical utility.

Perhaps I shall be excused for introducing at the close

of this chapter a figure (269) of a Cypriote vase of glazed red ware, which properly should have been placed in an earlier part of the work. There is a very similar vase to this in the Archaic Vase Room of the British Museum. It belongs to the class already spoken of as *telina*; the mouth is closed, but a pipe opens from the base, and the vessel required to be inverted when it was to be filled, and then turned back upon its base. By these means the object could be filled with perfume for sprinkling the hands of distinguished visitors to the house of its owner

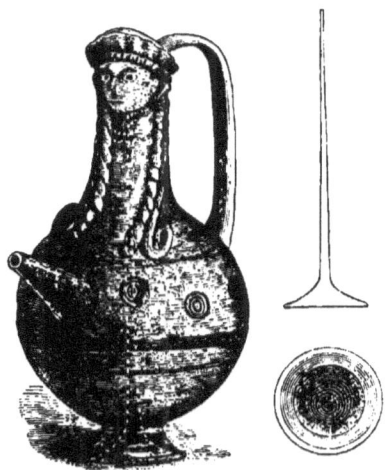

Fig. 269.   Cypriote Vase.   Terra cotta.

on festive occasions. The treatment of the curled hair of the figure, the concentric circles which constitute the decoration, and the very shape of the vessel, speak of the archaic times to which it must be referred. In respect of the hydrostatic arrangement of the interior, I believe this vessel is of the utmost rarity. I am indebted to Signor Vondiziani, a native of Larnaca, ex-Consul of Russia in Cyprus, for carefully restoring this vessel, which was broken to pieces when it was found.

CHAPTER XXI.

LAMPS.

HE number of lamps recovered from Cypriote sites is very large indeed. Their variety is almost equal to their number, for very rarely are two found to correspond in every particular.

According to the writer Clemens of Alexandria, the Egyptians[1] claim the credit of the invention of lamps. And Herodotus not only speaks of the "Feast of Lamps" at Sais on the Nile, but also of the lamp which was kept burning before the cow-shaped sarcophagus of the ancient King Mycerinus, of whom I have already given some account in an earlier chapter;[2] but no lamps, either of terra-cotta or any other substance, have been found which can justly be ascribed to ancient Egyptian times, nor, indeed, older than the Roman times. Lamps, *lychni* or *lucernae*, were made both by Greeks and Romans, and have been found in all sites occupied by these two important races of the old world.[3] They are almost always of terra-cotta (a few, of better class, being of bronze), and usually of circular shape, with one nozzle, termed *musus*, or *mykter*, for the wick, *myxa*, *thryallis*, *ellychnion* or *phlomos*, and a small handle, *ansa*;

---

[1] There is an often-quoted legend that Vulcan invented lamps, Minerva supplying the oil, and Prometheus the fire that kindled them.

[2] See pp. 137, 138.

[3] They were probably imported to the island of Cyprus in the age of the Consuls or during the reign of those native rulers who were dependent on the Imperial rulers of Rome.

the upper part, *discus*, being furnished with a hole for pouring in the oil, or *infundibulum*, anciently fitted with a stopper, of which there are but few specimens now extant. The word *myxa* gave the appellations *dimyxos* (fig. 270), *trimyxos, polymyxos* to lamps of two, three, or many

Fig. 270.   Dimyxos or Lamp for Two Wicks.   *Terra-cotta.*

nozzles. The *dimyxos* was also termed *bilychnis*. Greek lamps are to be distinguished from the Roman by their greater fineness, smaller size, paler material, and more delicate art, and above all by the inscriptions which they bear. Dr. Birch mentions, in his book on ancient pottery, a lamp formed in shape of two human feet in sandals. This may be compared with one in the Lawrence-Cesnola

Fig. 271.   Lamp.   *Terra-cotta.*

collection, found at Salamis (see fig. 271), which is here drawn to one-fourth the size of the original. It represents a human leg and foot, sandalled, with a Cupid or

Eros reclining on the instep. Another (fig. 272) shews a drunken actor—perhaps Silenus—masked, reclining on an amphora, and pointing in an explanatory and sug-

Fig. 272.   Lamp.   Terra-cotta.

gestive manner to his open mouth. Another (fig. 273) is the grinning head of a negress, with a gold earring in the right ear, to which I have already drawn attention.[1] Compare one in the Museum, the head of a negro, or

Fig. 273.   Lamp, with a Gold Earring in it.   Terra-cotta.

Nubian, with open jaws, through which the wick was inserted (Birch, *Hist. of Ancient Pottery*, new edition, 536). Most of the lamps with fanciful shapes are attributed by Dr. Birch to a period between the age of Augustus and that of Constantine. Some are in form of a human foot, or of a slipper. Many are of phallic design.

The earliest lamps have an open circular body, with a curved projecting rim (fig. 274), to prevent the oil from

[1] See page 36.

being spilled. They are found, not only in the ordinary terra-cotta, but also in the black glazed ware which we

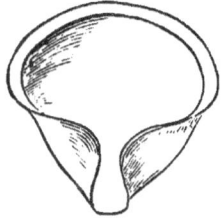

Fig. 274.　　　　Early Open Lamp.　　　　*Terra-cotta.*

are accustomed to associate with the sepulchral *fictilia* found at Nola. Many of them have a projecting hollow

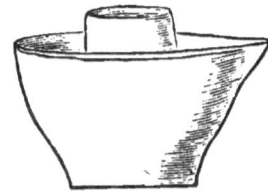

Fig. 275.　　　　Lamp with Hollow Pipe.　　　　*Terra-cotta.*

pipe in the centre, placed there in order to fasten them to a stick or upright peg upon the top of a candelabrum.

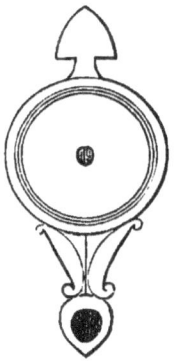

Fig. 276.　　　　Greek Lamp.　　　　*Terra-cotta.*

(fig. 275). These have no handles. Such a kind is shewn in the accompanying illustration.

Some of the larger sized lamps, and especially those of Greek origin, have a flat, triangular handle,[1] not unlike the barb of an anchor, which is either plain (fig. 276) or ornamented in various ways. Another in the collection has two nozzles. Among those of this class in the present collection are, one (fig. 277) having a bust of the

277.   279.

278.   280.
Figs. 277, 278, 279, 280.   Ornamented Lamp Handles.   *Terra-cotta.*

Moon-God placed upon a crescent enriched with spirals; another (fig. 278) with a galley and mariners; a third with an antefixal ornament and two dolphins naiant (fig. 279); and a fourth (fig. 280) with a similar antefixal and two palm branches.

Fig. 281 represents a circular lamp of the Roman

Fig. 281.   Circular Lamp.   *Terra-cotta.*

[1] One has a crescent-shaped handle, like that figured in Birch's *Hist. of Ancient Pottery*, New Edition, p. 506.

period, adorned with ten lancet-shaped cusps around its outer border, and a rosette or circular flower in the centre. This lamp, like the others, must be ascribed to a Roman period.

Fig. 282 shews an elegant lamp for four wicks, and having two *infundibula*, or holes for replenishing with oil. This was probably intended for use upon a can-

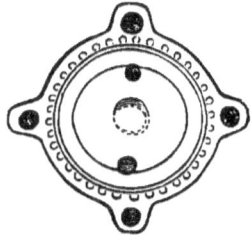

Fig. 282.　　　Four-wicked Lamp.　　　*Terra-cotta.*

delabrum. Round the *crater* or bowl of this lamp is the *limbus*, or decorated border of floral or other ornament.

Another Roman lamp of circular form (fig. 283) has an eagle rising, with the wings expanded, and the head turned over the back to the right. The eagle was a

Fig. 283.　　　Roman Lamp.　　　*Terra-cotta.*

favourite subject of ornamentation among the Romans on account of its connection with victory and military superiority.

O O

The annexed woodcut shews an oval lamp (fig. 285), perhaps of the Christian period, with an ornamental

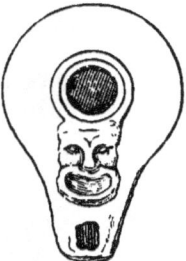

Fig. 284.   Lamp with Comic Mask.   *Terra-cotta.*

device, which may be a candlestick or a sacred mono-gram. The small figures appear very like Cypriote syllables.

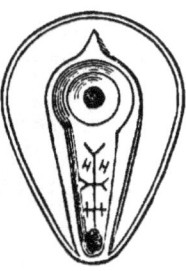

Fig. 285.   Oval Lamp.   *Terra-cotta.*

Among the lamps of later date and unconventional style may be mentioned that seen in fig. 286, where

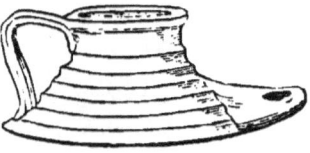

Fig. 286.   Late Lamp.   *Terra-cotta.*

the body is constructed in form of decreasing rows or bands, and is fitted with a handle, not unlike those seen on amphorae of a much older period.

I will conclude this short account of the numerous lamps with an illustration of the terra-cotta mould of a lamp (fig. 287), the device upon which is a head of considerable merit as a work of art. Fig. 288 represents a cast taken from it on a surface similar to that which

Figs. 287, 288.   Mould of a Lamp.   Terra-cotta.

would be afforded by a lamp. The other moulds (figs. 289, 290), of beautiful design, one of which has a figure of Mercury or Hermes, with caduceus, and a helmeted warrior, armed with a short sword, may be conveniently placed here.

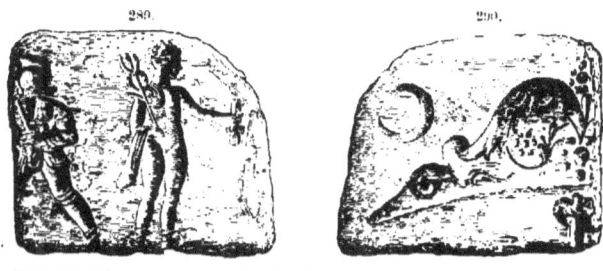

Figs. 289, 290.   Mould of a Lamp.   Terra-cotta.

Among the inscriptions I may record the subjoined list, among which occur names, in the genitive case, of

makers, some of them slaves, or of places and towns where
they were made, that of the pottery or the proprietor,
dedications, and private trade marks.

1.   CΦTPI   and   CΦT
      ΔΩΝOC   PIΔΩ
                              ΝOC

for CΦTPIΔΩΝOC.

2.   EΦT
      PIΔΩΝOC

The same with an E by mistake for the initial C.

3.   CΩTHPIΔΛ

4.   HΛTΛOT   and   HΛTΛ
                              OT

5.   EIP   and   EIPH
      HΛC   Λ   C

6.   EPMI   for EPMIΛΝOT.
      ΛΝO

7.   ΘEOΔO   and   ΘEOΔΩP
      POT

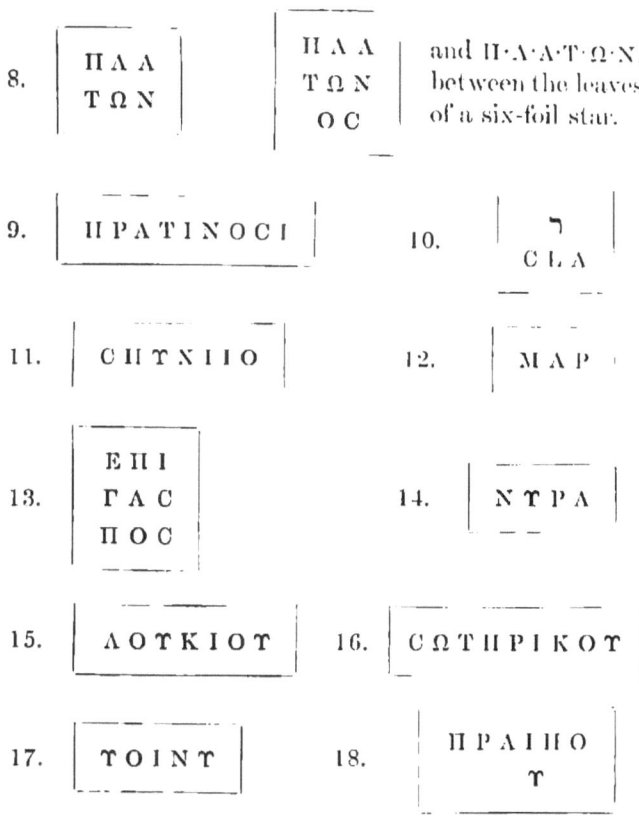

| 8. | Π Λ Λ
Τ Ω Ν | Π Λ Λ
Τ Ω Ν
Ο C | and Π·Λ·Λ·Τ·Ω·Ν.
between the leaves
of a six-foil star. |

9. Π Ρ Α Τ Ι Ν Ο C Ι

10. C L Λ

11. C Π Τ Χ Ι Ι Ο

12. Μ Α Ρ

13. Ε Π Ι Γ Λ C Π Ο C

14. Ν Τ Ρ Λ

15. Λ Ο Τ Κ Ι Ο Τ

16. C Ω Τ Π Ρ Ι Κ Ο Τ

17. Τ Ο Ι Ν Τ

18. Π Ρ Λ Ι Π Ο Τ

Among the private marks, or initials only, are:—A
hatched parallelogram; a diamond or lozenge; a human
foot, on the base of fig. 286; a bunch of grapes, on that
of fig. 281; a human hand, on that of fig. 284: X, I, T·N·.
A, ΠΝΟ, CE, M, Γ, I, ΠΝΤ, ΕΤΡ; COΘ, T, Λ. //, Π, Ɔ,
↓, A.M., and many others.

CHAPTER XXII

COINS.

OINS of a variety of types and countries, and in great numbers, are constantly found by the watchful excavator in Cyprus, for every dominant power has, in turn, left behind it these ancient and almost imperishable testimonies of its existence, buried in the soil where they were in former times the tangible and outward representative of wealth and all that empire possesses of resource and unity. I found numerous examples, in fairly good states of preservation, but generally very much clipped,[1] of Phœnician, Cypriote, Greek, Roman, Venetian, and Lusignan numismatics; but, inasmuch as most of these classes are well known, and have been treated exhaustively in works especially devoted to their elucidation, it is unnecessary for me to describe these coins on this occasion. I shall, however, here put on record a short notice of some of the Cypriote coins, because the knowledge which numismatists at present possess on this branch of Cypriote antiquities is very unsatisfactory, and for the most part tentative.

The only works on the subject of Cypriote coins which I have been able to consult are—that by M. le Duc de Luynes, entitled *Numismatique et Inscriptions Cypriotes*,

[1] This circumstance has been noticed by the writers on Cypriote coins.

fol. 1852 ;[1] a tractate by Mr. R. H. Lang, late Consul at Larnaca, upon two hoards of coins found at Larnaca or Kitium, in the *Numismatic Chronicle*, New Series, vol. xi; and a paper by M. le Comte de Vogüé, in the *Journal Asiatique*, August 1867, entitled " Inscriptions Phéniciennes de l'Ile de Chypre", with some further " Notes Épigraphiques" on the same subject, at p. 479, *et seq.*

Mr. Lang, describing the early specimens, states that to the coinage which has a punch-mark on the reverse, as in the earliest coins of Athens, numismatists generally assign a date anterior to B.C. 600 ; and as Cyprus was, at that distant period, in no way behind her neighbours in knowledge and practice of the arts, we may safely assume, he says, a similar date for the Cypriote coinage of that character. I believe, however, that all numismatists do not agree with this assumption.

Of these, I have a coin, bearing on the obverse a sphinx, seated, to the right, the wings expanded ; on the reverse a punch-mark (fig. 291). The sphinx was a common emblem of Assyria, and its use upon a Cypriote coinage may reasonably indicate the time when the

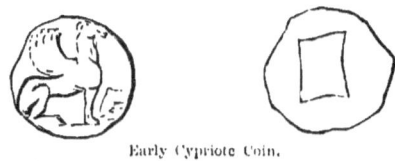

Fig. 291.   Early Cypriote Coin.   Silver.

Island of Cyprus was under the government, or a dependency of that mighty empire. This period may, perhaps, be about contemporary with the well-known and oft-recorded visit of the seven Kings of Cyprus to Sargon at Babylon B.C. 707. The same number of kings are said to have contributed towards the embellishing of the palace of Esarhaddon at Nineveh, about 670 B.C. Mr. Lang

---

[1] A fine work, as far as the numismatics and history are concerned, but greatly marred by the erroneous readings of the Cypriote characters.

gives their names as Ægisthus, King of Idalium; Pythagoras, King of Kitium; Ithodagon, King of Paphos; Eurylus, King of Soli; Damastes, King of Kurium, and the anonymous Kings of Salamis and of Tamissus. Several variants of the sphinx and punch-mark type are given by Mr. Lang, and the Duc de Luynes figures others. I cannot say whether my type is variant from these or not.

The ram was a favourite Cypriote emblem. It occurs on a coin of Evelthon, King of Salamis, which bears on the obverse a ram couchant to the left, with indistinct

Fig. 292.   Early Cypriote Coin.   *Silver.*

characters in the field. The reverse is a plain surface, or punch-mark. Mr. Lang mentions a type which bears a ram on the one side and a ram's head on the other, and the Duc de Luynes figures several other types, on which the ram or ram's head occurs.

Another coin of Evelthon in the collection bears (fig. 293) on the obverse a ram couchant to the right, with an

Fig. 293.   Coin of King Evelthon.   *Silver.*

inverted crescent enclosing a pellet and Cypriote characters in the field overhead, and in the exergue. On the reverse, within a cushion-shaped depression, an ornamental *crux ansata*. The devices of this type were known to the Duc de Luynes and to Mr. Lang. Another, probably of this class, is undetermined. The reverse is the same as that of the previous coin.

Fig. 294.   Cypriote Coin.   Copper.

The coins of Azbaal, King of Gebal, or Gabala, and Baalmelek, of which I possess several types (figs. 295, 296), are attributed, according to Mr. Lang, by the M. Le Comte de Vogüé, to Kitium, in the *Journal Asiatique*. They date about B.C. 560, according to Mr. Lang. In the British Museum collection of coins, a date of B.C. 448-410 is attributed to Baalmelek, and B.C. 410-387 to Azbaal. We have in this class (which bears

Fig. 295.   Coin of Azbaal or Baalmelek, King of Kitium.   Silver.

on the obverse a full-length figure of Hercules to the right, wearing a cloak, and lifting up a weapon in the right hand over his head, the left hand being stretched

Fig. 296.   Coin of Azbaal.   Silver.

out at full length; on the reverse, within a pearled or beaded square, is a lion devouring a stag, with Phœnician inscriptions in the field above them) the currency of Tyre, a currency which naturally was in large circulation

P P

in the Phœnician colonies of Cyprus, and, indeed, generally throughout the island. "The extensive number
and variety of the coins," says Mr. Lang, "both in silver
and gold, which have for reverse a lion devouring a stag,
seem to me to indicate a currency far greater than the
little colony of Kitium could pretend to. This is also the
only class of ancient coins which can with any likelihood
be attributed to Phœnicia; so that, in giving it to
Kitium, we remain without any known currency for
Tyre, then the chief emporium of commerce, and naturally
needing most largely a circulating medium. In assigning
to the coins of Azbaal and Baalmelek so early a date as

Fig. 297.   A Variant.   Silver.

B.C. 560, I am opposed to the views of the Duc de
Luynes; but the learned Duke himself expressed some
doubts upon the subject." Mr. Lang then proceeds to
examine the history of Tyre contemporaneously with
that of Cyprus during the sixth century B.C.

With respect to the origin of the device exhibited on
the reverse of this type, no satisfactory explanation has
been arrived at. Legends state that stags were accustomed to swim over to the rich pastures of Cyprus from
the mainland of Syria.[1]

Another of these coins is a variant of this type. Many

Fig. 298.   A Variant.   Silver.

[1] "Agri enim fertilitatem Ælianus prodit, cum scribat cervos ex
Syriâ in hanc insulam ad bonam pastionem transnatare."—*Ortelius.*

of them have been figured by the Duc de Luynes,[1] and by Mr. Lang in the works already referred to.

Fig. 299.   Early Cypriote Coin.   Silver.

A class not far removed from the foregoing bears on the obverse a ram couchant, to the left; reverse, a punch-mark. The ram appears to be a device pre-eminently of Cypriote use, but I am unable to conjecture the reason, unless the comparison of the form of the Island of Cyprus to that of a fleece[2] be connected with it. This type was not included in any of the coins found in the treasured hoards which I have already spoken of.

Another coin of this class, probably of Evagoras I, who liberated the Island of Cyprus from the Persian yoke, and restored the pure Hellenism of the country, which had been forgotten under the barbarian rule, bears on the obverse, within a pearled or beaded square, the forepart of a lion with open mouth, to the left; on the reverse an

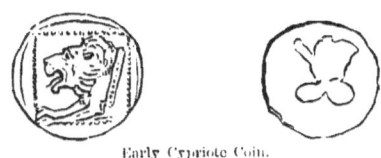

Fig. 300.   Early Cypriote Coin.   Silver.

[1] The Duc de Luynes accounts for the device of Hercules on the obverse of later coins as follows:—"Hercule, qui fut aussi le libérateur de ses contemporains, est un type naturellement choisi par Evagoras et peut-être la légende devant la tête du dieu y fait-elle allusion. Les lettres EY pour Evagoras sont ici le premier exemple de cet usage suivi depuis par les rois Cypriotes Nicoclès, Puytagoras, Evagoras II, et même Menelaüs, qui placèrent seulement quelques initiales sur leurs monnaies."

[2] " Formam ejus *velleri* comparari auctor Eustathius."—*Ortelius.*

uncertain device (fig. 300). It is of silver. This type was not included in Mr. Lang's hoards. I may here with propriety introduce the following extract, which gives a graphic and succinct account of the influence of Evagoras I on the history of Cyprus :—

"Citium, bien moins religieuse que commerçante, conserva son caractère primitif : le culte, la langue, les habitudes mercantiles de la mère patrie s'y maintinrent sans altération, ou du moins suivirent la même marche que sur le continent phénicien. Elle eut ainsi une existence distincte de celle des villes indigènes et des colonies grecques établies de toute antiquité sur différents points de la côte. Néanmoins elle suivit toujours le sort de l'île dans ses rapports avec les puissances voisines ; c'est-à-dire que, tout en conservant une certaine autonomie, elle fut successivement vassale des grands empires que se partagèrent la domination de l'Orient, l'Assyrie, l'Égypte, la Perse. Elle fut des premières à se soumettre à Salmanasar et à Nabuchodonosor, quand ces monarques envahirent le littoral Méditerranéen. La preuve matérielle de la conquête Assyrienne a été trouvée aux portes mêmes de Citium. C'est la stèle de Sargon, aujourd'hui conservée au musée de Berlin. Plus tard quand l'Égypte, sous la vingt-sixième dynastie, entra dans le concert Européen, les flottes de Citium, jointes à celles de Tyr et de Sidon, furent battues par les vaisseaux d'Apriès ou d'Amasis, et l'île subit la douce domination des souverains Égyptiens, jusqu'au jour où la victoire de Cambyse la fit passer sous la suzeraineté de la Perse.

"Dans les grandes guerres qui mirent aux prises les États naissants de la Grèce et les vieilles races de l'Asie, Cypre ne resta pas neutre, et les galères de Citium se mêlèrent aux flottes Phéniciennes qui portaient en Europe les hordes du grand roi. L'île fut le théâtre de luttes violentes dans lesquelles les villes Phéniciennes prirent parti pour les Perses contre les Athéniens, que soutenaient les colonies helléniques. L'avantage finit par rester aux Asiatiques : mais leur puissance sortit affaiblie de la lutte, et, pendant la seconde moitié du Ve. siècle, l'autorité du grand roi fut presque nominale. Les petits dynastes locaux, Grecs ou autres, prirent une plus grande importance, battirent monnaie en leur propre nom comme les Azbaal de Citium, et quand l'esprit hellénique se réveilla de nouveau sous la vigoureuse main d'Évagoras, il combattit avec avantage contre l'Asie. La lutte fut longue ; Citium, alliée naturelle des Perses, fut la dernière à se soumettre à Évagoras, mais elle eut la consolation de le voir perdre dans sa rade la victoire navale qui sauva au moins la suzeraineté persane.

"Évagoras fut le précurseur d'Alexandre par l'impulsion qu'il donna à la propagande hellénique en Orient ; avec lui, les lettres, les arts, les sciences de la Grèce prirent en Cypre un développement nouveau. Le mouvement se continua après sa mort, si ce n'est peut-être à Citium, où la petite dynastie des Melekiathon et des Pumiathon revint à la langue, aux types, aux usages nationaux. Cette réaction toute locale ne pouvait arrêter le courant qui poussait l'Occident en Asie, et quand Alexandre le Grand, porté par ce courant, eut envahi la Syrie, les rois grecs de Cypre, conduits par Pnytagoras, vinrent se joindre à lui et prendre leur part des victoires qui consacraient définitivement le triomphe de la Grèce sur la Perse. Citium ne put concourir à l'envahissement de la Phénicie à la prise de Tyr, mais elle dut sans doute à sa neutralité de perdre une partie de son territoire ; néanmoins elle conserva son autonomie jusqu'au jour où l'île entière fut annexée à l'unité gréco-égyptienne, en attendant le moment où elle devait disparaître dans l'unité de l'Empire Romain."—M. de Vogüé, *Journ. Asiatique*, 6 Ser., tom. x, pp. 113-115.

Coins of the type with a lion's head have been placed next to those bearing the punch-marked reverse. They are also probably to be ascribed to Evagoras I. Of these, I have one (fig. 301) upon which the obverse has a lion's head, with open mouth, to the right ; reverse, the fore-

Fig. 301.   Early Cypriote Coin.   *Silver.*

part of a lion, with the paws elevated, and the head reclining in a somewhat unusual manner.

Fig. 302 represents a class of coin of great interest for the bilingual inscription on it. The Cypriote characters are BA, NI, and correspond with the B.N. in Greek

Fig. 302.   Cypriote Bilingual Coin.   *Copper.*

capitals below. It is to be referred to Nicocles, or Nicocreon, son of Evagoras I, King of Cyprus.

The accompanying figure (303) represents a very beautiful silver coin of Nicocreon, or Nicocles, King of Cyprus, inscribed on the obverse ΝΙ; on the reverse ΒΑ. for ΒΑΣΙΛΕΤΣ.

Fig. 303.   Cypriote Coin.   Silver.

Next in order may be placed the undetermined and uncertain coins of Cyprus, among which is the type which bears on the obverse a bull statant to the left, with or without the so-called *mihir*, or flying bird, in the field overhead; on the reverse, with a rectangular counter-sunk compartment, a flying dove, a bird for which Athenæus says Cyprus was celebrated,[1] or an eagle. It is not very unlike the coins of Aristokypros, one of the earliest

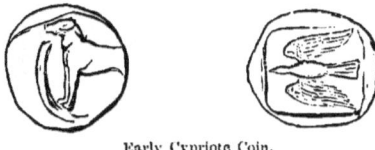

Fig. 304.   Early Cypriote Coin.   Silver.

rulers of the island. Another coin in the collection is a variant of this type (fig. 305). They are known to and

Fig. 305.   Early Cypriote Coin.   Silver.

described by the authors to whom I have already frequently made reference.

[1] " Eximias ejus columbas celebrat Athenæus."—*Ortelius.*

Another undetermined type is that shewn in fig. 306. On each side is a head in profile to the right.

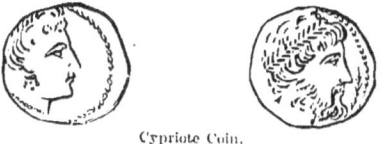

Fig. 306.   Cypriote Coin.   *Silver.*

The following figure (307) gives another undetermined type, the reverse bearing a wheel of four spokes.

Fig. 307.   Cypriote Coin.   *Silver.*

A coin with the same head of a lion as in fig. 301, to the left, on the obverse, and having a head of Pallas with a casque to the right on the reverse (fig. 308), I place

Fig. 308.   Early Coin.   *Silver.*

here, although it may be hereafter shewn to be of later date than many which come after it in the series.

The type of coinage which bears on the obverse a lion's head, and on the reverse a cross of the kind called *croix ancrée*, is described by Mr. Lang, and probably comes next in order of date.

An uncertain coin of common occurrence in Cypriote

Fig. 309.   Coin of Cyprus.   *Copper.*

diggings (fig. 309) bears on the obverse a lion ; on the
reverse a horse, with a star of eight points in the field.

The following is an electrum coin (310), the obverse of

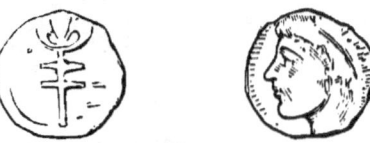

Fig. 310.   Coin of Cyprus.   Electrum.

which bears the head of Apollo, and the reverse a device
called the *croix ancrée* by Mr. Lang. The position in
the series of Cypriote coins is as yet undetermined.

The following coins, although of no great especial
value, are of considerable importance, as shewing how

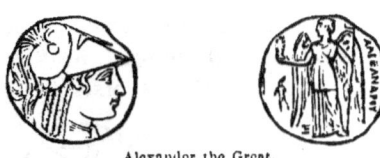

Fig. 311.   Alexander the Great.   Gold.

numerous were the currencies that passed in the Island
of Cyprus in the earliest days of the history of the
island. Staters of Alexander the Great (fig. 311) are of
frequent occurrence, and another coin of Alexander the
Great was found, of silver, the reverse being a seated
figure of Zeus to the left, holding a bird on his hand.

Fig. 312 represents a coin of Massicytes, in Lycia, in

Fig. 312.   Lycian Coin.   Silver.

fine preservation, found by me at a great depth of earth
in Salamis. It is interesting, not on account of its type.

which, I believe, is known to numismatists, but as shewing what coins were current in Cyprus at an early period.

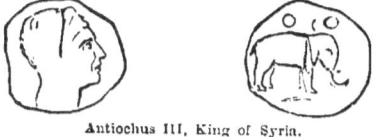

Fig. 313.   Antiochus III, King of Syria.   *Electrum.*

The coins of Antiochus III (fig. 313); of Corinth (fig. 314);

Fig. 314.   Corinth.   *Silver.*

of Eretria in Euboea (fig. 315); and many of uncertain and

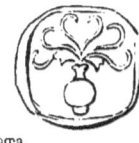

Fig. 315.   Eretria in Euboea.   *Silver.*

undetermined localities (fig. 316), are in the Lawrence-

Fig. 316.   Uncertain Greek Coin.   *Silver.*

Cesnola collection. Among others, I may refer to one of

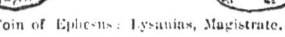

Fig. 317.   Coin of Ephesus: Lysanias, Magistrate.   *Silver.*

Ephesus (fig. 317), with the name of Lysanias, the magis-

Fig. 318.   Coin of Celenderis in Cilicia.   Silver.

trate; others of Celenderis in Cilicia (fig. 318); of

Fig. 319.   Coin of Miletus.   Silver.

Miletus (fig. 319); of Soli in Cilicia (fig. 320); of Judæa

Fig. 320.   Coin of Soli in Cilicia.   Silver.

(fig. 321), with an inscription purporting that the coin is

Fig. 321.   Coin of Judæa—the sixth part of a Shekel.   Copper.

the equivalent of a sixth part of a shekel; a coin of the

Fig. 322.   Coin of Rhodes.   Silver.

Island of Rhodes, with the name of the magistrate, Diognetus, ΔΙΟΓΝΗΤΟΣ, on the reverse, the obverse being designed with the beautiful portraiture of Phœbus Apollo in his character of the Sun God; a coin of a city of Phœnicia (fig. 323), perhaps Aradus; and lastly I will

Fig. 323.   Coin of a Phœnician City.   Copper.

mention a coin (fig 323) of Valerian the Elder, A.D. 253-260, for Attaleia in Pamphylia, bearing on the obverse figures of Nike, Artemis, and Athene. This last coin is believed to be of the greatest rarity. There is no specimen of it in the British Museum.

Fig. 324.   Coin of Attaleia.   Copper.

The legends are—*Obv.*, ΑΤ ΚΑΙ ΠΟ ΛΙ ΟΤΑΛΑΕΡΙ-ΑΝΟΝ ΕΤ . C. *Rev.*, ΑΤΤΑΛΕΩΝ.

Passing over, for the reasons already given, intermediate currencies of Byzantium and other places, which are well known to numismatists, and all of which are copiously represented by the result of my excavations, I shall conclude with the following observations upon the Latin Kings of Cyprus, of whose coins I found many fine examples. They form an interesting and unbroken series in the numismatics of that island. The

Lusignan dynasty held possession from A.D. 1192 to A.D. 1489, or for nearly three hundred years, eighteen princes having reigned during that time, of whom six are represented by coins in the Lawrence-Cesnola collection. The events which led to Guy de Lusignan, founder of the dynasty, becoming master of the island, are related in the valuable little volume on Cyprus, published in 1878 by Captain Savile, of the Intelligence Branch, Quartermaster-General's Department, Horse Guards. Abridged, and with slight alterations, the narrative is as follows :—

In the spring of 1191, Richard Cœur de Lion left Messina to join King Philip of France in the third Crusade. A storm dispersed his fleet, and a vessel which carried his sister, Queen Dowager of Sicily, and his *fiancée*, Berengaria of Navarre, was driven to Limassol, and, being refused entrance to the port, anchored in the roadstead. Cyprus was then under the rule of Isaac Comnenus. He had been appointed "Duke" by the Greek Emperor of Byzantium, but declared his independence, and assumed the title of "Emperor of Cyprus". This treacherous prince, who had already imprisoned the crews of three other English ships wrecked on the south coast, tried to seize the vessel containing the royal ladies ; but, Richard coming up from Rhodes with the remains of his fleet, frustrated the attempt, and avenged it by landing his troops and occupying Limassol. The arrogance and bad faith of Isaac obliged Richard to attack and defeat him at Colossi. The Cypriote army fled into the interior, and rallied again in the Messarian plain. Richard, meanwhile, in the presence of Guy, Lord of Lusignan in Poitou, ex-king of Jerusalem, and the Princes of Antioch and Tripoli, newly arrived in Cyprus, celebrated, on May 12th, 1191, his marriage with Berengaria. The history of the succeeding events is not clear. Probably some new treachery on Isaac's part determined Richard to follow and punish him. Guy de Lusignan occupied Famagusta.

Richard himself defeated and captured Isaac at Tremi-
tusia, marched upon Nicosia, which surrendered without
a blow, and reduced, one by one, the famous castles, Ky-
renia, Hilarion, Buffavento, and Cantara. Shortly afterwards, Richard sailed with his prisoner from Limassol to
S. Jean d'Acre, leaving the island in charge of R. de Can-
ville and Robert de Turnham. Isaac was confined and
died at Tripoli. Cyprus was now sold by Richard to the
Templars for 100,000 gold bezants, about £300,000 ster-
ling. The rule of the knights was severe and unpopular,
and, weary of their bargain, they begged that they might
be permitted to restore the island to Richard, and to
receive back the 40,000 bezants already paid on account.
The latter condition the king would not agree to; but at
last, Guy de Lusignan intervened, and, on paying Richard
60,000 bezants, was invested by him with the sovereignty
of the island, of which he took possession May 1192. Guy
now resigned his claims to the throne of Jerusalem, and
devoted himself to restoring order and tranquility in the
island. But he reigned scarcely two years, and, perhaps,
never actually assumed the title of King of Cyprus. He
died in April 1194, and was succeeded by his brother
Amaury.

I may appropriately conclude this chapter upon coins
with fig. 325, which represents a broken and imperfect jar

Fig. 325.   Hoard of Coins in a Jar.   Terra-cotta.

found at Salamis, containing a mass of bronze coins encrusted together so thoroughly, that very little could be

deciphered upon them. The jar was closed with a flat stone (fig. 326) of irregular shape, having upon it several lines of Greek capital letters, which I am inclined to believe were inscribed upon it to resemble an

Fig. 326.   Cover of Fig. 325.   *Stone.*

exorcism or anathema, in order that ignorant and superstitious finders might be deterred from robbing the hoard which the owner and depositor hoped at some future time to recover.

Larnaka (Kitium).

APPENDIX.

HE ancient map of which I give a reproduction is derived from that of Abraham Ortelius, and shows very clearly the principal sites of antiquity in Cyprus. With respect to the extant maps of the Island, I may refer to an article entitled, "The Cartography of Cyprus", in the *Athenæum*, No. 2647, July 20, 1878, pp. 84, 85; in which the writer, after disproving the widespread belief as to general want of correct information on the matter, refers to the *Recherches Scientifiques en Orient, entreprises par les Ordres du Gouvernement (Français) pendant les Années* 1853 *et* 1854, *par M. Albert Gaudry*, Paris, 1855, grand 8vo. In this work is contained the best information on Cyprus, as well as one of the best known and most elaborate maps of the island. The earliest detailed maps are of the sixteenth century, made in the time of the Venetian rule, one of the oldest being engraved by Bertelli, Rome, 1562; then follow those of the general atlases and other works of Ortelius, 1570; Mercator, 1595; Bleau, 1635; Coronelli, 1696; De Lisle, 1726; Dapper, 1688; Pococke, 1743; Drummond, 1754; Ali Bey, 1816; and M. Marcel Cerruti, Sardinian Consul at Larnaka, in 1844-1847, still, it is believed, unpublished. Then comes the Chart of Cyprus, by Captain Thos. Graves in 1849, republished with corrections in 1874. The map of the *Recherches* already mentioned, and that contained in the *Essai d'une Carte Agricole de l'Ile de Chypre, par MM. Albert Gaudry et Amédée Damour, dressé d'après la Carte Géographique inédite de M. de Mas Latrie,*

Paris, 1854. The last mentioned map was reproduced and geologically coloured in the *Mémoires de la Société Géologique de France*, 2me série, tom. vii, Mém. 3, Paris, 1859, 4to., but dated 1860. In 1862, the map of M. de Mas Latrie was published in his *Histoire de l'Île de Chypre sous le Règne des Princes de la Maison de Lusignan*, with a statistical table which forms a complete "Index Geographicus" of the whole of the island. The geological map above mentioned was reproduced by Unger and Kotschy in their work entitled, *Die Insel Cypern*, considerably reduced. There is also a good map in Von Löher's *Cyprus*. The writer of the *Athenæum* article also draws attention to the thirteenth century map in the *Peutinger Tables* at Vienna, and passes some strictures upon some recently published maps of the island.

The reader will observe a province or district in the ancient map that I have introduced at page 4, to which Ortelius has applied the name of SALAMINIA. Of this district, Salamis was the centre, or chief city. Now, as my discoveries and excavations were, with few exceptions, carried on within this area, I have selected, and I trust appropriately applied, the name for the title of my work. But, if the reader be inclined to criticise the use of this name in classical or ante-classical times, he may consider the word to be a neuter plural of the adjective Σαλαμίνιος, and to refer to the *Salaminian things* of which the Lawrence-Cesnola collection is composed.

The use of the golden foil of larger or smaller dimensions, and resembling one or other of the organs of the face, to lay upon the faces of the dead, a practice which has been well illustrated by my discoveries, and referred to at page 17, has been lately shewn to have prevailed in Egypt, by the discovery of a golden mouth modelled to represent the lips, upon a mummy of a somewhat late period, unrolled by Mr. C. Park of Russell Square. These golden lips are considerably thicker than the very thinly beaten foil which I and others have found in Cypriote tombs.

According to Ebers,[1] the late Mariette Pacha found in an older portion of the Apis catacombs of Memphis, a human body, with a golden mask on the face, and with many costly ornaments and amulets on the breast. From the accompanying inscriptions, it became known that these were the remains of Khamûs, the eldes

[1] *Egypt*, vol. i, p. 164.

son of the monarch Rameses II, who was high priest at Memphis, and is often mentioned as a particularly pious prince. He died during the lifetime of his father, and seems to have been buried among the sacred Apis Bulls as a special distinction above others.

I am indebted to Mr. William Chappell, F.S.A., the author of *The History of Ancient Music*, for the following notes on the flute figured at p. 56.

"The Greek *bronze* flute discovered by Major di Cesnola, during his excavations in the Island of Cyprus, is the only one of the kind that has been found, but it is in too fragile a state to be played upon. Nevertheless, by careful measurements, an exact copy has been made in brass, by Mr. R. Carte, the celebrated flutist, and his son, Mr. Henry Carte, and this reproduces the notes of the original instrument. They are nearly those of the modern chromatic scale, the lowest note being C in the bass staff, while the treble extends to G, an octave and half above it. The notes produced by the model are thirteen: C, C sharp, D, D sharp, E, F, G, A, B flat, B, C, E, G.

"This scale is very like that of the ivory flutes found in the excavations at Pompeii, and now in the museum at Naples. However, one of the latter has a B below the bass C, and it has both F sharp and G sharp, which seem to be deficient in the bronze flute. Again, the Pompeian flutes ascend from the upper C to C sharp, and stop there, while the bronze flute ascends from upper C to E and G.

"These Greek instruments would now fall rather under the denomination of pipes than of flutes, because they were not held transversely, as is the modern flute, but longitudinally, and they were played from the end by a reed held in the mouth, as is the clarionet. The bore is cylindrical, as in the flute and clarionet, in contradistinction to hautboy and bassoon, which are slightly conical, and thereby require another form of reed to sound them. Cylindrical pipes require the flapping reed, one form of which is found in the clarionet, and another in the bagpipe. The latter kind is enclosed within the mouth, the lips extending beyond the vibrating part, and reeds of this kind are used in Egypt to this day in the little *arghool* or double flute. Dr. Stainer was kind enough to lend one of the *arghool* flutes in his collection to Mr. Henry Carte, who made an exact copy of the reed, and by proper adjustment, as to length, for the model he had taken, he succeeded in producing the above named scale.

"In place of the keys used in modern flutes to sound extra notes

R R

which the fingers do not cover, the Greeks used flat rings of
metal round the tubes of their flutes, and bored through them into
the tube.[1] Then the rings could be turned slightly round, so as
to cover or uncover the holes in the body of the flute, and thus
the notes which were to be used in the scale that the player had
selected, were adjusted to his requirements, and all others were
temporarily stopped. The Greek chromatic scale had only seven
notes in the octave, not twelve, as in the modern chromatic
scale."

An interesting experiment[2] was made about four years ago
by M. Victor Mahillon, Conservator of the Museum attached to
the Conservatoire of Music at Brussels, with a view to determining the tone and compass of the ancient *ivory* flutes found at
Pompeii, of which there are four in the museum at Naples. The
simplest of the four was selected by M. Mahillon for an experiment for reconstruction, which he undertook with the double
object of preserving these precious instruments from the too frequent handling of the curious, and of determining their tone and
compass. The pipe in question measures exactly twenty-one
English inches, and it is composed entirely of ivory, the bore
cylindrical in its whole length, and the ivory tube covered with
metallic rings of bronze and silver, which turn to the right and
left, but are kept from moving up or down by a fixed ring below
them holding them in their respective positions. By means of
these turning sockets, which are each pierced with a side-hole
establishing communication with the corresponding hole in the
ivory tube, the executant was able to suppress at will those he did
not wish to employ. It is plain from the shape of the cup of the
bore, that it was destined to contain a reed ; but the question was
" What sort of a reed ?" M. Mahillon fortunately was acquainted
with the Egyptian *arghool* flutes, an instrument of reed-cane,
described by Villoteau, a specimen of which is in the Brussels
Museum. The *arghool* is of cylindrical bore, pierced with
lateral holes, like the Pompeian flute. The latter is of Greek
origin, the Greeks, again, having borrowed the greater number of
their instruments from Egypt. M. Mahillon therefore chose the
reed of the *arghool* flute, which is a striking reed, with which to
make his experiment ; and, after one or two trials as to the dimen-

[1] A careful examination of the flute shows several rings of this nature
upon it.   [2] *Musical World*, March 1878.

sions to be given to it, he succeeded in making the pipe speak as he desired. The problem seemed to him to be solved for the following reasons :—The double-reed (hautboy and bassoon) is, it is stated, always connected with conical pipes, never with cylindrical. The striking reed makes the cylindrical pipe of the clarionet vibrate. It was, therefore, the sort of reed which ought to be selected. The mouthpiece of the clarionet was unknown to the ancients, therefore it was necessary to find a different mode of application, which M. Mahillon discovered in the *arghool*, the reed of which is let entirely into the mouth, the lips being applied on the pipe where it is introduced. When blown into, the tongue of the reed vibrates, and provokes the vibration of the column of air. Admitting that the chromatic scale was known to the ancients, and the division of the tube by thirteen rings being given, it was permissible, therefore, to believe that the right reed was found if the thirteenth sound was the octave of the first. This M. Mahillon found to be the case when he had discovered the correct length of which to make the reed. By this means, he gives B second line in bass clef as the grave note of the instrument ; and, by the opening of the successive lateral holes, the following sounds are produced :—C sharp, D, E, F, F sharp, G, G sharp, G sharp, A, B flat, B natural. The absence of C and of D sharp is accounted for by the fact that the second and fifth of the rings are not bored. The hole of which the open- ing gives B flat is on the other side of the instrument, and is closed by the thumb of the left hand. When the ring which opens the A is turned to the other side, it puts in communication with the air a lateral hole pierced in the ivory tube, a little above that which gives G sharp, and which produces a second G sharp, a little higher in pitch than the preceding one. The second G sharp establishes two quarters of a tone between G and A. The G is too low by nearly a quarter of a tone. The defect M. Mahillon thought it necessary to reproduce, in order to make the copy exact ; and he thinks that possibly the cause of it may be a restoration which has been visibly made in the model at the exact place of this hole. To produce the sound, the performer intro- duces the reed and a part of the ivory mouthpiece into the mouth, so that the lips rest on the widest part of the mouthpiece. When blown into in this position, the side holes being closed, the lowest sound is obtained. It is curious that the tone of this instrument corresponds exactly with that of an instrument of which M.

Gavaert, Director of the Conservatoire at Brussels, in his researches, was led to conjecture the existence, but of which he could find no precise indications in the ancient authors. Its compass he imagined to be from D, third line in bass clef, to F, second space in treble clef, corresponding, allowing for the elevation of pitch, to one D in the great octave to D in the small octave. M. Gavaert requested M. Mahillon to construct an instrument of this compass, which was practicable, and confirmed the former's suppositions as to the tibia *plus que parfaite* of the ancients. This was done in the summer of 1877; and in the following October, M. Gavaert and M. Mahillon went together to Naples, where they had occasion to study the Pompeian flutes, with the interesting results which are here described. Since then, M. Mahillon has reconstructed the most perfect of the four flutes, applying again the striking reed of the arghoul in connection with the cylindrical pipe, and has got the following sounds from B, second line in bass clef: C, C sharp, D, D sharp, E, F, F sharp, G, G sharp, A, B flat, B natural, C, C sharp. It may be interesting to know that M. Mahillon has also made an exact copy of the Roman trumpets in the museum at Naples, and has found them to have the following compass, starting from G below the line in treble clef:—B, E, G, B flat, C, D, E, F sharp, G, of which the real effect is just a quarter lower than the note written.

As a curious survival of ancient forms, the broken head of a musician, part of whose double pipe still remains carved on his lips, and held in position by the φορβειά, or φόρβιον, figured at p. 93, represents the practice of a kind of music even yet in vogue among the swains of the Mediterranean islands. In a communication recently inserted in the *Standard* (February 7), Mr. II. John states:—"I have frequently seen the player of the tibia contriving to play upon two pipes at once in Sicily. In that island, the pastoral life of ancient Europe is mirrored, or, at least, represented with little change. I once lived in a farmhouse in the province of Messina, and I remember how much I was struck with the skill of one of the farmer's sons in constructing and playing on the double flute. The two members of the instrument were fashioned out of the local reed with his pruning-knife. One was designed for the sharp notes, the other for the droning accompaniment. He inserted the two mouthpieces between his lips, close together, the ends spreading out in the manner that is familiar to every one in classical paintings. The music was rude, and, perhaps, to ears that have been over-cultivated with the mosaic melodies of the present day, it might sound barbarous; but to me, in the short twilight, with the mountains behind, the Straits of Messina and the Calabrias in front, these rustic airs, simple and plaintive—perhaps the same notes that might have been heard in the days of Virgil, and perhaps even of Homer—were inexpressibly beautiful."

My readers will, I am sure, pardon my introducing here, *apropos* of the "double pipe", a charming sonnet, recently published by Mr. Gosse, in which that poet, like Mr. John, recognised the plaintive sweetness of the music :—

> " Cool, and palm-shaded from the torrid heat,
>   The young brown tenor puts his singing by,
>   And sets the twin-pipe to his lip to try
> Some air of bulrush-glooms where lovers meet.
> O swart musician ! time and fame are fleet ;
>   Brief all delight, and youth's feet fain to fly !
>   Pipe on in peace ! To-morrow must we die ?
> What matter, if our life to-day be sweet !
> Soon, soon, the silver paper-reeds that sigh
>   Along the Sacred River will repeat
>   The echo of the dark-stoled bearers' feet,
> Who carry you, with wailing, where must lie
> Your swathed and withered body, by and by,
>   In perfumed darkness with the grains of wheat."

As a strange coincidence which occurred during the progress of my excavations, I am desirous of recording that the interesting

Coin of Queen Cleopatra.   *Silver.*

terra-cotta statuette of a genius riding on a cock, having the plinth furnished with the Greek inscription given on p. 207, was taken from a spot not many feet from that wherein I found the coins of a Queen Cleopatra figured above. There is little doubt as to the age of the terra-cotta, or the motive which prompted the addition of the inscription to it, when we bear thus in mind the peculiar circumstance that a coin shewing a similar inscription should be found in such close contiguity to the fictile relic.

The native characters and language used by the early inhabitants of Cyprus are not yet completely understood, although much has been done to settle their position among the alphabets and dialects of the world. The first antiquary who appears to have attempted the decipherment of the Cypriote inscriptions was the Duc de Luynes, in his *Numismatique et Inscriptions Cypriotes*, published privately in 1852. In this work, we are told,[1] he gave an elaborate account of all the then known Cypriote inscriptions, with plates of the texts, and a list of all the Cypriote forms and characters. They consist of legends on coins, bronze objects, rocks, stone slabs, and other antiquities. One group or word of very frequent occurrence on these inscriptions, especially on the coins, the Duc de Luynes proposed to identify with the name of Salamis, the name of the principal ancient city in the island; another group he identified with the name of Amathus, another city, and he proposed readings for several other words, but his attempts failed, owing to his having assumed a wrong basis in the supposed identification of Salamis and Amathus.

The next attempt to read the Cypriote inscriptions was made by Professor Röth of Heidelberg, who, following in the same track as the Duc de Luynes, published a memoir, entitled *Proklamation des Amasis*, in 1855, under the auspices of the Duc de Luynes, who had already published a *facsimile* of his inscription in the work mentioned above. Professor Röth, however, unfortunately accepted as proved the identification of the words Salamis and Amathus, and, starting from this erroneous point, proposed phonetic values for all the Cypriote characters, and applied his system to the long inscription known as the "Tablet of Idalium", of the whole of which he published a supposed translation. According to the Professor, this was a decree of Amasis, King of Egypt, B.C. 571-527, addressed to the inhabitants of Cyprus.

[1] *English Cyclopædia—Arts and Sciences* (supplement), col. 1369.

After this attempt at decipherment of the inscriptions, a considerable number were added to the known list by Mr. R. H. Lang, formerly British Consul at Larnaca, the Comte de Vogüé (in the *Journal Asiatique*, 1868), Helfferick in 1869, and others. To these it has been my good fortune to contribute a goodly number, sculptured, engraved, or painted, upon tablets, gems, and other objects of antiquity, as will be seen on reference to the articles described in the text of this work, on which they occur.

But, just as in the case of the Egyptian language, which baffled the attempts of philologists to unravel its meaning until an ancient side-by-side translation had been discovered in the Rosetta stone; in like manner, a stone formerly the pedestal of a statue, inscribed with a bilingual inscription, consisting of three lines of Phœnician and four lines of Cypriote, was discovered by Mr. Lang, whose collection of seven inscribed stones and a number of coins is now in the British Museum; and this discovery proved to be of the greatest importance, for it formed the key to the deciphering of the hitherto undiscovered language. To Mr. Lang belongs the honour of discovering the group of characters which the Duc de Luynes had read *Salamis*, to signify *king*;[1] but, at the time, the sound of the Cypriote word, and therefore the nature of the language, was yet unknown.

The next step in the progress of discovery I will venture to quote in the words of the work already mentioned: "Mr. George Smith, of the Department of Oriental Antiquities, British Museum, simultaneously discovered the word *king*, and read the proper names. . . . . . From these proper names he found the phonetic values of about forty of the Cypriote characters, and came to the conclusion that these characters formed a syllabary, consisting in all of about fifty-four characters, of which about twelve represented different forms of the vowels, while the others were used for the consonants. There were about three forms for each consonant, each one representing it combined with a different vowel. Mr. Smith gave a translation of the opening passage on the bilingual inscription, but he could not give any reading for the bronze plate inscription; he, however, conjectured the language to be allied to the Greek. Mr. Smith's results were also published at the Society of Biblical Archæology, 7 November 1871."

The next link was added by Dr. Birch, Keeper of the Oriental Antiquities in the British Museum, into whose charge the stone

---

[1] These observations were laid before the Society of Biblical Archæology on the 7th November 1871.

which occupies the same important relation to Cypriote philology
that the Rosetta Stone does to the philology of Egyptian Hieroglyphics, passed. He established the fact that the language of
the Cypriote inscriptions was closely allied to the Greek:—

" Κύπρος¹ πόλις μεγάλη· δῆμοι τὴν γλῶτταν ἀκριβῶς "Ελληνες",

and published, in the *Transactions* of the Society already mentioned,² tentative translations of the bilingual text and the inscription upon the bronze tablet of Dali, in which he makes a number
of comparisons between the Cypriote words and their Greek equivalents.

Subsequent attention has been given to this interesting subject
by M. Halévy, whose researches, now rejected by scholars, were
published in 1872; in the *Sammlung Kyprischer Inschriften in
Epikorischer Schrift* of Moriz Schmidt, Professor at Jena, published
at that city in 1876; and in Dr. W. Deecke's *Der Ursprung der
Kyprischer Syllenschrift*, Strasburg, 1877, as well as in several other
works.

Mr. Hyde Clarke has kindly furnished me with some philo-
logical notes on the early language of Cyprus, which I regret I
am unable to introduce on this occasion. I will be content to
quote the concluding sentences of his communication, which are
as follow:—"With regard to the comparative philology and
grammar of the Palæocypriote, the Akkad, of course, supplies
materials, as also do the living languages which are allied to the
Akkad. Although the old languages of the Mediterranean were
related, they differed greatly in vocabulary and development.
Thus I know that Cypriote differed from the Etruscan and Palæo-
Latin on the west, and from the Cretan and the Khita, the
Canaanitic and the Lydian on the east. The Cypriote characters
are, like all others, derived from an earlier stock, of which even
the Khita only constitutes a secondary representative, and it has
most probably only a general relationship to those characters
which we now know as cuneiform; the approximations of Professor Deecke proving the community of origin without always
establishing identity."

For the convenience of reference I subjoin a table of the characters and their equivalents as far as they are at present deciphered:—

¹ Himerius, *Ecl.*, xviii, 1. (Schmidt).
² Vol. i, Part ii (read January 2nd, 1872).

EQUIVALENTS.	CYPRIOTE CHARACTERS.
a.	✳ ✳ ✳ ⟩⟨ or ⟩⟨ (leaden plate)
e. {	✳ ⟩⟨ ⟩⟨ ⟩⟨ ⟩⟨ ⟩⟨ K K K (P.) ¥
	⧊ ⧊ ⧊ ⦙⦚ ⦙⦚ ⧧ (Hissarlik) ⊣⦙ (Dali)
i.	⅄ ⅄
o, ω.	⧬ ⧬ (⊥ ro at Paphos) ↓ ↓ ↓ ⧬
u.	⋎ ⋎ ⋋ ⌣ ∧ (∧ Ktima) ↲
ka, ga, or χa.	⊥ ⊥ ⊥ ⌂ ⊥ △
ke, ge, or χe.	⧦ ⧦
ki, gi, or χi.	⊻ ⊻ ⩲ ⩲
ko, go, or χo.	∩ (∧K) ∧ ⊓ ⊓
ku, gu, or χu.	⧬ ⧬ ⧬
ta, da. or θa.	⊢ ⊣ ⅄
te, etc.	⅄ ⅄ (G.)² ⅄ ⅄ ⅄
ti, etc.	⇑ ⇑ ⇑ ⋏ ⋏ ⋏
to, etc.	F F F ⊼ ⊼ ⊼ ⋌ T ⊼ (K) ⋌ ⋌ ⋌
ba, pa, or φa.	⧻ ⧻
be, etc.	S ⋨ ⋨
bi, etc.	⩒

EQUIVALENTS.	CYPRIOTE CHARACTERS.
lo, etc.	Π Λ Λ $\int$ (P.) $\int$
lu, etc.	ω ω
la.	$\asymp$ $\asymp$ $\triangle$
le.	8 (G.) $\cancel{\chi}$ ($\cancel{\pi}$ Γ) $\widehat{T}$ (P.) $\widehat{\omega}$ (K.) $\wedge$
li.	$\angle$ $\sqsubset$ $\sqsubset$
lo.	$+$
lu.	$\widehat{\cap}$ $\widehat{\cap}$ $\overline{\pi}$ (l.p.)
ra.	$\triangledown$ Ω Ω ϱ
re.	$\widehat{\cap}$ $\widehat{\cap}$ $\widehat{\sqcap}$ $\overline{\sqcap}$ $\wedge$ (G.) $\cancel{\varkappa}$ (l.p.)
ri.	$\cancel{7}$ $\cancel{7}$ $\nwarrow$ $\nwarrow$ $\flat$
ro.	ℓ ℓ χ $\cancel{\chi}$ $\cancel{\chi}$ $\cancel{\chi}$ (K.)
ru.	$\rangle$ $\supset$,c $\ll$ $\Vdash$
na.	$\top$ $\top$ $\mp$
ne.	$\cancel{\text{\char}}$ $\cancel{\text{\char}}$ $\cancel{\text{\char}}$ $\cancel{\text{\char}}$ $\cancel{\text{\char}}$ $\cancel{\text{\char}}$ (G.)
ni.	$\angle$ $\cancel{Z}$ $\cancel{Z}$ ш лг
no.	$\gamma\gamma$ $\cancel{\gamma}$ $\gamma\gamma$ V (l.p.)
mа.	$\cancel{)(}$ $\cancel{)(}$
me.	$\cancel{\lambda}$ Υ $\cancel{\lambda}$ $\cancel{\lambda}$ $\cancel{\lambda}$ $\times$ $\cancel{\lambda}$ $\cancel{\lambda}$ $\cancel{\lambda}$ $\cancel{\lambda}$
mi.	Υ $\Upsilon\Upsilon$ $\Lambda\Lambda$

¹ Ktima.

Equivalents.	Cypriote Characters.
mo.[1]	
mu.	
ja.	
je.	
ji.	
ϝa. (digamma).	
ϝe.	I I I H (G.) Z (P.)
ϝω.	(K.) ⊥ (P)
sa.	V ∨ Y γ
se.	
si.	
	(P.)
so.	
su.	
xe.	
ζa.	
ξω.	

---

¹ To this may be added ⊟ the rectangle with *horizontal* bar, instead of perpendicular, as seen in the inscription given by me at page 89, fig. 83, which I read provisionally as *mo*, also.

Terra-cotta Statuette.

INDEX.

LIST OF FIRST SUBSCRIBERS.

Five Hundred Copies only have been Printed. This list includes only those Subscribers whose names were received before the Printing was completed.—A. P. C.

Adams, J. S., Esq., 88, Holland Park, W.

Baxter, Mrs., The Tower, Fitzjohn's Avenue, Hampstead.
Baglioni, Leopoldo, Esq., 20, Via Roma, Turin, Italy.
Barker, T. J., Esq., Avon House, Steele's Road, Haverstock Hill, N W.
Bennoch, F., Esq., F.S.A., 5, Tavistock Square, W.C.
Best, W. M., Esq., Gresham Club, E.C. (*Two copies*).
Biehl, Thomas, Esq., Muswell Hill, London.
Birch. Samuel, Esq., LL.D., F.S.A., British Museum.
Birch, Walter de Gray, Esq., F.S.A., F.R.S.L., British Museum.
Bird, P. Hinckes, Esq., F.R.C.S., F.L.S., 1, Norfolk Square, W.
Blair, Robert, Esq., South Shields.
Boase, Charles W., Esq., M.A., Exeter College, Oxford.
Brayshaw, T. H., Esq., Manager of the Eastern Telegraph Company, Larnaca, Cyprus.
Brent, Cecil, Esq., F.S.A., 37, Palace Grove, Bromley.
Brent, Francis, Esq., F.S.A., 19, Clarendon Place, Citadel Road, Plymouth.
Brock, E. P. Loftus, Esq., F.S.A., 19, Montague Place, Russell Square.
Brooke, Thomas, Esq., F.S.A., Armitage Bridge, Huddersfield.
Browne, Mrs., Gloucester Villa, Somerset Road, Ealing.
Burroughs, T. Procter, Esq., F.S.A., The Priory, Great Yarmouth.

Caruana, Dr. A. A., Librarian to the Public Library, Malta.
Carter, Mrs., 8, Powis Square, Bayswater.
Chapman, Thomas, Esq., 37, Tregunter Road, West Brompton.
Clark, George T., Esq., F.S.A., 44, Berkeley Square, W.
Clarke, Hyde, Esq., 32, St. George's Square, S.W.
Cobham, C. Delaval, Esq., Commissioner, Larnaca, Cyprus.
Cole, Mrs., 64, Portland Place, W.
Coles, Jno., Esq., 4, Kensington Park Gardens, W.
Cotton. F. S., Esq., The Knoll, West Hampstead.

Davis, Rev. Edwin John, English Episcopal Chaplain at Alexandria.
De Martino, Cav. Eduardo, 2, College Crescent, Belsize Park.

Evans, John, Esq., D.C.L., F.R.S., F.S.A., 65, Old Bailey, E.C.

Gamba, Professor Alberto, Corso Vittorio Emanuele, 30, Turin.
Gancia, R., Esq., 13, Southwark Street, S.E.
Gosselin, Hellier, Esq., 28, Cranley Gardens, South Kensington.
Greg, R. P., Esq., F.S.A., Coles, Buntington, Herts.

Hardy, W. B., Esq., 92, Portland Place, W.
Harrison, Charles, Esq., F.S.A., 17, Queen's Gate Place, S.W.
Hay, Lord John, Admiral of the British Royal Navy, Fulmer Place
    Fulmer, Slough.
Haynes, Henry W., Esq., 239, Beacon Street, Boston, Mass., U.S.A.
Hall, Isaac H., Esq., 725, Chesnut Street, Philadelphia, U.S.A.
Herbert, J. R., Esq., R.A., The Chimes, West Hampstead.
Hildebrand, Herr Hans, Antiquary of the Kingdom of Sweden, Stockholm.
Hill, Charles, Esq., F.S.A., Rockhurst, West Hoathly, Sussex.
Hill, Henry, Esq., F.S.A., 2, Curzon Street, W.
Holman, George, Esq., 5 and 6, Great Winchester Street, E.C.
Horn, G., Esq., 150, Sloane Street, S.W.

Johnston, Alexander, Esq., 1, College Villas, South Hampstead.

Klincksieck, M. C., Esq., Paris.
Killerby, B. F., Esq., 65, Cornhill, E.C.   (*Three copies.*)

Lambert, George, Esq., F.S.A., 10, Coventry Street, Piccadilly
Lawrence, Edwin Henry, Esq., F.S.A., 84, Holland Park, W.
Layard, Sir Austen Henry, K.C.B., 3, Saville Row, London.
Lewis, Rev. S. S., M.A., F.S.A., Corpus Christi College, Cambridge
Liebleim, Professor F., Christiania, Norway.
Library of the Corporation of the City of London, Guildhall.
Lyndon, Miss J., Clinton, British Columbia.

Manchester Free Library, Chas. W. Sutton, Esq., Chief Librarian.
Mann, Richard, Esq., 5, Charlotte Street, Bath.
Mauleverer, Miss A., The Mall, Armagh, Ireland.
Menabrea, Marquis de Val Dora, General of the Italian Army and
    Italian Ambassador, 35, Queen's Gate, South Kensington.
Merrill, Moses, Esq., Public Latin School, Warren Avenue, Boston,
    Mass., U.S.A.
Moore, W. B., Esq., 62, Belsize Park Gardens, N.W.   (*Two copies.*)
Morgan, Thomas, Esq., F.S.A., Hill Side House, Palace Road, Streatham
    Hill

Moss, Robert, Esq., Moreland House, Seaforth, Liverpool.

Nixon, Edward, Esq., Saville House, Methley, Leeds.

Ogle, Harman Chaloner, Esq., Magdalen College School, Oxford.
Orgill, Mrs., Springmead, Rosslyn Park, Hampstead. *(Two copies.)*

Parker, J. H., Esq., C.B., F.S.A., Ashmolean Museum, Oxford.
Palmer-Stone, H., Esq., 7, King Street, St. James's.
Pellas, Eugenio, Esq., 67, Cornhill, E.C.
Picrides, Demetrius, Esq., Larnaca, Cyprus.
Phené, J. S., Esq., LL.D., F.S.A., Oakley Street, S.W.
Phillips, Rev. George, D.D., Queen's College Lodge, Cambridge.
Pitt-Rivers, General A., 4, Grosvenor Gardens, W.
Powis, the Right Hon. the Earl of, 45, Berkeley Square, W.
Price, John Edward, Esq., F.S.A., M.R.S.L., 60, Albion Road, Stoke
    Newington, N.

Rasch, F. C. S., Esq., 8, Burwood Place, Hyde Park.
Redman, Mrs., 6, Belsize Park, Hampstead, N.W.
Ressman, Baron C., Conseiller de l'Ambassade de S. M. le Roi d'Italia,
    35, Queen's Gate, S.W.
Ricotti, Professor Ercole, Italian Senator, Turin.
Richardson, Dr. B. W., M.A., F.R.S., F.S.A., 25, Manchester Square, W.
Robinson, Thomas W. U., Esq., F.S.A., Houghton-le-Spring, Durham.
Roofe, William, Esq., B.A.S., Craven Cottage, Merton Road, Surrey.
Rylands, W. H., Esq., F.S.A., 11 Hart Street, Bloomsbury.

Sayce, Rev. Professor A. H., Queen's College, Oxford.
Science and Art Department, Cromwell Road, South Kensington.
Serrao, Paolo, Esq., 39, Lombard Street, E.C.
Simms, S. W., Esq., George Street, Bath.
Simpson, Rev. Dr. W. Sparrow, F.S.A., 9, Amen Court, London.
South, Rev. E. W., Proprietary School, Blackheath.
Spottiswoode, W., Esq., P.R.S., 41, Grosvenor Place, S.W.
Steet, G. Carrick, Esq., 130, King Henry's Road, N.W.
Stirling, Mrs., 73, Ladbroke Grove, Notting Hill.
Stuart, Robert, Esq., Grand Hotel, Palanza, Lago Maggiore.
Stephens, F. G., Esq., 10, The Terrace, Hammersmith, W.
Stevens, Henry, Esq., F.S.A., 13, Upper Avenue Road, South Hampstead.
Strickland, Edward, Esq., 2, All Saints Court, Bristol.
Sutton, Charles W., Esq., Manchester Free Library.
Swainson, Rev. C. A., D.D., Christ's College Lodge, Cambridge.

Thomas, Watson, Esq., 79, Lansdowne Road, W.

Thring, Rev. Edward, School House, Uppingham, Rutland.
Trist, J. W., Esq., Master of the Skinner's Company, 62, Old Broad Street, E.C. (*Three copies.*)
Trübner, Nicholas, Esq., Publisher, 57, Ludgate Hill, E.C. (*Three Hundred and Twelve copies.*)
Tübingen, Germany, Königliche Universitäts Bibliotheke, R. Roth, Chief Librarian.
Turin, Italy, La Reale Accademia Albertina, Signor C. A. Aufossi, Librajo.

Vincent, Samuel, Esq., Cressy Cottage, Sutton, Surrey.
Vize, George, Esq., 4, Loraine Road, Holloway, N.

Wadmore, J. F., Esq., 35, Great St. Helens, E.C.
Wallace-Dunlop, Miss, 5, Connaught Square, Hyde Park.
Wallis, George, Esq., F.S.A., 4, New Residences, South Kensington.
Walker, Dr. E. J., Trinity College, Cambridge.
Watkins, Charles, Esq., Manager of the Imperial Ottoman Bank, Larnaca, Cyprus.
Westminster, His Grace the Duke of, Eaton, Chester.
Whitaker, J. Vernon, Esq., Paternoster Square.
Wilkinson, C. H., Esq., Maitland Villa, Finchley.

Yuill, Wm., Esq., 3, Fenchurch Avenue, E.C.

The Editor of *The Times.*
,, ,, *Daily Telegraph.*
,, ,, *Athenæum.*
,, ,, *Academy.*
,, ,, *Builder.*

Palma Villa, Woodchurch Road,
West Hampstead, N.W.
28th June 1882.

T. RICHARDS, PRINTER, 37, GREAT QUEEN STREET.

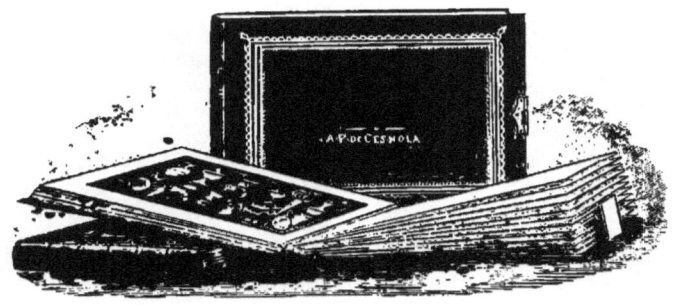

www.ingramcontent.com/pod-product-compliance
Lightning Source LLC
Chambersburg PA
CBHW030950110726
47900CB00004B/1207